Interacting
with Virtual
Environments

Interacting
with Virtual
Environments

Edited by

Lindsay MacDonald
Crosfield Electronics Ltd, UK

John Vince
Hughes Rediffusion Simulation Ltd, UK

Foreword by

Ben Shneiderman

JOHN WILEY & SONS

Chichester • New York • Brisbane • Toronto • Singapore

Designations used by companies to distinguish their products are often
claimed as trademarks. In all instances where John Wiley & Sons Ltd.
is aware of a claim, the product names appear in initial capital or all
capital letters. Readers, however, should contact the appropriate
companies for more complete information regarding trademarks and
registration.

Other Wiley Editorial Offices

John Wiley & Sons, Inc., 605 Third Avenue,
New York, NY 10158-0012, USA

Jacaranda Wiley Ltd, 33 Park Road, Milton,
Queensland 4064, Australia

John Wiley & Sons (Canada) Ltd, 22 Worcester Road,
Rexdale, Ontario M9W 1L1, Canada

John Wiley & Sons (SEA) Pte Ltd, 37 Jalan Pemimpin #05-04,
Block B, Union Industrial Building, Singapore 2057

Library of Congress Cataloging-in-Publication Data

Interacting with virtual environments / edited by Lindsay MacDonald,
John Vince.
     p. cm.
   Includes bibliographical references and index.
   ISBN 0 471 93941 2
   1. Human-computer interaction. 2. Virtual reality.
I. MacDonald, L. W. (Lindsay W.), 1950– . II. Vince, John (John
A.)
QA76.9.H85I592 1994
006—dc20   93-33676
                                                                CIP

British Library Cataloguing in Publication Data

A catalogue record for this book is available from the British Library

ISBN 0 471 93941 2

Produced from camera-ready copy supplied by the editors using MS Word
Printed and bound in Great Britain by Bookcraft (Bath) Ltd.

Contents

Foreword

For more than 5000 generations men and women have enjoyed discovering patterns in nature and teaching each other how to interpret what they saw. Sharp-eyed visionaries recognised that leaves changing colour from green to brown were harbingers of winter and a signal to move south. Tracks in the mud were understood as clues to where enemies had been or where game might be found to feed a hungry family.

For more than 500 generations early artists endeavoured to record and share what they saw with charcoal drawings on cave walls or with colourful glazes on clay pots. Everywhere on our planet the passion to create images and ornaments flourished, even though the media required great skill to master. We still treasure these images of ornate Egyptian royalty, fierce Chinese warriors, or fertile African goddesses.

For more than 50 generations artisans devoted their lives to refining image-making technology and art. They evolved increasingly precise pictures with depth, perspective, shadow, texture, and detail, not only to convey reality but to influence opinions, lift the spirit, and evoke emotional responses. Creative individuals developed methods for drawing maps, sketching plans for buildings, and making religious symbols. Learning to make images took many years and an artist might only produce a few hundred works in a career.

During the past 500 years printing was perfected, giving trained professionals the power to produce high-quality and low-cost images that could be shared by many people. Then in the past 150 years photography offered universal access to the creation of high-quality images. Realistic portraits, precise records of news events, accurate aerial views of cities, and diagnostic X-rays became common. Our memories of childhood, parents, experiences, and remote places could be preserved. Film and television intensified the viewer's experience with animation and furthered the principle of mass distribution on a global scale.

And now in our generation several technologies further restructure our relationship with images. While photography became a mass culture tool early in this century, only in the past decade has the video camcorder enabled large numbers of individuals to create animated images. Computers began as number crunchers, but new designs enable easier creation, capture, editing, searching, and viewing of still and moving images. Electronic networks promise universal and rapid dissemination of images. Grandparents will use videophones to see their newborn grandchildren while honeymooning couples will preview their destinations and choose among hotel rooms by seeing the furnishings and layout. These technologies allow us to overcome our limited capacity to create, disseminate, and access images.

Future scenarios include include access to vast libraries of images from online National Galleries of Art, medical histories including X-rays, sonograms, and electrocardiographs, massive environmental image databases from NASA's Earth Orbiting System of satellites, and entertainment resources such as 50000 videos on demand. On a personal basis, digital photography and video offer users the chance to capture, edit, store, and send family experiences. For learning and business, multimedia/hypermedia tools with user controlled 3-D animations will become normal. Authors of papers in this volume are exploring important paths in all these imaging technologies.

There are ample challenges for scientists and technologists in creating these new tools in a way that serves human needs at low cost. For scientists exploring novel user interfaces, the rigour of psychologically-oriented controlled experimentation seems to be the path to rapid progress. This hypothesis testing approach, based on the desire to validate theories and predictive models, requires courage and commitment. These reductionist methods can go astray, but the objective feedback from focused experiments quickly steers the researcher back on the track in pursuit of broad theories and big breakthroughs. For technologists developing commercially viable products the three pillars of success appear to be: iterative usability testing, User Interface Management Systems, and a guidelines document process.

There are also ample challenges for communicators with messages and artists with imaginative visions in learning how to use these new media. The daring impressionist painters of the 1880s and the counter cultural abstract expressionists of the 1950s created revolutionary images that reshaped our concepts of what images should be. Now, post-modernist cyber-artists and virtual realists are challenging basic assumptions about time and space, object and subject, fact and fantasy, and private and public. The scientists and technologists will have succeeded only if the communicators and artists are attracted to create with these tools.

There are seductive possibilities but there are also unsettling questions. How will we respond when art is no longer "fixed in a tangible medium of expression" (to use the phrase from copyright law), and our notions of limited access, ownership, and permanence vanish? How will the criteria for quality change when everyone can create images and broadcast them universally? Will some authoritative alternative emerge as photography loses its role as trusted witness to history? Art and ideas usually stem from a single individual, but can we accept communal creation through Computer Supported Cooperative Art? How will social and political structures change as centralised control gives way to distributed sources of influence?

Finally, how can we balance our attraction to these new technologies with our sensitivity to human values? Can we ensure that the benefits of our efforts are not compromised? The authors of the papers in these volumes do not answer all these questions, but they are part of the community that is exploring and creating exciting new paths for all of us to follow.

Ben Shneiderman © 1994
University of Maryland
College Park, MD 20742 USA

Preface

Ten years ago computer-based systems for interacting with images were in their infancy. Most computers could not display images at all and relied for their user interfaces on keyboard input and character displays. Systems capable of image display were large and expensive, being purpose-designed for specific turnkey applications such as electronic page composition, aircraft cockpit simulation or satellite image analysis. Interaction possibilities were usually limited to a small number of functions selected from a customised keypad plus zoom and scroll of the image under the control of a joystick or trackball. The systems were invariably closed environments, with all components being supplied by the one vendor.

Several influences over the past decade have dramatically changed the situation. The first has been the inexorable rise in the power of desktop computers. From 1983 to 1993 we have seen an increase of approximately one hundred times in both the processing power and memory capacity of personal computers for about the same end-purchase price. Ten years ago a typical desktop computer was a PC-AT running at about 0.1 million operations per second with 640 kbyte random access memory (RAM) and a 10 Mbyte hard disk; now it is a Sun SPARC-10 running at about 10 million operations per second with 64 Mbyte RAM and a 1 Gbyte hard disk.

The second influence has been the continuing development of colour peripherals. CRT monitors have not changed much in terms of the basic technology but they have become cheaper, more reliable and available in a variety of convenient sizes for desktop use. What has changed radically is the cost and size of frame stores to drive a monitor with a high-quality 24-bit image. In 1983 a 1024 by 1024 pixel frame store occupied about 3 cubic feet, was mounted in a 19-inch rack and cost about $100 000. Today it fits on a postcard-sized plug-in circuit board and costs about $2000. Simple palette-mapped 8-bit frame stores are now included as standard equipment on the motherboard of most current personal computers, so that colour displays are almost ubiquitous.

The third influence has been the evolving capabilities of software — not only the operating systems (Unix instead of MS-DOS in our example), but also networking, distributed file systems and client−server remote operation. These have all served to demystify computing for the average user and to provide the means for building configurable systems. Many professional users prefer to purchase heterogeneous system components from a number of suppliers and then "plug and play" in the privacy of their own offices, rather than pay a premium to a systems integrator. Pressure from users to make systems more open has fuelled the adoption of image interchange standards such as Postscript and TIFF, which provide system-independent methods for specifying page description or image file formats.

The last but by no means least influence has been the growing sophistication of user interfaces, both graphical (GUI) and others. From the first incarnations ten years ago of the WIMP user interface (Windows, Icons, Mouse, Pointer) by Xerox and Apple, the interfaces of today offer the user multiple input channels to access and control multiple displays, combining text with graphics, sound, imagery, video and remote communications. Two-dimensional desktops with static widgets are evolving into three-dimensional animated metaphors. Andries van Dam predicts that by the end of this decade we can expect to see 3-G computer platforms (ie. Giga-flops, Giga-bytes and Giga-baud) as the norm, with most of their horsepower being used to support a user interface of the SILK variety (Speech, Image, Language, Knowledge).

This book brings together the leading developers of human−computer interaction and image display methods to provide a valuable insight into how the two disciplines are being synthesised in practical applications. The objective has been to give readers an understanding of the state of the art, whilst also offering generic techniques that can be taken away and deployed in other applications. We believe that this book will be welcomed in the office of every research and development engineer engaged in the design of interactive systems.

Lindsay MacDonald
John Vince

July 1993

About the Editors

Lindsay MacDonald is a Senior Consultant with Crosfield Electronics. He holds B.Sc. (Hons) and B.Eng. (electrical engineering) degrees from the University of Sydney. He has been with Crosfield for 16 years and has been one of the principal architects for three generations of computer-based workstations for electronic page layout and digital image manipulation for the graphic arts industry. His work brings together human-computer interface design, computer graphics and colour image processing. He holds 19 patents for inventions in these fields.

He has been responsible for Crosfield's involvement in three collaborative research projects. Two of these were funded by the UK Department of Trade and Industry under the Alvey and IEATP programmes and focused on the development of an optimal model of colour appearance and methods of colour device characterisation, based on extensive psychometric experimental work at Loughborough University. Currently he is working with the ESPRIT IIIMARC project, developing methods for direct digital imaging of fine art paintings and printing with an increased colour gamut.

He has lectured extensively in recent years on all aspects of colour, bringing together the perception of colour with its reproduction on displays and in print. He has co-authored two other books: *Computer Generated Colour* and *Human Factors in the Design of IT Systems*. He sits on the Advisory Boards of the journals Displays and Applied Image Processing and is a member of the professional bodies BCS, IEE, IEEE, ACM, SPIE, SID and the Colour Group of Great Britain.

John Vince is Chief Scientist at Hughes Rediffusion Simulation. He holds a M.Tech. in computer science and a Ph.D. in computer graphics from Brunel University. Prior to taking up an industrial appointment, he had been with Middlesex Polytechnic (now Middlesex University) for 16 years, where he taught computer graphics and computer animation. During this time, he established a successful computer animation unit which undertook a wide variety of animations for television and film special effects. His PICASO and PRISM computer graphics systems were used for this work and for teaching computer graphics to students and professional graphic designers.

He has written five books: *A Dictionary of Computer Graphics, Computer Graphics for Graphic Designers, The Language of Computer Graphics, 3D Computer Animation,* and *Computer Graphics.*

His interests are in graphics algorithms, real-time image generators, computer graphics technology, display technology, mathematics for computer graphics, virtual environment systems, and teaching issues in computer animation.

He has given many presentations on all aspects of computer graphics and computer animation, and has become an active member of the Virtual Environment community. He is a fellow of the British Computer Society, and is a Visiting Professor at the University of Brighton.

Contributors

Dr John Brooke
Digital Equipment Company
P.O. Box 39
Newbury RG13 2QA
United Kingdom

Prof William A. S. Buxton
University of Toronto
83 Cairns Avenue
Toronto
Ontario M4L 1X6
Canada

Dr Matthew Chalmers
Rank Xerox EuroPARC
61 Regent Street
Cambridge CB2 1AB
United Kingdom

Mr Sean Clark
LUTCHI Research Centre
Loughborough University of
Technology
Loughborough
Leicestershire LE11 3TU
United Kingdom

Prof Gillian Crampton Smith
Royal College of Art
Kensington Gore
London SW7 2EU
United Kingdom

Mr John Cupitt
The National Gallery
Trafalgar Square
London WC2N 5DN
United Kingdom

Mr Allan Davison,
Paul Otto and David Lau-Kee
Canon Research Centre
Europe 17-20 Frederick
Sanger Road
Surrey Research Park
Guildford
Surrey GU2 5YD
United Kingdom

Prof R. J. Lansdown
Middlesex University
Cat Hill
Barnet
Hertfordshire EN4 8HT
United Kingdom

Mr William Latham and Dr
Stephen Todd
IBM UK Scientific Centre
Winchester
Hampshire SO23 9DR
United Kingdom

Mr Lindsay MacDonald
Crosfield Electronics
Three Cherry Trees Lane
Hemel Hempstead
Hertfordshire HP2 7RH
United Kingdom

Prof Nadia Magnenat
Thalmann
Centre Universitaire
d'Informatique
University of Geneva
12 rue du Lac
CH-1207, Geneva
Switzerland

Mr Kirk Martinez
Department of History of Art
Birkbeck College
University of London
Gower Street
London
United Kingdom

Dr Norman Richards and P.
Rankin
Interactive Systems Group
Philips Research Laboratories
Cross Oak Lane
Redhill
Surrey RH1 5HA
United Kingdom

Dr Neil Robinson
CN Services
The Old Post Office
Worthing Road
Southwater
West Sussex
United Kingdom

Prof Stephen A. R. Scrivener
University of Derby
Kedleston Road
Derby DE3 1GB
UK

Prof Daniel Thalmann
Computer Graphics
Laboratory
Swiss Federal Institute of
Technology
CH-1207, Lausanne
Switzerland

Dr David Travis,
T. Watson and M. Atyeo
Human Factors Division
BT Laboratories
Martlesham Heath
Ipswich IP5 7RE
United Kingdom

Prof John A. Vince
Hughes Rediffusion Simulation
Gatwick Road
Crawley
West Sussex RH10 2RL
United Kingdom

Prof Dave Zeltzer
Sensory Communications
Group
Massachusetts Institute of
Technology
Room 36-763
50 Vassar Street
Cambridge MA 02139-4307
USA

Acknowledgements

"Interacting with Virtual Environments" is based upon the proceedings of the two-day conference "Interacting with Images" held in the Sainsbury Wing of the National Gallery, on the 10th and 11th February 1993. This event was organised by the British Computer Society's, Computer Graphics and Displays Group, and the conference theme reflected the state-of-the-art in real-time image interaction.

Speakers at the conference were faced with the challenge of preparing their papers to provide a stimulating live presenation, and a coherent chapter of this book, and we gratefully acknowledge their work in making the conference a success, and this book possible. As speakers had devoted so much time preparing their original papers, only slight editorial changes were necessary to prepare this book; nevertheless, we thank them for the time and effort they devoted to this task.

We would also sincerely acknowledge the advice and support from Dr Rae Earnshaw, the Chairman of the BCS Computer Graphics and Displays Group - Rae's considerable experience in publishing previous proceedings was extremely useful in preparing this book.

Finally, we would like to record our thanks to Jane Preston who was responsible for formatting the book from the electronic data files submitted by the authors. It was her first attempt at a large-scale desktop publishing project, and she performed a magnificent task.

Trademarks

Amiga is a trademark of Commodore Computers, Inc.
BattleTech is a trademark of Virtual World Entertainments, Inc.
CAMNET is a trademark of British Telecom plc
Colorspace is a trademark of Crosfield Electronics, Ltd.
Data Browser is a trademark of VPL Inc.
DECvoice is a trademark of Digital Equipment Corporation, Inc.
Legend Quest is a trademark of Virtual Reality Design & Leisure, Inc.
Microsoft is a registered trademark of Microsoft, Inc.
MS-Windows is a registered trademark of Microsoft, Inc.
SimGraphics is a registered trademark of SimGraphics Engineering Corp.
Smalltalk-80 is a trademark of ParcPlaceSystems, Inc.
SonicFinder is a trademark of Apple Computer, Inc.
Spaceball and Spaceball 2003 are registered trademarks of Spaceball Technologies Inc.
SunOS, SunSPARCstation, OpenWindows, NeWS, VIEW-Station, VideoPix, V-Sugar are
trademarks of Sun Microsystems, Inc.
UNIX is a registered trademark of AT&T Technologies, Inc.
Virtuality is a registered trademark of W Industries Ltd.
MS-Windows is a trademark of Microsoft, Inc.

Many of the designations used by manufacturers and sellers to distinguish their products are
claimed as trademarks, and some of these used in this book may not appear in this list. The
absence of a designation from this list does not imply that the designation is not claimed by
its respective user.

1

Human Skills in Interface Design

William A.S. Buxton

1.1 Introduction

In an earlier work (Buxton 1986), I speculated on what conclusions a future anthropologist would draw about our physical make-up, based on the tools (namely computers) used by our society. The objective was to point out that these tools reflect a very distorted view of our physiology and the motor/sensory skills. For example, the near absence of pressure sensors reflects a failure to exploit a fundamental and well-developed capability of the hand. The impoverished use of sound reflects a waste of our ability to use audio to make sense out of our environment.

The paper dealt primarily with the domain of the visible and tangible. Nevertheless, things have changed very little in the intervening years. Furthermore, it can well be argued that things are even more distorted if we look at how the technology reflects less visible human traits such as cognition, or social interactions.

In what follows, we use a technology-as-mirror metaphor. One intent is to provide some *human-centred* criteria for evaluating designs. Another is to help foster a mind-set that will lead to improved designs in the future.

1.2 Three mirrors

The thesis of this chapter is that we should consider technology in terms of the fidelity with which it reflects human capabilities on three levels:

- *physical:* how we are built and what motor/sensory skills we possess;

Interacting with Virtual Environments Edited by Lindsay MacDonald and John Vince

- *cognitive:* how we think, learn, solve problems and what cognitive skills we possess;

- *social:* how we relate to our social milieu, including group structure and dynamics, power, politics, and what social skills we possess.

Our metaphor is one of three separate mirrors, each reflecting one of these levels. In order to be judged acceptable, designs must provide an acceptable degree of fidelity in how they reflect each of these three aspects of human make-up and activity. The benefit is in how the model can provide a simple but valuable test that can be used during the design process. We now look at each of these mirrors in turn.

1.3 Mirror one: how we sense and control

Look and feel

The notion of *Look and Feel* primarily encompasses aspects of the user interface that are reflected by our first mirror. The term has had a lot of recent attention, largely because of the efforts of various manufacturers to protect their own approach. Looking into our first mirror, however, what we see is something distorted and unworthy of protracted protection.

First, the very term reflects a lack of concern with a primary sense - sound. And if we look at the interfaces in question, then something like:

look   feel   sound

would be a more accurate representation of what is actually there. Look dominates, feel is impoverished and sound, while used, is almost a "throw-away". In short, the balance is out of all proportion with human make-up and capabilities.

One of the first priorities of the next generation of user interface, therefore, is to correct the current distortions in mirror one. How some emerging systems and technologies can lead the way in doing so forms the basis of the next few sections.

Multimedia

Multimedia is one of the topics that inevitably arises when discussing emerging technologies. As likely or not, the discussion has two main components: "Multimedia is the future!" and, "What is multimedia?" The results are generally more than a little confused.

I think that a lot of the excitement about multimedia is well founded. However, by definition, "Multimedia" focuses on the *medium* or *technology* rather than the *application* or *user*. Therein lies a prime source of confusion.

If we take a user centred approach, we quickly see that it is not the media *per se* that are important. The media are transitory, one to be replaced by another as technology evolves. What makes these technologies different are the human sensory modalities and channels of communication that they employ. Rather than focusing on the media, therefore, more appropriate and focused terms might be:

- *multi-sensory:* design that utilises multiple sensory modalities;
- *multi-channel:* design that utilises multiple channels, of the same or different modalities;
- *multi-tasking:* design that recognises that (as driving a car demonstrates) humans can perform more than one task at a time.

Multimedia is simply design that makes better and broader use of the human's capabilities to receive and transmit information. However, since the vast majority of the literature has been technocentric, confusion has resulted. Without an understanding of the properties of the various sensory modalities, the associated channels, and the way in which they work together, how can effective use of the technology's potential be motivated or achieved?

Let's look at some examples that provide counter-examples to the mainstream, and point to what can be achieved when one breaks away from the *status quo*.

Bidirectionality of the senses

An interesting attribute of most human-computer interaction is that it uses a different sensory modality in each direction of communication: primarily *visual* from computer to human, and *motor/tactile* from human to computer. This is almost taken for granted. But it is contrast to almost all human-human communication.

This is brought up because recognising and balancing asymmetries is a good heuristic for uncovering new design alternatives. Let's take the visual system, for example. Everyday we use our eyes not just to see, but to direct the attention of others to what we are looking at. Here is a well practiced human skill which is a candidate for use in human-computer interaction. Here is an opportunity that systems such as that by LC Technologies Inc.[1], shown in Figure 1.1, have exploited.

Similarly, we think of the things that we touch and move as being input devices, only, and spend very little time thinking about their use as tactile *displays*. In one way, virtually all input devices are also output in that we can feel their size, shape, action, and movement. But while important, this is generally passive display. Force-feedback devices are one approach to coming closer to taking advantage of our capabilities of touch. Examples of such devices are described by Brookes *et al.* (1990) and Iwata (1990), which is illustrated in Figure 1.2. But much of the same effect can be achieved by smaller tactile displays, such as Braille displays designed for visually disabled users. Another example is the tactile display mounted in the button of the SimGraphics mouse, shown in Figure 1.3.[2]

---

1 LC Technologies, Inc., 4415 Glen Rose St., Fairfax, VA, USA 22032

2 SimGraphics Engineering Corp., 1137 Huntington Dr., Suite A-1, South Pasadena, CA, USA 91030

Figure 1.1. A Non-Intrusive Eye Tracker. A video camera mounted under the display tracks the position of the eye's pupil and translates the data into screen coordinates. Thus, the eyes can be used for pointing. (Photo: LC Technologies, Inc., Fairfax, VA).

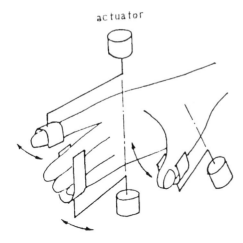

actuator

Figure 1.2. A force-feedback hand controller (Iwata, 1990). The device is a stationary exo-skeletal mechanism. The schematic shows the actuators that provide the feedback.

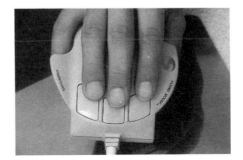

Figure 1.3. This 6D pointing device has an array of computer-controlled pins in the button that rise and fall under computer control in order to provide a degree of tactile feedback, such as to simulate the feeling of crossing a border, or coming into contact with an edge. (SimGraphics Engineering Corp.)

The SonicFinder and beyond

One of the most interesting pieces of software circulating in the research underground is something called the *SonicFinder* (Gaver 1989). It was developed at Apple Computer's *Human Interface Group* by Bill Gaver. The SonicFinder is a prototype version of the Macintosh Finder that is based on the novel proposition that we can hear. This may seem a fairly obvious fact, until we look at the sonic vocabulary used by most computer systems.

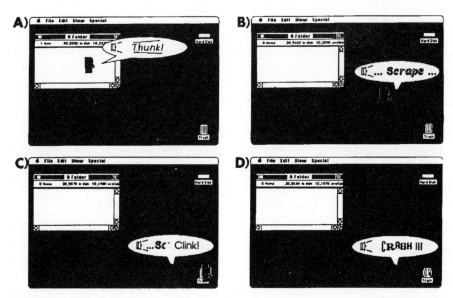

Figure 1.4. The SonicFinder. The example illustrates the use of sound during four stages of dragging a file to the trash can. (A) The user selects the object and hears the impact. (B) The user drags the object and hears it scrape along the desktop. (C) The user drags the object over the trash can; the scraping sound stops and the trash can makes its noise. (D) The user releases the object; a crash provides confirmation of the deletion (Gaver, 1989).

What the SonicFinder does is use sound in a way that very much reflects how it is used in the everyday world. You can "tap" on objects to determine their type (application, disk, file folder, etc.) and their size (small objects have high pitched sounds, large objects are low). When you drag an object, you hear a noisy "scraping" sound. When a dragged object "collides" with a container (such as a file folder, disk, or the trash can), you hear a distinct sound.

Now all of this may seem to suffer from terminal "cuteness" or frivolity. After all, aren't sounds for video games and cyber-wimps? But how many times have you missed the trash can when deleting a file, or unintentionally dropped a file into a file folder when dragging it from one window to another? Frequently, I would guess, yet these are precisely the kinds of errors that disappear through such use of sound.

We have ears and are pretty good at using them. Machines that have the capability to exploit their potential are finally becoming more common. Starting with the Commodore *Amiga,* which comes with rich audio and text-to-speech, we are now seeing audio as an important ingredient in other platforms. The challenge now is to learn how to use audio effectively, not just for music or to provide some acoustic lollipop, but as a means to provide a sonic landscape that helps us navigate through complex information spaces.

Hands-on computing?

Every day we turn pages with one hand while writing with the other. We steer our car with one hand while changing gears with the other. We hold a ruler or drafting machine with one hand and use a pencil in the other. All of these tasks employ the performance of everyday motor skills that have potential in human-computer interaction, but are largely ignored by computer systems.

Computers like the Macintosh were designed for Napoleon: unless you are typing, you can work all day with one hand tucked into your jacket. Fine if you are one-handed - a waste if you are not. The image of the user reflected in the technology is lopsided to the extreme.

"Hands-on" computing is largely a myth. It would be better called "hand-on" or even "finger-on." If we are accurately to reflect human potential, we should be able to scroll through a document by manipulating a track ball with one hand, while pointing with a mouse using the other. We should be able to scale an object using a potentiometer in one hand, while dragging it into position with the other. Or, in a program like *MacDraw*, we should be able to move the drawing page under the window using a trackball in one hand, while still keeping our "pen" in the other.

To a certain degree, high-end interactive computer graphics systems have used this type of interaction for a number of years. This is seen, for example, in systems that provide a potentiometer box which enables the non-dominant hand to perform transformations such as *rotate, scale* and *translate*. To date, however, such use of two-handed input has not penetrated the mainstream market. This is about to change.

Can you deal with the pressure?

Using two hands is not enough, however. Another property that we all have - but which is not reflected in the computer technologies that we use - is the ability of our hands to control and sense pressure. Gradually, designers are beginning to recognise this capability and design for it. One lead comes from electronic musical instrument keyboards. There - unlike your mouse - keys are not simple switches. Each key has what is known as *aftertouch:* the ability to sense continuously how hard the key is being pressed.

Soon (hopefully), aftertouch will be standard on mouse buttons, thereby providing natural control for line thickness, scrolling speed, or the speed of fast-forward or rewind on videos or CD-ROM. Already, a few manufacturers, such as *Wacom* and *Numonics* make styli for tablets that are pressure sensitive.

But no matter how well the look, feel and sound of a user interface is developed, it still may not fit in the way we think or work, and therefore fail. To gain a better understanding of this, and see how emerging technologies might help, we can now look into a different mirror.

1.4 Mirror two: how we think and problem solve

The myth of the information revolution

There are would-be sages and futurists who will tell you that we are in the middle of an information revolution - the impact of which is matched only by that which followed the invention of the printing press or the industrial revolution. Unfortunately, this notion is false, and illustrates a serious lack of understanding of the nature of information.

By definition, information is that which *informs*, and which can serve as the basis for informed decision making. Rather than an information revolution, what we are currently experiencing is a data explosion. The combined advances in contemporary telecommunications and computational technologies have helped to spawn an era where true information is ever more difficult to find at all, much less in a timely manner.

Information technologies that deserve the name are less computational engines than technologies to filter and refine data into a form where it does inform, and warrants the name *information* (Tufte 1983, 1990). Just as we want systems to reflect how we hear, see and touch, we want those same technologies to accurately reflect and support how we think, learn, problem solve, and make decisions.

One of the biggest successes of the personal computer world is the spreadsheet. One of the main reasons for this is that it "fits" the way that people think about certain problems. Rather than generate masses of new numbers, it helped users refine data into information by enabling them to explore and understand new relationships.

A similar notion is behind one of the emerging "hot" topics of computer science, namely *scientific visualisation*. The objective of visualisation is not to make pretty pictures. It is to render complex data in a visual form that enables us to understand better the underlying phenomena. Notation is a tool of thought, and what these emerging technologies provide is a notational engine *par excellence*. One way to apply our second mirror is to look at the notations used to represent various problem domains, and like a "cognitive anthropologist," attempt to infer what assumptions are implicit in the representation as to how people think, solve problems, etc. In most cases, it is likely that the assumptions thus derived will be a significant distortion of reality.

Scientific visualisation is an important attempt to eliminate the distortion; however, science is not the only field of endeavour to which the technology's notational powers can be applied. A good example of using the power of visualisation in other domains is the *Information Visualizer* (Card, Robertson and MacKinlay 1991) which is used to represent data used in the context of office work. An example of the system is shown in Figure 1.5.

So far, visualisation has been primarily a means of presentation. Data is rendered and displayed, but the degree of interaction is minimal (largely due to the computational overhead of the rendering process). People are not sponges, and do not learn by absorbing information. Rather, they construct knowledge intentionally and actively. Simply put, one learns by experience: exploring and doing. If systems are to reflect better this learning process, then they must, like the Information Visualizer be interactive and support active exploration. "Interactive visualisation" rather than scientific visualisation is the better objective, but there is one thing still missing.

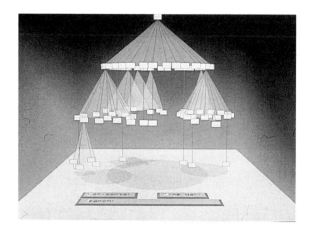

Figure 1.5. Representing hierarchic data in a "cone tree." From Card, Robertson and MacKinlay (1991).

From the criteria of our first mirror, there is a problem with focusing just on the visual sense. Both our tactile and aural senses are appropriate channels for representation. Hence, where our path should be heading is towards *Interactive Perceptualisation*.

Such a base will lead us to systems that enable us better to explore and understand relationships, test hypotheses and deal with the complexity of our lives.

1.5 Mirror three: social context

Alone in the corner

Back in grade-school, if I misbehaved, I was taken out of the group and forced to sit alone, usually facing the wall or corner. Now that I've grown up and have a computer, where do I find myself? - out of the group, sitting alone, usually facing the wall or a corner. The reasons are different, but the punishment is the same.

The point is that the design of the technologies that we use in the workplace have largely ignored the social dynamics of how we work. We face walls because the backs of our machines are so ugly and full of cables, that we hide them. We are anchored to our designated position by the umbilical cord connecting our computer to the wall socket. We sit alone because virtually all of our systems assume that we interact with computers in a missionary position: one user and one computer face-to-face - no other position allowed.

Instruments of change

Technologies have had a large impact on how we work, with whom we work and who has what power. That will never change. What can change, however, is who or what is in the driver's seat.

In the past, work has been automated and technologies introduced based on what was possible. If a new technology became available, it was placed in the work place and the organisation adjusted accordingly. Since they were the easiest to program, routine tasks were the first to have technological support.

Of all of the user-related changes emerging today, perhaps the most significant is a change from this approach. Organisations and systems designers are beginning to recognise that rather than have the technology dictate the organisational structure, the organisation should dictate the technology. People and how they work are beginning to be recognised as the key to improved productivity.

The importance of this change cannot be overemphasised. No matter how perfectly your icons and menus are designed, or how well a system supports the user in performing their job, if they are doing the wrong job, the system is a failure.

For example, placing computers into patrol cars is intended to help police perform his or her job. But if the technology means that the police now devote more time to apprehending the minor offenders than the technology affords (stolen vehicles, unpaid traffic fines, etc.), the system may be a failure. The courts are clogged with minor offences, and little has been done to help investigate serious crimes.

From birthing rights in central America to PARC

The past ten years have seen the development of a new profession: applied psychology. Traditionally, psychology has been a discipline which analysed and tried to understand and explain human behaviour. Now, largely due to problems encountered in human-computer interaction, there is a new branch of psychology which attempts to apply this understanding in the context of a design art. The shift is from the descriptive to the prescriptive.

What we are seeing today is a very similar phenomenon in the discipline of socio-anthropology. If we want the society and social structures of work (and play) to drive technology, rather than the reverse, the obvious place to look for expertise is in disciplines such as sociology and anthropology. Like psychology, these are traditionally analytic, not design disciplines. However, change is coming, and a new discipline is being born: *applied socio-anthropology.*

Hence, we have a new breed of anthropologists like Lucy Suchman and Gitte Jordan (who last studied birthing rites in Central America) stalking the halls of Xerox PARC. There, they study the structure of organisations and work, with the intent of laying the foundation for a design art that takes into account the larger social context. Like psychology, socio-anthropology is becoming a prescriptive as well as an analytical science.

Groups and the instruments

Perhaps these social concerns are most visible in the rapidly emerging areas of *groupware* and computer supported cooperative work (CSCW). The convergence is from two directions. On the one hand we have the theory growing out of the applied social sciences, and at the other, we have the emergence of important enabling technologies, such as local area networks, new displays technologies and video conferencing.

Telecommunications, video and computer LANS are converging, thereby enabling new forms of collaboration, such as Xerox's *Mediaspace* (Stults 1986), *EuroPARC* (Buxton and Moran 1990), and *Ubiquitous Computing* (Weiser 1991). By integrating a range of technologies, both systems permit a degree of *telepresence* previously impossible.

Telepresence

By "telepresence," we mean the use of technology to support a sense of social proximity, despite geographical and/or temporal distance. Through telepresence, workers who are at remote sites will, ideally, be able to share a degree of collegiality and interaction that would otherwise only have been possible by being co-resident at the same site. Likewise, telepresence technologies will permit those who missed key meetings or classes to attend "after the fact." Thereby, they will be able to capture not only the content of what passed, but also the shared references and organisational culture from which that content grew. As such, telepresence technologies can be thought of as a kind of *social prosthesis* that can help overcome gaps and weaknesses within organisational structures.

Slowly but surely, the emerging technologies are going to let us out of the corner, and permit us to take a full and active role in the group, whether co-located or not.

1.6 Conclusions

The backdrop for this chapter is the high complexity but limited functionality of current systems. Our strong view is that for systems to reach their full potential, their design must be altered to provide a better match to the skills and potential of their intended users. We have tended too long to try and overcome shortcomings of design through training and documentation. Technology must adapt to the user, not the contrary.

Hopefully, the three mirrors model presented in this paper helps provide some catalyst to rethinking how we approach the design of computer systems. Humans have a vast repertoire of skills which they have accumulated from a life time of living in the everyday world. These skills are largely ignored and wasted in current practice. Nevertheless, they are a resource waiting to be exploited by innovative designers. By doing so, designers will greatly improve the fidelity of the reflection in each of our three mirrors, and in so doing, they will provide us with technologies which afford us to do that which we do best, namely, be human.

Acknowledgements

The work which underlies this chapter has been supported by the Natural and Engineering Sciences Council of Canada, Xerox PARC, Apple Computer Company, Digital Equipment Corp., and the Information Technology Research Centre of Canada. This support is gratefully acknowledged. In addition, I would like to acknowledge the contribution of the Input Research Group of the University of Toronto and my colleague Ron Baecker, who planted the seed for many of my ideas. I would also like to thank Lindsay MacDonald who made many helpful comments on the manuscript. Finally, I would like to thank the Friend21 workshop in Japan which was the initial catalyst for this chapter.

References

Brooks F.P. Jr., Ouh-Young M., Batter J. & Kilpatrick P.J. (1990). Project GROPE - haptic displays for scientific visualization, *Computer Graphics* **24(3)**, Proceedings of SIGGRAPH '90, 177-185.

Buxton W. (1986). There's More to Interaction than Meets the Eye: Some Issues in Manual Input. In Norman, D. A. and Draper, S. W. (Eds.), *User Centered System Design: New Perspectives on Human-Computer Interaction.* Lawrence Erlbaum Associates, Hillsdale, New Jersey, 319-337.

Buxton W. & Moran T. (1990). EuroPARC's Integrated Interactive Intermedia Facility (iiif): early experience, In S. Gibbs & A.A. Verrijn-Stuart (Eds.). *Multi-user interfaces and applications,* Proceedings of the IFIP WG 8.4 Conference on Multi-user Interfaces and Applications, Heraklion, Crete. Amsterdam: Elsevier Science Publishers B.V. (North-Holland), 11-34.

Card C., Roberston G. and MacKinlay (1991). Proceedings of CHI'91, 461-462.

Gaver W.W. (1989). The SonicFinder: An interface that uses auditory icons. *Human-Computer Interaction* **4(1)**, 67-94.

Iwata H. (1990). Artificial reality with force-feedback: development of desktop virtual space with compact master manipulator, *Computer Graphics* **24(3)**, Proceedings of SIGGRAPH '90, 165-170.

Stults R. (1986). *Media Space.* Systems Concepts Lab Technical Report. Palo Alto, CA: Xerox PARC.

Tufte E. (1983). *The Visual Display of Quantitative Information.* Cheshire, Connecticut: Graphics Press.

Tufte E. (1990). *Envisioning Information.* Cheshire, Connecticut: Graphics Press.

Weiser M. (1991). The computer for the 21st century. *Scientific American,* **265(3)**, 94-104.

2

Designing Flexible and Adaptable Interfaces

John Brooke

2.1 Introduction

For the last six years or so I have been a member of an advanced development group in Digital Equipment Corporation, working on a programme of research known as the Jabberwocky project. The programme derives its name from Lewis Carroll's "Through the Looking Glass". When Alice passes through the looking glass, one of the first things she finds is a looking glass poem, which, when held up to the mirror she is able to read but not to understand, since it starts:

JABBERWOCKY
" 'Twas brillig and the slithy toves
Did gyre and gimble in the wabe;
All mimsy were the borogoves,
And the mome raths outgrabe."

The poem is eventually explained to Alice by Humpty Dumpty, who is obviously a past master at interpretation of words:

"I don't know what you mean by "glory"" Alice said.

Humpty Dumpty smiled contemptuously. "Of course you don't - till I tell you. I meant "there's a nice knock-down argument for you!""

"But "glory" doesn't mean "a nice knock-down argument"" Alice objected.

Interacting with Virtual Environments Edited by Lindsay MacDonald and John Vince
© 1994 John Wiley & Sons Ltd

"When I use a word," Humpty Dumpty said, in rather a scornful tone, "it means just what I choose it to mean - nothing more or less."

"The question is," said Alice, "whether you can make words mean so many different things."

"The question is," said Humpty Dumpty, "which is to be the master - that's all."

To the non-technical user, the user interface presented by most computer systems - even in these days of such supposed universal panaceas as graphical user interfaces - is about as comprehensible as the Jabberwocky poem is to Alice. The goal of the Jabberwocky programme has been to develop tools and methods which allow us to build computer systems which are appropriate to the needs of the user.

In this chapter, I will explore the degree to which the problem of building appropriate systems is affected by, and affects, the way in which people interact with information through the use of language, images and other symbols, and the implications this has for the way in which we build systems. In particular, I will look at the idea of separating form from function, and will argue that from the point of view of producing appropriate technology it is necessary to make this separation, since language and images can only be interpreted in terms of their context and that for a designer to assume that particular images and symbols will be interpreted in particular ways will make it difficult to produce systems appropriate to the needs of the user.

2.2 Appropriate technology

At first sight, the two photographs in Figure 2.1 would seem to have little in common. What, after all, is the connection between a farmer with a donkey cart in the Gambia, and people trying out high-technology workstations

Figure 2.1. Two illustrations highlighting the importance of appropriate technology.

The connection lies in the notion of appropriate technology. Aid agencies and governments have often failed with overseas aid programmes because they have attempted simply to transplant western technology to Third World countries. Western technology, however, does not necessarily work in the environment where aid is being delivered. If you offered a Gambian farmer a choice between a donkey cart and a Ferrari - or even a Land Rover - then he would probably be better advised to take the donkey cart as it is a much more appropriate technology for his needs and his environment. It is cheap, simple, capable of carrying out the tasks that a farmer wants to do, can be easily repaired - or, indeed, built - by the farmer, doesn't need expensive refuelling, and can negotiate the rough and rutted roads. A high-performance sports car would probably cover the total amount of paved road available in the country in a matter of minutes, can't carry a single goat to market, and spare parts would not be available. Even all-terrain vehicles are inappropriate because of the high cost of fuel and repairs (although they may well be appropriate technology for representatives of aid agencies because they have the wherewithal to fuel and repair them, and their jobs require them to cover much more ground than would be possible in a donkey cart).

In just the same way, the users of computer systems need appropriate technology. Too often, computer systems do not fit in with the user, the tasks users do, or the environment in which they carry out those tasks.

2.3 Fashion in user interface design and determinants of usability

There is a fairly simplistic view of usability which assumes that a system can be made usable by endowing it with certain characteristics. For instance, it is common to see software products advertised as having "user-friendly point-and-click interface". What is interesting about this approach to usability is that the characteristics which supposedly endow a system with this quality of usability are apparently subject to the whims of fashion. Ten years ago, the magic recipe for "user-friendliness" was to ensure that an application should have a menu interface. Natural language enjoyed a short vogue. The current fashion is for graphic UIs. The fact that all of these have been touted as the answer to making a system usable and that they have been superseded indicates that they weren't, in fact, the answer; they were merely an answer, the nature of which was determined by the technology available at the time and the problems to which technology was being applied. As technology changes, new panaceas are promoted; old user interface technologies get relegated to the status of an also-ran.

An alternative view of usability is much more closely related to the notion of appropriateness. For instance, the current draft of international standard ISO 9241-11 (Guidance on Usability Specification and Measures) defines usability as

"The effectiveness, efficiency and satisfaction with which specified users achieve specified goals in particular environments"

This definition emphasises that usability is changed by context; what is usable by one user doing a particular job in a certain environment may be unusable for a different user doing a different task in a different environment. It is possible to argue that there is, in fact, no such thing as an unusable system; there are only systems used in appropriate or inappropriate contexts. As context changes systems may become less usable.

For example, when many computer operating systems were first developed, the technological context involved low-speed electromechanical terminals with no graphics capabilities. Also, computers were available only to a very few people, all of whom were highly trained and, most probably were using computers in disciplines which relied heavily on the use of symbolic expressions and languages to represent their solutions to problems. In this sort of context, it is hardly surprising that the interfaces that developed to operating systems were command languages which were capable of representing complex ideas very economically. The expressiveness of the command languages reflected the type of language used in mathematics, physics, chemistry and engineering, and the economy helped when the I/O devices were slow, noisy and expensive to run.

As computers began to be applied to new and less esoteric domains, such as text processing and financial calculations, they also began to be used by a wider range of people to whom such languages were neither familiar nor useful ways of expressing the problem domains. For these people, new styles of interface were needed, and technology also changed to allow the representation of objects more appropriate to the new domains, such as documents, filing cabinets, and spreadsheets without having to spend vast sums of money.

However, the problem that seems to arise every time a new user interface technology arrives is that everybody tries to apply it to all problem domains and all users. The fact that graphic UIs are a better way of representing some (not all!) text processing problems and that they are also more acceptable to people who do not tend to use symbolic languages does not mean that the older styles of user interface are wrong and should be thrown away. They may very well still be appropriate to the types of people for whom they were developed in the first place, and, in fact, many people familiar with interfaces such as command languages will frequently use them in preference to graphic UIs.

2.4 Understanding language and symbols

Everybody has their own interpretation and understanding of the meanings of words, symbols and images. When we use symbols in a social milieu, the demands of communication mean that there are commonly agreed interpretations of words and symbols among groups of people, but this does not guarantee that somebody from outside that group will necessarily share that understanding. Part of the understanding arises from a common set of assumptions about the context in which language or images will be interpreted.

On a linguistic level, similar problems arise. For example, the word "timpani" has very different meaning to a musician and to an anatomist. However, a music loving anatomist is also quite capable of interpreting the same word in two different ways depending on whether they are dissecting the auditory system of an organism or attending a concert.

This problem is particularly pertinent to the way in which computer systems are developed, since computer systems are, more than anything, systems for manipulating information. Thus the assumptions made by the designers of information systems about the users of the systems, the tasks those users will be doing, and the environment in which they will be doing it, are crucial to the way in which they represent the workings of the information system. If these do not correspond to the way in which the end users actually use the system, then there will be problems.

Unfortunately, it seems as though at present, most computer systems do not represent information in ways which represent the way that individuals think and work. This is perhaps not surprising, since most information systems are designed and built by software engineers. In the past, software engineers were often designing and building systems for other software engineers to use, and there was the occasional coincidence between the intentions of the designer and the way the system was used by the user. However, this is much less likely to be the case nowadays. As Gentner and Grudin (1990) point out, "from the engineer's perspective, the ideal interface reflects the underlying mechanism and affords direct access to the control points of the mechanism". Many computer systems are, in fact, rather like cars where it is necessary to understand the workings of the internal combustion engine in order to be able to drive them.

2.5 Change

The Jabberwocky programme has focused on how to build systems appropriate to a context. One therefore has to begin by understanding who is to be the user of the system, what task or tasks they will be doing with the system, and the nature of the environment in which they will use the system. Furthermore, given that context, one needs to understand how users would measure whether the system was useful to them (i.e. what do the terms effective, efficient and satisfying mean in this context?).

The situation is complicated by the fact that all of these things are in a state of continual change. Because of this, there needs to be a continual tracking of the state of the user, task and environment, and of the fit of the application to the context.

Building systems that are appropriate to a well-specified context (and a continually changing one, at that) inevitably means that one will probably finish up building small, highly targeted applications. Low cost is essential, since there will have to be many small applications and they will have to be continually redeveloped as the context changes. This has implications, in turn, for the development methods used in producing software. The computer industry, by and large, produces software on the shotgun principle, i.e. large generic products which contain many different functions. Typically, users of software actually employ only 5-10% of the functions available in a product; see, for instance, the work of Whiteside *et al.* (1982). They found, when studying text editors, that individual users employed 5% of the functions available in a variety of text editors. When you surveyed a broad range of users then, apart from a small core of functions used by everybody (typically cursor movement and text insertion and deletion) then everybody used a different 5% of the total functions available.

The arguments in favour of producing generic applications are generally couched in terms of minimising the costs of software development. Unfortunately, this then places the costs of making the applications appropriate to a particular context on the user rather than on the developer. For instance, many word processing packages provide "styles" of document.

However, the user must either adopt these standard styles, or must learn how to modify them to suit their particular needs. What an end user needs is the style they want to use delivered as part of the application so that they do not have to learn how to modify the application in the first place.

2.6 Form and function

One of the key factors in producing applications which are appropriate to a user's needs is to ensure that the functionality of that application is presented in a form which the user finds acceptable. Users may have strong preferences or special needs in how they want to view and to manipulate their system.

The relationship between the form which things take, and the functions which they can accomplish, are inextricably intertwined. The form-function relationship is a topic that has been discussed in a variety of contexts throughout history. For instance, the Aristotelian doctrine of teleology states that the form of natural objects is determined by their final ends or purposes. The Darwinian explanation of evolution focuses on the preferential selection of characteristics of organisms that are appropriate to the environment in which they exist, through the mechanism of reproduction. In the built, rather than the natural, world, the relationship has also been much studied. The modern movement in architecture until the 1960s was guided by Louis Sullivan's statement "form follows function" (which, contrary to the evidence of much recent architecture, was not meant to mean that utilitarian designs were intrinsically beautiful, but that form and function must be considered as one in the design process).

The difference between form in the natural world and form in the built world is that in the former, there is a large variety of potential new forms, new instances of which can be generated at any time. Thus, if an organism has characteristics which are inappropriate for the environment in which it lives, new organisms with different combinations of characteristics are generated by breeding and mutations, and future generations will tend to be better adapted to the environment because they will survive and reproduce more successfully. In the built world, the ability of an artefact to be appropriate to a variety of environments depends on the choice of characteristics built in by the designer in the first place, since it is usually difficult to add new characteristics once an artefact has been built. Thus, for instance, many American automobiles built in the late 1960s and early 1970s became inappropriate during the oil crisis of 1973, since they were designed with an assumption of low oil prices in the environment in which they would be used; there was no way to change the characteristics of these cars (and indeed it was very difficult to change the production lines which developed them) to cope with a new environment which placed different constraints on these artefacts.

The same problem occurs in information systems, although the possibility of modification is slightly higher than with actual physical objects. However, in terms of the variety of forms currently available, software has a "gene pool" akin to that found in remote Appalachian communities or European royal families, in that there is very little variety available to allow the development of new systems appropriate to new environments. (A recent survey by Myers and Rosson (1992) for instance, covered 74 applications, almost all of which were developed to run in an environment using a direct manipulation windowing interface.)

The underlying assumptions of the way software will operate, and the tools available for building systems also restrict the possible forms in which a user may interact with a system. Development tools of today provide the software engineer with very easy routes to producing a particular style of interaction with information, but in the process of making development of that form easy, restrict the ability to produce alternative forms of interaction. For instance, many of the graphic user interfaces of today (e.g. X-11, MS-Windows) use an event-driven programming model. When programming these systems, the software engineer creates user interface objects such as dialogue boxes, which contain other objects such as push buttons, form fields, check boxes and the like. The programmer then sets up a continuous program loop which calls particular routines when events occur in objects contained by the user interface. Thus, for instance, one routine will be called when an event such as a mouse movement or a button press takes place inside one object; another routine will be called when a different event takes place inside another object.

Unless the programmer is extremely careful this usually means that the routines will be structured in such a way that each one corresponds to an event in a particular user interface object. If the style of the interface is changed, so that the user interface now contains completely new objects, then the partitioning of logic may all need to be changed. What, in effect, has happened is that the form of the interface has determined the underlying functions of the information system. If, however, the surface form is not appropriate to a context, then both the surface form and the underlying functions have to be changed. This is inefficient and costly.

2.7 Separating form and function

From the point of view of building adaptable systems, it is highly desirable that a system should provide access to functionality in a variety of different forms, so that users can access functions using a style of interaction appropriate to the context of their task, environment and personal preferences. Ideally, functional services should be developed with no user interface. This idea, in fact is incorporated into mechanisms such as APIs (application program interfaces), shared code libraries, dynamic link libraries and runtime code libraries. However, all of these mechanisms are still linked irrevocably to the user interface when the code of an application is compiled. In a truly adaptable system, the relationship between user interface and functionality would never be completely defined, so that styles of interaction can be added and removed as the need arises, without affecting the operation of any of the functional services.

The following sections contain a description of the Jabberwocky tool kit which has been designed and developed following the principles described above.

2.8 User interfaces as translators

In the Jabberwocky tool kit, all user interfaces act simply as translators between one form of expression and another. User interfaces have no functional purpose whatever, and all are interchangeable. However, they allow the user to express their requirements in a form acceptable to them, and then transform it to a form required by a functional service.

As an example, many operating systems require commands in various arcane languages. To get a listing of stored files, for instance, the user usually has to issue a command which looks like "dir *.*" or "ls *". This, not surprisingly, is not intuitively obvious to most users. Given that they have to type in commands, they might prefer to say something along the lines of "list files", or "show me my files".

A user interface in the Jabberwocky tool kit allows the user to do just this. It takes their preferred form of expression such as "list files" and transforms it into a message such as "dir *.*" Alternatively, if the user is talking to, say a calculator function, then it should equally well be able to transform "add 23.55 to 99.6, then divide by 3" into a series of commands such as "(23.5+99.6)/3=" to be sent to the calculator. Since a translator is not an integral part of any particular application, it is equally capable of talking to a file management system as to a calculator, and should indeed be able to talk to either in subsequent translations.

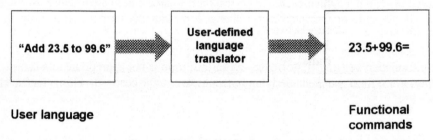

User language   **Functional commands**

Figure 2.2. A simple translator.

Having performed the translation, however, the transformed command must now be passed on from the translator to the functional service. The Jabberwocky tool kit therefore connects the translator and the functional service together via a software bus. Just as the only purpose of the translator is to transform messages from one form to another, the only purpose of this software bus, known as the dialogue bus, is to transport messages from one service to another, whether the service is a translator or a functional service.

In Figure 2.3 the translator and the functional service can be seen attached to the software bus, as well as an input channel (a keyboard) and an output channel (a screen). Input from the user is routed to the translator, output from the translator is routed to the input of the calculator functions, and the output from the calculator functions is routed to the screen. It may seem that this has actually achieved very little, Why, after all didn't we just build the translator into the functional services and save the overhead and computer resources involved in the software bus? There are several reasons. Firstly, we wouldn't be able to respond to change if we tied the functional services and the translator together. Secondly, we may have no way of actually getting at the functional services except through its interface. Many computer systems are running applications that have been in existence for a long time, and nobody knows any longer how it works or dares to touch it. Thirdly, we now have a new capability which we didn't have before, because the software bus which forms the backbone of the tool kit is asynchronous, and we can therefore connect multiple functional services together, or multiple user interface translators, or indeed both.

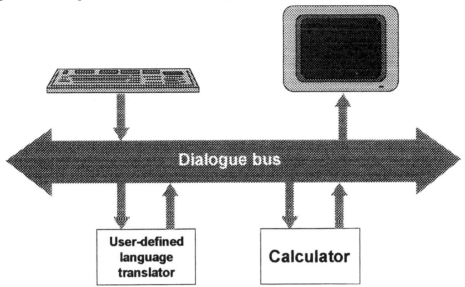

Figure 2.3. The data paths showing information flow from the keyboard to screen via the software bus.

2.9 Multiple ways of accessing the same functions

Given the notion that a user interface is merely a translator between one form of expression and another, it is possible to develop a variety of different forms of user interface to communicate between the user and the functional services connected to the dialogue bus. For instance, in order to create a graphic UI, we need to create a translator which manages graphic user interface objects and translates events taking place in them into messages for the functional services (Figure 2.4).

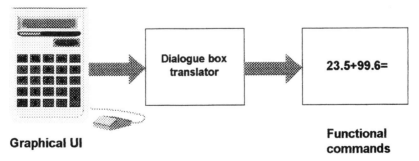

Figure 2.4. A dialogue box translator.

Alternatively, rather than using a graphic user interface tool kit to construct a representation of a calculator, we might decide that what we want to do is to take an actual image of a calculator such as a photograph, and use that as the mechanism for interacting with the functional services. We could specify that when certain regions in the image (such as the calculator keys) are activated with a pointing device, then appropriate messages should be sent to the calculator functions (Figure 2.5).

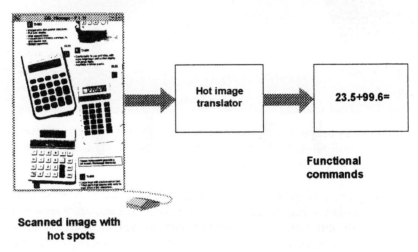

Scanned image with
hot spots

Figure 2.5. A scanned image translator.

2.10 Translating translated messages

Since multiple translators and multiple functional services can be plugged into the dialogue bus simultaneously, it is possible to direct the output of one translator into the input of another. This can be a very useful way of "amplifying" the capabilities of a system, since it allows reuse of translation mechanisms. Thus, for instance, one can minimise the amount of work needed to build a translator for speech input if a translator for user-defined language already exists. All that needs to be added is a translator that will take speech input and translate it into an ASCII stream, which can then be routed into the user-defined language translator and subsequently routed on to the appropriate functional services.

This technique has been successfully used in the Jabberwocky tool kit, for instance, to integrate the DECvoice speech recognition system, which can perform both speaker dependent and limited speaker independent speech recognition (Figure 2.6).

Similar translations can be applied on the output side. One obvious translation is to pass the output of the calculator, for instance, through a text-to-speech synthesis system, and this can indeed be done. Given speech recognition on the input side, and speech synthesis on the output side, it is possible to switch immediately from having a calculator with a graphic interface to having a speech-driven and speech-generating one. This means that the same calculator functions could be used by people with normal vision and by people with impaired

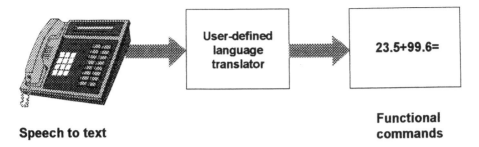

Figure 2.6. Chaining translators together.

visual function; or by people who need to use the tools in a hands-off environment as well as those with a desk available on which to place a monitor and a pointing device; and the switch could be made simply by plugging different translators into the bus with the same calculator functions.

In developing a system to demonstrate the flexibility achievable by this structure of interconnected translators and functions, we have developed some translators which are not obviously useful in this context; for instance, one alternative form of output we have developed is a short animated sequence of pictures, where a hand holds up appropriate numbers of fingers to signal the output of the calculator. See Figure 2.7. There are probably very few people who would want a calculator that displayed its results like this, but it can also easily be seen that the same technology could be applied in other contexts where users have special characteristics and where such output may be more appropriate to the tasks being performed. Thus, for instance, an animated sequence of mouth shapes might make a useful adjunct to a speech channel when the user is hearing-impaired.

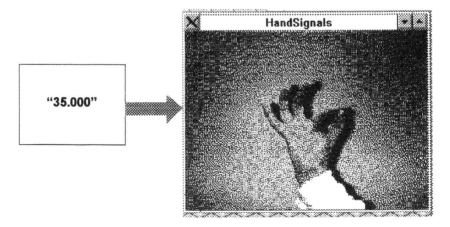

Figure 2.7. Animated hand signals as a form of output.

2.11 Multiple interfaces to the same functions or the same interface for different functions?

In the preceding sections we have seen how many different user interfaces can be mapped on the same functions simply by creating a translator which takes one form of expression and transforms it into another. The modular nature of the Jabberwocky tool kit also allows us to either provide a multiplicity of interfaces which are simultaneously available, or to provide a standard interface to many different pieces of functionality. Which of these options the designer chooses to provide once again depends on the context; in some circumstances it is important to provide a common interface, in others rapidly changing circumstances require the availability of different ways of accessing functions. The important thing is that the technological environment should provide the flexibility to offer both alternatives, rather than restricting the systems capability to be adapted to different environments.

2.12 Future proofing

The flexibility offered by this tool kit also future-proofs the designer to some extent against changes in fashion and technology. Since user interface technology - and fashion in user interface technology - is also constantly changing, when new technologies become available, they can simply be incorporated into the environment by building a new translator and plugging it into the bus. See Figure 2.8. The existing functional services do not have to be changed in order to carry on working with the new technology. Thus, in the unlikely event that a telepathic interface to information systems could be developed, it would be extremely simple to incorporate it into existing systems.

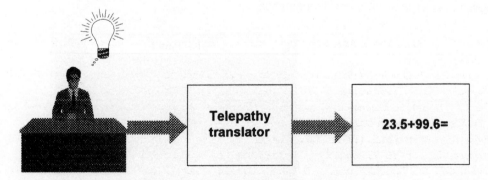

Figure 2.8. A multi-interface, four-function calculator.

Of course, this also works the other way round. As the technology for the underlying functional services changes and improves, it can be built into the system without disturbing the way in which the user interacts with it, since the translators merely have to be changed to transform the user's expressions into a different form of functional commands. The user need not be aware that any change has taken place behind the scenes.

2.13 Conclusions

This chapter has tried to raise some of the issues which bear on whether we can build systems which are appropriate to the needs of users. In order to do this, there needs to be a movement away from the development of large generic applications towards much smaller, more highly targeted applications. Large, generic applications place the onus on the user of a) working out what functions it offers which are relevant to them and to their tasks and b) changing the way in which they work in order to fit in with the design of the application. This is hardly a recipe for user-centred design. There is, however, a downside to building small, user-centred applications, in that software developers will have to be much nimbler on their feet in the way that they develop applications and in the way they respond to the changing needs of users.

The Jabberwocky tool kit, described in this chapter, has proved to be very successful in providing a flexible environment where applications can be tailored to fit the needs of users. It achieves this flexibility by modularising the tools and functions needed to create applications, and particularly by separating the representation of information and of access to functions from the functions themselves. While this chapter has focused on the flexibility achieved by allowing multiple styles of interaction to be mapped onto multiple functional services, the tool kit provides a number of other benefits beyond the scope of the chapter. The tool kit has allowed very rapid and flexible development of applications in both internal and external projects, and is being further developed to increase its range of capabilities.

References

Carroll L. (1971). *Alice's Adventures in Wonderland and Through the Looking Glass.* Oxford University Press.

Gentner D.R. & Grudin J. (1990). Why good engineers (sometimes) create bad interfaces. SIGCHI special bulletin. *Proceedings of CHI 90 conference, Seattle Washington.* pp 277-282.

ISO CD 9241-11.2 *Ergonomic Requirements for Office Work with Visual Display Terminals (VDTs)- Guidance on Usability Specification and Measures.*

Myers B. & Rosson M.B. (1992). Survey on user interface programming. SIGCHI special bulletin, *Proceedings of CHI 92 conference,* Monterey California. pp 195-202.

Whiteside J., Archer N., Wixon D. & Good M. (1982). How do people really use text editors? *SIGOA Newsletter 3,* 1, pp 29-40.

3

Visual Programming

Allan Davison, Paul Otto and David Lau-Kee

3.1 Introduction

User interfaces have become more visually oriented. The motivation for this trend is, generally, to make applications easier to use for people who are computer literate but not computer experts. There is now a reasonable amount of evidence to suggest that the judicious use of graphics and direct manipulation interaction are important techniques in producing powerful and expressive application interfaces.

Much research has gone into applying visual interface techniques to computer programming. Text based programming languages, although compact and familiar in representation, are essentially one dimensional representations. The display of such programs can be enhanced by pretty printing techniques, such as indenting statements within language constructs. But this form of representation still leaves all interpretation of the flow of data or control through the program to the user.

Visual programming attempts to exploit two or more dimensional graphical representations in the programming process. For instance, programs can be specified using icons to represent language constructs, such as loops and conditional statements. An example of this is the Proc-BLOX (Glinert 1987) system, which uses jigsaw puzzle pieces to represent language constructs. The pieces can only be put together in ways that produce syntactically correct programs.

Program visualisation, on the other hand, makes use of graphics to illustrate, or possibly animate, some aspect of a program i.e. its execution state or data. This chapter concentrates on application of visual programming and program visualisation to image processing. In particular, the design and implementation of the VPL (Lau-Kee *et al.* 1991) image processing system.

Our goal, for VPL, was to develop a system that could be used by people who had an image processing background but were not necessarily computer programmers. Traditional image processing tools have consisted of libraries of image transformation functions. To exploit

Interacting with Virtual Environments Edited by Lindsay MacDonald and John Vince
© 1994 John Wiley & Sons Ltd

them the user must become a programmer. In general such libraries do not provide support for the display and interaction with data.

VPL provides an integrated set of tools for the construction and execution of programs and the management of data and functions. Graphical objects, representing data and functions, are active and can be manipulated using drag and drop interaction.

The next section introduces some of the issues of visual programming: styles of programming language and the interactive nature of visual programming environments. The remainder of the chapter concentrates on the VPL image processing system.

3.2 Issues of visual programming

Visual programming systems can be characterised by the type of program specification they use. Typical specification styles that have been used are flowcharts, graphs and icons. A number of image processing visual programming systems, including VPL, AVS (Upson *et al.* 1989), HI-VISUAL (Hirakawa *et al.* 1987), and Khoros (Williams and Rasure 1990), use a variation of graph specification called data flow.

Data flow programs are typically presented as a set of nodes, representing functions and data, connected together by links, or wires, to form a graph that specifies the flow of data through the program.

This style of specification contrasts with that of imperative languages, where language constructs are used to specify the control flow within a program. For example, in VPL, the data flow *if* equivalent function has three inputs. The value on the first input determines whether the data on the second or third input will appear on the output.

One of the issues of visual program specification is that of granularity. The use of nodes to represent primitive operations is known as fine-grain data flow. With coarse-grain data flow, nodes represent high level operations that are specified as a collection of primitive operations

Programs specified with fine-grain data flow quickly become large and unmanageable. However, to add new functions to a system using coarse-grain data flow requires the user to program in a different language. This will often be a textual language such as C or Fortran.

In VPL, both fine and coarse-grain data flow are supported in a seamless fashion. A form of procedural abstraction allows users to develop new functions by incrementally constructing program graphs from existing functions, by direct manipulation, and without having to use a conventional text based programming language. Hence programs can consist of a set of hierarchical graphs, where nodes in a graph represent functions or graphs.

An important factor in the attractiveness of visual programming systems is the interactive nature of their user interfaces. The use of direct manipulation allows objects to be operated on directly by using a pointing device, typically a mouse. Crucial to the success of this form of interaction is the quality of the feedback provided by the interface.

Tanimoto (1990) adopts a measure of the interactive nature of a programming environment, in particular, the amount of feedback provided to the user during the construction of programs, or the *liveness* of the system. He proposes four levels of *liveness*:

- 1 - is an *informative* level, the system provides a visual representation of a program but it is not used by the computer in executing the program, it exists only as documentation.

- 2 - is a *significant* level, the visual representation is an executable specification for the program.

- 3 - is a *responsive* level where user modifications of the visual representation trigger re-computation of the program.

- 4 - at this level the system automatically generates results as they are required but allows the user to modify the program specification whilst computation is in progress.

The VPL system is level 4 live. Programs, even partially constructed ones, will execute when there is a demand that can be satisfied. The progress of the computation is made visible to the user by highlighting the functions in the graph that are executing. Modification of an executing graph will terminate the computation and trigger re-evaluation if necessary.

If the reader is interested in finding out more about visual languages references (Myers 1990), (Glinert 1990a) and (Glinert 1990b) provide a comprehensive introduction to the subject as well as discussing a wide range of existing systems.

3.3 VPL design aims

The original goal of the project was to develop an easy to use graphical user interface to the V-Sugar (Sato *et al.* 1990) image processing library. In particular, the system was to support users who had knowledge of image processing but were not necessarily expert programmers.

The interests of the research team led to the development of a prototype (Lau-Kee *et al.* 1990), using Smalltalk-80 and C, in order to explore the use of visual programming techniques. This experience led to the following design requirements:

- to produce an environment that would support an incremental, exploratory form of programming;

- to support a direct manipulation interface based around a consistent drag and drop interaction mechanism. Significantly, this has to be more than a graphical operation, the action should have some meaning. For instance, dropping a function on the Book tool (described in the next section) should cause the tool to display a description of the function;

- to preserve the quality of interaction. This is particularly important given the application domain, image processing, which is computationally expensive. We wanted the user interface to remain *active* at all times, even during image processing;

- the system should be extensible, in particular, users should be able to define new functions without resorting to conventional text-based programming languages.

These design aims led to a system which presents the user with a highly integrated set of tools. With a simple, consistent drag and drop interaction mechanism for moving functions and data between the tools.

3.4 VPL system tools

The main VPL tool is the Workspace. The Workspace is where program graphs are constructed, by linking together functions and data, and executed. The other VPL tools support the program development process by providing data and function management, image viewing and on-line information facilities.

If required the user can have multiple invocations of any tool. For instance, this allows the user to have several Workspaces active. The following subsections describe each of the VPL tools in more detail.

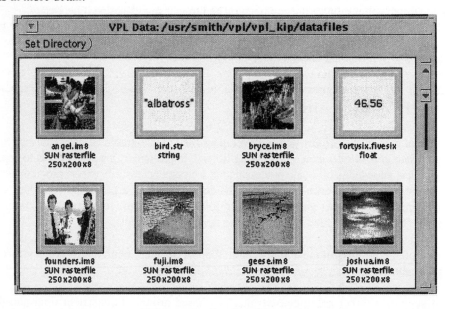

Figure 3.1. The Data Browser.

The Data Browser

The Data Browser provides a view onto VPL data items that are stored in a directory of the UNIX file structure. These data items are typed and, as well as images, contain data of any type supported by the VPL system i.e. strings and numbers.

The Data Browser displays data items in iconic form, as illustrated in Figure 3.1. The centre of an icon shows the content of the data item, a thumbnail version in the case of images. Displayed underneath the icon is information about the type and size of the item. The Data

Browser allows the user to change the directory being viewed through a directory pop-up window.

The user makes data *live* by selecting and dragging a data item from the Data Browser and dropping it onto the Workspace. At this point the data is automatically encapsulated into a *Producer* component. A Producer (discussed in more detail in the Workspace section) is a source of data. It is always ready to produce data on demand.

Data can be saved by dragging the selected data and dropping it onto the Data Browser. A dialogue prompts the user for item name etc. The copying and deletion of data items is also supported.

The Book

The interactive and exploratory nature of the VPL environment encourages users to experiment by building programs and observing their results. For this approach to work in practice, however, it must be possible for the user to quickly obtain information about a function.

Through a menu attached to each function, the system allows the user to display a dialogue containing information about the types of data a function will accept as input and produce as output. This information represents a definition of the programmatic interface to a function.

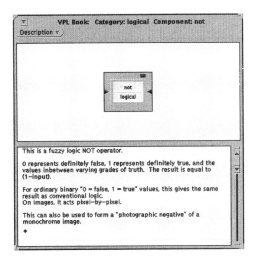

Figure 3.2. The VPL Book.

The Book, on the other hand, is an interactive tool that provides on-line retrieval and management of descriptions of functions in the library and supports:

• presentation of information on the purpose of each function

- customisation of this information on a per user basis
- addition of descriptions for user defined functions

As shown in Figure 3.2, the Book consists of two panels. The top panel displays function icons and the lower panel, a scrollable text description of the selected function. Descriptions are accessed by selecting a component from the Component Browser, or Workspace, and dragging and dropping it onto the Book.

The Book provides cut and paste and general text editing facilities to allow descriptions of functions to be added or changed. This allows the user to annotate or enhance existing function descriptions with their own notes. Once the user has created a new function a description of the operation of the function can be added to the Book.

Component icons displayed in the Book can be selected and dragged to other tools, such as the Workspace, for use.

The Component Browser

The pre-defined library components provided by VPL are stored in a database. This database is structured, grouping components into categories. Each user has their own copy of this database which represents a persistent store of functions and descriptions that can be modified and extended by the user.

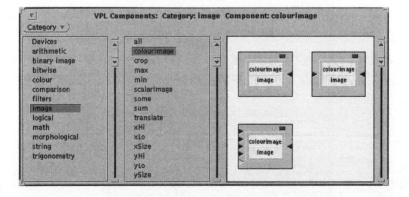

Figure 3.3. The Component Browser.

The Component Browser provides access to functions in the database through category and component lists. The user can view component icons by selecting the appropriate category and component names from these lists. Figure 3.3 shows the *colourimage* component icon. The arrows on the icon represent input and output ports for the component and the square in the top right hand corner is a copy button. To use a component it must first be selected and then dragged from the Component Browser and dropped onto the Workspace. A menu associated with a component's icon allows the user to display the type signature information of the inputs and outputs for that component.

Programs created in the Workspace can be packaged as components and stored in the database. The Component Browser supports management of the database by allowing the creation and renaming of categories and the creation and copying of components.

The Workspace

The Workspace is where programs, in the form of executable graphs, are interactively constructed. Such graphs contain three major types of components:

- *Producers* - represent a source of data for a program graph. There are specific Producers for integers, floats, strings and enumerated data items, that allow their values to be interactively modified. When data, for instance an image, is dragged from the Data Browser and dropped onto the Workspace it is packaged as a generic Producer.

- *Consumers* - generate demand for data in the program graph and display the result when it has been calculated. There are two main Consumers, called probes. A data probe, which displays the data on its input, and a type probe which allows the user to see the specific type of the data on its input. A probe's input can be connected to any component's output port to generate demand at that point in the graph.

- *Functions* - represent the bulk of the components in the database. They have input and output ports. They operate on the input data, producing results on output ports.

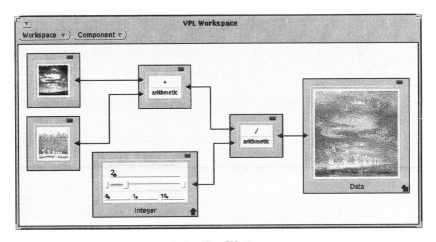

Figure 3.4. The Workspace.

Figure 3.4 shows the graph of a program that adds two images together and scales the resultant pixel values. Program graphs are generated by dragging components and data onto the Workspace and then interactively linking their input and output ports together. As the user builds a program, changes to the graph are communicated to a Graph Evaluator. If the Graph Evaluator determines that it can satisfy a demand in the graph, even in a partially completed graph, then it will initiate execution of the appropriate functions.

Feedback on the progress of execution through the graph is made visible to the user by highlighting the boundary of executing component green. If an error is detected within a component its boundary is made red and, through the component's menu, a dialogue box can be displayed giving information about the type of error.

An important issue of error handling is how to deal with multiple errors, in particular the case where one error produces multiple symptoms. It is all too easy to swamp the user with error messages or present errors in a fashion that is not useful to the user. If multiple errors occur, VPL highlights the boundaries of all the components that generated errors and leaves the user to select the errors they wish to see.

When a program has been constructed and tested it can be turned into a component function and stored in the user's database. This then makes the new function available for inclusion as a component in other programs the user may wish to develop.

The Image Viewer

The results of programs in the Workspace are displayed in data probes, as in Figure 3.5. For image data this representation will often be too small, obscuring detail of interest to the user.

The Image Viewer provides the functionality needed for the viewing of multiple images at different resolutions and orientations.

As shown in Figure 3.5, the left-hand side of the Image Viewer is an image docking area. Images are added to the Viewer by dragging and dropping them onto an empty icon dock which then displays a thumbnail version of the image. An image can then be displayed in the image pane. Once in the image pane an image can be interactively panned, scaled and rotated.

When an image from the Workspace is dragged to the Viewer it remains *live* or *hot-linked* to its source. Updates of the source image in the Workspace are dynamically reflected in the *hot-linked* image. It is possible to *freeze*, and subsequently *unfreeze*, live images in the Viewer.

3.5 Architecture of VPL

The architecture of the VPL system, as illustrated in Figure 3.6, consists of the following major modules:

- The *front end* which provides the user interfaces of the tools, such as the Component Browser, Workspace and Image Viewer.

- The *middle* controls program evaluation through a Graph Evaluator module. Changes to the program graph made in the front end are communicated to the middle where the Graph Evaluator checks for any data that may have been made invalid as a result. If inconsistencies are detected the front end is informed ensuring rapid feedback to the user. The Graph Evaluator then initiates evaluation of new data values.

- The *Hub* handles communications between the major system processes i.e. the front end, middle and the database.

- The *database* process provides management and access to the components and their descriptions. It presents a persistent information store to the rest of the system.

- The *back end* contains the image processing library and performs data computations under the control the middle.

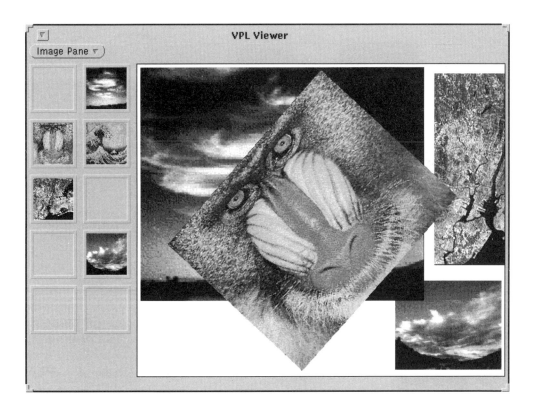

Figure 3.5. The Image Viewer.

The VPL system was implemented on Sun SPARCstations using C++ for the middle and the database. The front end was written in NeWS, which is the extended PostScript language provided by Sun's OpenWindows window system. The VPL system is implemented with multiple processes and uses both synchronous and asynchronous communication mechanisms to connect them. The benefits of this are:

- the ability to distribute VPL processes to other machines on a network. This allows VPL to take advantage of any specific hardware capabilities that might exist on a network. For instance running the image processing on a machine with large memory and computational resources.

- the front end can remain responsive even while image processing is in progress. This satisfies one of the requirements discussed in the Design Aims.

- to a large degree the front end can be isolated from, and provide immediate feedback on, errors in other parts of the system.

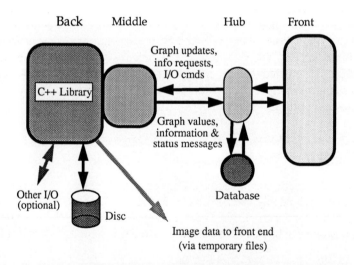

Figure 3.6. Architecture of the VPL System.

VPL provides a declarative language that supports function overloading. For example the add function can be used to add two numbers together or a number to an image. To support this a dispatcher is needed to determine, at runtime, the particular function that should be called based on the types of the arguments.

However, for a large image processing library, such as VIEW-Station (Tamura *et al.* 1989) which consists of over 1000 functions and 75 types, developing and testing such a large dispatcher is a considerable problem. Our solution was to automate the process by machine-analysing the library header files and automatically generating the dispatching code.

As well as greatly reducing the work required to upgrade and maintain the dispatcher code, this method also has the advantage that it makes the task of adapting to other compatible image processing libraries easier. To date we have built two versions of the VPL system, one using the V-Sugar library from VIEW-Station system, and the other using an image processing library developed at CRE.

3.6 VPL as a programming language

As has already been highlighted, VPL provides a powerful programming language. Functions in VPL are *first class* objects and as such can be referenced in the same ways as data objects. In addition, VPL supports higher-order functions i.e. functions can take functions as arguments or return them as results. These two capabilities provide the mechanisms by which the generality and flexibility of the programming model can be enhanced.

Before presenting an example of the creation of a program control structure it is necessary to explain the operation of the following higher-order functions:

- the *Select* component has three inputs and one output. When a *Select* component is executed the output value it generates is dependent on the value on its first input port. If this has the value "true" then the value on the second input port is forwarded to the output. If the value is "false" then the output value is obtained from the third input port. It should be remembered that this is a demand driven system and as such demand on the *Select* component's output will first cause demand to be propagated to the first input and only then to the second or third input.

- the *Apply* component takes a function on its first input and applies it to the argument list on its second input.

- the *Generic Producer* component is a Producer (as described in the earlier Workspace section) that can hold any VPL data item. Because VPL functions are first-class objects it can also hold a function. This component then provides the basic mechanism by which a function can be passed to other higher-order functions such as Apply.

The Repeat Component

As an example of the capability to build new control structures consider the *Repeat* component. A definition for this component is that it should apply the function on its second input to the argument list on its third input the number of times specified by the value on its first input.

Figure 3.7 shows the program graph representing the *Repeat* function as defined above. Briefly the operation of the graph is: while the first input of the *Select* component is "true" i.e. while the value on the first input of the *Repeat* component is greater than zero, demand is generated on its second input. This causes a recursive call of the *Repeat* component with the value on its first input reduced by one and the argument list on its third input processed by applying the function on the second input of the current invocation of *Repeat* to that argument list.

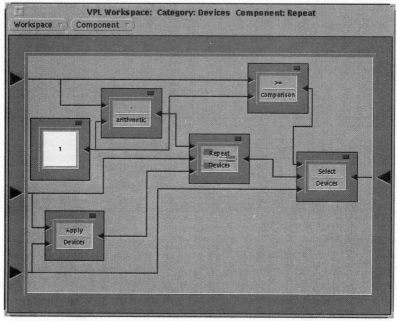

Figure 3.7. Specification of the Repeat function.

3.7 An example

This section gives an example of a simple image processing operation. The set of Figures 3.8-3.12 illustrate the sequence of interactions performed by the user in building a program. The purpose of this program is to allow the user to interactively modify the colour balance of an image. In this example we want the user to be able to individually control the amount of red, green and blue in the image. For example, setting the green and blue controls to 0 will leave only the red component of the image displayed.

To achieve this we scale the colour values of the image with the multiply operator. One argument to the multiply function being an image and the second the user defined colour value.

The sequence of actions required to create and execute this program is as follows:

- Find the float producer in the Device category of the Component Browser and drag it into the Workspace. The producer is edited so that its range is between 0.0 and 1.0 with a step of 0.1. This modified instance of the float producer in the Workspace is now copied twice by dragging and dropping from its green copy button.

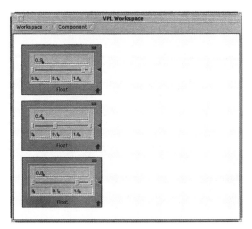
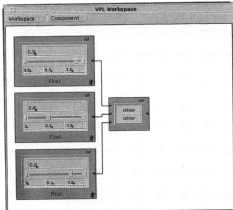
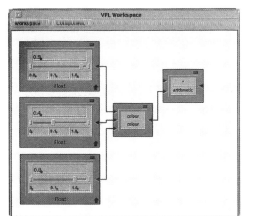
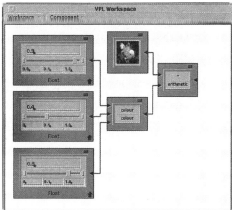
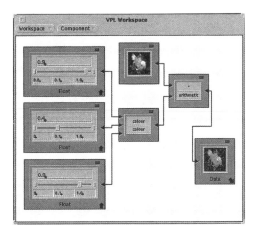

Figures 3.8-3.12. Illustrate the sequence to build an image colour balance program

- The colour function in the Colour category of the Component Browser is selected and dragged to the Workspace. Its input ports are wired to the output ports of the float producers. The output of this function is a red, green and blue (RGB) colour triple.

- Next, the multiply function is located in the Component Browser and dragged to the Workspace. One of its inputs is connected to the output of the colour function. The other input of the multiply function will be connected to a producer containing the image to be modified. The function will multiply the colour image, pixel by pixel, with the colour triple. The result of this will be a version of the input image with its red, green and blue colour components scaled appropriately by the colour triple.

- The image the user wishes to modify is located with the Data Browser and dragged onto the Workspace. The output port of the image producer is wired to the remaining input port of the multiply function.

- The program graph is now ready to execute. All that is required for the program to start executing is for a demand to be placed on the output of the multiply function. This is achieved by wiring the input port of a data probe to the output port of the multiply function.

When execution of the program is complete a new image will appear in the data probe. If the user changes the value of any of the colour controls, the program will generate a new colour triple and apply this to the input image. Thus a new image, with a different colour balance, is generated. The order in which the program graph was created in this example is not important.

3.8 Conclusions

The example given in the previous section demonstrates the nature of the programming process in VPL. Programs can be constructed and executed using simple mouse-based interaction techniques. Taken together with the interactive input and data display support, the VPL programming environment leaves the user free to concentrate on performing the required task.

The tools provided by VPL present a structured access to functions, definitions of their input, output interface and descriptions of their operation. The ability to package program graphs as functions enables the user to create new functions and extend the library. This packaging also aids in managing the complexity of larger programs by presenting the program in a hierachical, black box style.

From the user's point of view there are two areas where VPL could be improved. The first is interaction with image data. Image processing is often performed on some part of an image, perhaps a set of lines from the image or a rectangular region. Although VPL has the functionality to perform these operations it should also let the user identify areas of interest by interactively selecting them on the image itself. Secondly, the functionality of the Book could be enhanced. The addition of searching facilities would allow the user to form queries to establish which functions produce data of type Colour for instance, or others based on the descriptions of the functions. This would allow users to explore the range of function available as well as identify functions that perform particular operations.

3.9 Future

VPL is an example of visual programming applied to image processing, but what of the future for visual programming? When will visual programming techniques be applied to more general programming and user interface environments?

Currently people use many different text based programming languages. This situation exists because no one language has proven "best" for all tasks. Program development on UNIX systems for instance, may involve the use of at least three different languages. A language, for example C or C++, to develop application algorithms and scripting languages as provided by "shell" and "make" utilities to support development and installation of the application. It is not likely, in the near future, that a single visual language could replace all of these.

Our experience from developing VPL is that using current interface and systems technologies, highly interactive visual programming environments are difficult to generate. Clearly more research is required to determine:

- when visual programming and direct manipulation techniques can be usefully applied
- the possibility of providing multiple forms of program specification
- underlying mechanisms required for such systems and to determine how best to provide them.

Acknowledgements

The VPL project was sponsored by the VIEW-Station image processing group at Canon Information Systems Research Centre in Japan. Recognition is due to the following people for their work on the VPL system over the last few years, David Lau-Kee, Paul Otto, Mark Smith, Ian Wilkinson, Yasuo Kozato and Adam Billyard.

I would also like to thank Colin McCartney and Ian Wilkinson for their help and suggestions for improving this chapter.

References

Glinert E. (1987). Out of Flatland: Towards 3-D Visual Programming, *Proceedings Fall Joint Computer Conference,* IEEE Computer Society, Dallas, Texas, pp 292-299.
Glinert E. (1990a). *Visual Programming Environments: Applications and Issues,* IEEE Computer Society Press.

Glinert E. (1990b). *Visual Programming Environments: Paradigms and Systems*, IEEE Computer Society Press.

Hirakawa M., Iwata S., Yoshimoto I., Tanaka M. & Ichikawa T. (1987). HI-VISUAL Iconic Programming, *Proceedings IEEE Workshop on Visual Languages*, IEEE Computer Society, Sweden.

Lau-Kee D., Kozato Y., Otto G.P. & Tamura H. (1990). Software Environment of Vision and Image Engineering Workstation - A Prototype Visual Programming Language for Image Processing, *Proceedings of 41st National Conference of the Information Processing Society*, Japan. (Published in Japanese).

Lau-Kee D., Billyard A., Faichney R., Kozato Y., Otto P., Smith M. & Wilkinson I. (1991). VPL: An Active, Declarative Visual Programming System, *Proceedings IEEE Workshop on Visual Languages*, IEEE Computer Society, Japan.

Myers B. (1990). Taxonomies of Visual Programming and Program Visualisation, *Journal of Visual Languages and Computing* 1, 97-123.

Sato H., Okazaki H., Kawai T., Yamamoto H. & Tamura H. (1990). The VIEW-Station Environment Tools and Architecture for a Platform-Independent Image Processing Workstation, *Proceedings of the 10th International Conference on Pattern Recognition*, Atlantic City.

Tamura H., Sato H., Yamamoto H., Okazaki H. & Kawai T. (1989). The Software Architecture of an Image Processing Workstation, *Proceedings of 6th Scandinavian Conference on Image Analysis*, Oulo, Finland.

Tanimoto S.L. (1990). Viva: A Visual Language for Image Processing, *Journal of Visual Languages and Computing*, 1(2).

Upson C., Faulhaver T., Kamins D., Laidlaw D., Schlegel D., Vroom J., Gurwitz R., Van Dam A. (1989). The Application Visualisation System: A Computational Environment for Scientific Visualisation, *IEEE Computer Graphics and Applications*, 9(7), 30-42.

Williams C.S., Rasure J.R. (1990). A Visual Language for Image Processing, *Proceedings IEEE Workshop on Visual Languages*.

4

Human Psychology in Virtual Environments

David Travis, Toby Watson and Mike Atyeo

4.1 Introduction

VRR: What do you think is the greatest obstacle facing the VR industry and why?
Latta: Lack of basic research. The issues of having the most intimate form of human computer interface in Virtual Reality necessitate a thorough understanding of human perceptual, muscle and psychological systems. Yet that research foundation does not exist.

Dr John Latta interviewed in *Virtual Reality Report*, 2 (7) p 4.

Why apply psychology?

It is an unfortunate truth that the first-time visitor to a virtual environment is frequently disappointed by the experience. The visitor usually expects to enter a world defined by state-of-the art graphic objects and begin to interact with them in an intuitive way. But with even the very best equipment, the image quality is poor and there are significant time lags when the visitor moves the head. Moreover, interacting with these images is akin to feeling for an object in the dark - while wearing boxing gloves.

McLellan (McLellan 1992) reviews the key design issues in virtual environments raised by leading industry analysts. Jonathan Waldern (of W Industries) argues that the most difficult issue is user considerations (including anthropometric, ergonomic and health and safety factors); Myron Krueger (Krueger 1991) lists nine factors in the design of artificial worlds, virtually all of which impinge on the domain of psychology, including visual expectations, optical flow as the user moves through space, motion sickness and resolution. Tom Furness, director of the Human Interface Technology Laboratory warns that VR companies designing

Interacting with Virtual Environments Edited by Lindsay MacDonald and John Vince
© 1994 John Wiley & Sons Ltd

products without an understanding of human factors principles are creating a problem for the industry.

The approach

It seems there is a general belief that behavioural science has something to contribute to the design of virtual environments. In the field of human-computer interaction, there is wide agreement that in order to design effective systems, the systems must be *user-centred*. In practice, this means the following objectives must be achieved: (see for example Gould 1988, Shneiderman 1987, Norman and Draper 1986, Chapanis and Budurka 1990):

- identify tasks users must perform
- learn user capabilities
- learn hardware/software constraints
- set specific usability targets in behavioural terms
- iteratively incorporate changes and test until behavioural targets are met (or a critical deadline is reached)

The first part of this paper considers immersion as a defining characteristic of virtual environments. It asks the question if this quality is a useful or necessary one. The second part of the paper addresses the tasks for which virtual environments are suited, *i.e.* the tasks users must perform and how virtual environments may help. The final part of the paper concentrates on user capabilities within the context of the hardware and software constraints, and considers the usability targets that should be met.

4.2 The great immersion debate

What is virtual reality?

There is a polarisation in the industry as to what constitutes virtual reality. Vendors of helmet-mounted display systems use this as a defining feature of virtual reality, whereas vendors of desktop or "through the window" systems are more generous in their definition of what constitutes virtual reality. The hub of the argument centres on what the system requirements are for true immersion. We call this discussion the Great Immersion Debate, but we argue in this section that it is specious because the debate fails to centre on the most important feature of these systems: the user. The user has a particular task to perform for which immersion may or may not be important.

It is straightforward to derive a set of theoretical parameters for the ultimate virtual environment technology. We know, for example, the resolution of the human eye in space, time and colour, and we could set these as the upper limits for what a head-mounted display should achieve. But what can the technology achieve now?

Cost, performance and resolution are the issues that are keeping VR from becoming a widely used engineering tool. Currently, the technology is of extraordinarily poor quality. On wearing a head-mounted display, the user becomes legally blind. Moreover, head-mounted displays reduce the user's sense of security, freedom of movement, and eye contact with the real environment. The user looks and feels isolated.

Health and safety issues

The key benefit of head-mounted systems is the freedom from the display screen bottleneck. Computer technology has an astonishing processing capacity but the output is limited to a two-dimensional display generally no larger than a sheet of A4 paper. VDU screens are cluttered because users want to keep the tools they use where they can get at them - on the screen itself. This produces screens that are messy and cluttered. Head-mounted systems help release this inherent processing capacity.

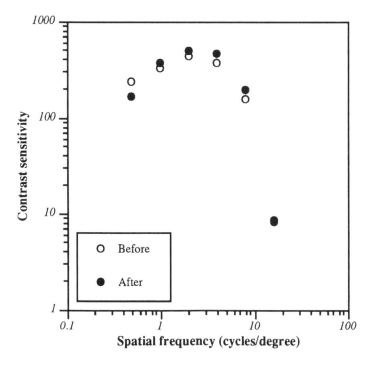

Figure 4.1. The effects of a head-mounted display on contrast sensitivity. Contrast sensitivity was measured to vertical sine-wave gratings using the method of adjustment. Thresholds were measured prior to using a W Industries Virtuality system and again 30 minutes after. Each data point is the average of four threshold settings. Both scales in this Figure are logarithmic.

However, there is some concern that the displays in head-mounted systems may cause eye strain and visual disorders. The concern is that prolonged use could make real-world activities (such as driving) potentially lethal. Such displays are generally viewed at a few centimetres, about ten times closer than the recommended viewing distance for VDUs. This means that the ciliary muscles must work hard to keep the image focused by the lens, and the extra ocular muscles must work hard to converge the eyes so that fusion of the images of both eyes can occur. It is generally accepted that the tension of the ciliary and extra ocular muscles produces visual strain (Jaschinski-Kruza 1988). In fact, there is some evidence (currently unpublished but reported in *Virtual Reality Report* **2** (9), p14) that head-mounted displays can induce deficits in binocular function.

Given the low resolution of the headsets with their clearly visible dot matrix structures, one might expect to find the type of contrast threshold elevations described for example by Lunn and Banks (1986) and Greenhouse, Bailey, Howarth, and Berman (1989) for conventionally viewed CRT displays. However, preliminary work in our own laboratory suggests that prolonged use of a W Industries head-mounted display appears not to affect spatial contrast sensitivity (see Figure 4.1).

Moreover, we know that any immersive system - and not just head-mounted displays - can cause nausea. This is due to the conflict between information from disparate senses (in this case visual and vestibular cues; for a more detailed analysis, see Oman 1991).

The case for non-immersive virtual reality

The fascination with reproducing real-world scenarios is based partly on the fact that "virtual reality" has defined itself by focusing on immersion, or head-mounted, technologies and partly by the most common visual demonstrations (for example, simulation, architectural design and telerobotics) for which the immersion technologies are ideally suited. For certain applications, reproducing reality is clearly a key feature of the application. But this focus means that other, more novel applications, may be excluded. This becomes clearer when we consider the types of application available for non-immersive systems.

One example comes from work we have been involved in at BT Laboratories. As part of a wider programme of work examining enhancements to visual telecommunications services, we have been looking at the potential for 3-D imaging systems for videotelephony and videoconferencing applications. The overall programme has the aim of improving current telecommunications visual services. This programme is long-term; the applications could be realised when the potential bandwidth of optical fibre systems can be exploited on a wider scale - unlimited by video systems which are forced to operate at 64kbit/s. One current 3-D system uses an optical multiplexing technique (Sheat *et al.* 1992) with a 2.5 metre diagonal, curved lenticular screen. Upon this screen we have projected both still (35mm slides) and moving images. Because the image contains true, stereoscopic information, the image appears convincingly three-dimensional, yet the viewer does not need to wear a head-mounted display or spectacles - the three-dimensional image is auto stereoscopic. Our initial approach was to attempt to reproduce exactly the same image as would be seen if the large screen were in fact a window on the world. However, we have found that viewers do not notice depth compressions of down to 50%. Since reducing depth effectively increases bandwidth (that is, more varied scenes may be shown within the "usable" 3-D volume of the display system) we have investigated the options for compressing depth. Intuitively, linear depth compression (where all depths are compressed by the same factor) would seem to be the most useful. In fact, compressing the depth non-linearly (that is enhancing either the foreground or the background, but not both) can give acceptable results. This work is being carried out with human factors involvement at the outset so that the opinions of users of the system are captured and used to drive system development.

For a second example, consider a visit to a virtual supermarket. The user might dial up this virtual shop using a digital communication line and a desktop computer. He or she can then browse through the aisles of the supermarket: this would be a 3-D representation of an idealised shop containing familiar, although not necessarily literal, metaphors. When the user finds the product that he or she wishes to buy, it is selected (perhaps with a mouse) and dragged into a shopping trolley. Finally, passing through the virtual check-out triggers an electronic order for the goods across the telephone line and simultaneously debits the user's credit card. The user benefits by having a simple way to shop; the retailer benefits by having reduced overheads and a market limited only by delivery area. The idea can of course be extended to a virtual shopping mall, which might include banking and insurance services, clothes shops and travel agents. This is a novel application for virtual reality and one for which a focus on reproducing the actual scene is unimportant. Rather, the virtual environment becomes the route to a host of products and services through the gateway of telecommunications.

The idea of using 3-D visualisations presented on a conventional display and interacting with them using a desktop mouse has been further developed at Xerox PARC. This new type of graphical user interface is characterised by the fact that it uses real-time, colour, 3-D, interactive animation (Clarkson 1991). The system has been christened "The Information Visualiser". In this system, information is distributed through a number of 3-D and 2-D rooms, each of which represents an overview of a virtual workspace. Rooms are connected to each other by doors, through which the user can walk from one workspace to another. Each room characterises information using novel visualisations. For example, the Cam Tree visualisation presents hierarchical information (such as an organisational chart or a file directory structure) in a 3-D structure that can be rotated, much as a carousel. The important point is that the information presented is not inherently 3-D in nature, unlike an architectural walk through or a molecular model. As well as allowing the user to grasp the information visually, the Information Visualiser also makes efficient use of the conventional display. For example, another visualisation, the Perspective Wall, resembles a view of a wall broken into thirds. The centre panel provides a detailed view of some linear information (for example, a timeline chart) while the two side panels provide only contextual information. When an object is selected, the wall scrolls around bringing the selected item to the front. This effectively increases the bandwidth of the conventional display.

Synthesising reality

There are several reasons why we must question if we really do want to recreate reality. The first is that the information from our perceptual system can be unreliable. There are numerous examples in the world of perceptual misjudgements: geometric visual illusions reveal conditions where our sensory apparatus misjudges objective facts about the world. A similar example comes from the classic study of Carmichael, Hogan, and Walter (1932). Subjects in this experiment were shown a simple picture (for example, O - O) and told it was one of two alternatives (in this example, either a pair of spectacles or a set of dumbbells). When they were later asked to redraw the picture they had seen, the representation was distorted towards the verbal description that they had been given. Further examples of distortions in visual memory can be found in Tversky (1991). Where we already know about these perceptual misjudgements, it makes sense to design them out of virtual worlds.

The second reason we should question the desire to create a carbon copy of reality is that there are positive advantages to enhancing reality. For example, when using perspective displays, many subjects show a perceptual bias, as if they were looking at the display through a telephoto lens (Ellis 1991). This perceptual bias can be corrected by introducing a "reality" bias - in this case, a compensating wide-angle distortion (McGreevy and Ellis 1986).

A third example comes from the world of training. Intuitively, it might be thought that trainee surgeons should be provided with highly realistic depictions of morphological structures. In fact, photographs taken in the operating room appear spatially flat, because operating lights are diffuse. In order to see depth, medical illustrators apply a directional light source that produces strong highlights and casts shadows. These depth cues produce a visualisation that has far greater clarity than the original scene itself (McConathy and Doyle 1991).

4.3 Task performance criteria

"Virtual reality" has frequently been accused of being a technology in search of an application. Those of us who have demonstrated virtual environments to business or academic colleagues are aware of the refrain "This is great, but what can you use it for?". This problem has been caused by placing the emphasis on the *technology* rather than the *customer*. The majority of the work has been on the development of VR world technologies rather than on meeting user requirements. Surely, the key question to ask is: "What does the user want to do with information?". An answer to this question helps the designer develop a bespoke system fitted to the user's needs. The emphasis then moves away from the technology towards the user. The industry emphasis on the technology is understandable, because the best solution to the customer's needs may not be a virtual environment at all.

Currently, few psychological studies have been carried out demonstrating exactly what tasks virtual environments facilitate (although see Ellis, Kaiser, and Grunwald 1991). It seems self-evident to say that they are good for visualising and understanding complex, 3-D environments, and for providing a sense of presence. The aim of this section is to review those specific areas where virtual environments appear to offer value.

Entertainment

Entertainment is currently the most active market for exploitation of VR. The main reasons for this are (a) image quality is not as important as in other applications; (b) standards and compatibility with existing equipment is not a significant issue resulting in a quick time to market and an atmosphere in which innovation is positively encouraged; and (c) the publicity surrounding virtual environments has primed the market.

W Industries have successfully sold both standalone and networked systems in the arcade market. Reports are of sales exceeding $11 million in 1992 (a 600% rise since its launch in 1991); the venture capitalist company Apax Partners recently invested £2.4 million in W Industries. Virtuality centres now operate in the USA, Japan, Germany, Hong Kong, Korea, Australia, Switzerland, Thailand and Israel, as well as the UK.

The first commercial application of interactive VR to the entertainment field was the BattleTech Center in Chicago (owned by Virtual World Entertainments). Participants pay $7 for a ten minute battle game, which involves them not donning goggles and gloves, but entering networked simulators. A demographic study has shown that most participants are males with an average age of 23. The centre is reported to be successful, with immediate plans to open about a dozen more. A Japanese installation reported that over 30000 games had been played on its 32-machine system in its first month. A similar example in the UK is the Nottingham "Legend Quest" centre. "Legend Quest", owned by Virtual Reality Design and Leisure (VRDL), is a Dungeons and Dragons entertainment, based on four networked W Industries Virtuality systems. The centre reached break even only six weeks after opening its doors at the end of January 1992. Within five years VRDL expect to have 150 centres in the UK and 320 in the USA.

W Industries' systems are currently very expensive (£25-30k), and clearly not aimed at the home market. The respected market analyst, Dr John Latta of 4th Wave, estimates that a home VR game could capture up to 25% of the homes games market. The value of the current games market is estimated to be £845 million (£470 million on hardware and £375 million on software). Dr Junji Nomura, leader of the Matsushita kitchen simulation (see below), has said that "VR in home entertainment systems will need a cost reduction of two orders of magnitude". One interesting development towards this end is the Mandala system. The Mandala system uses a video camera and a computer to allow the user to step into and interact with computer generated and video worlds, live, without physically touching or wearing anything. For example, users can assign sounds to a virtual drum kit, then integrate their own imagery into interactive scenarios of their own design. With the increasing availability of existing home video cameras, this may soon become the first VR system taken up widely by the home entertainment market.

Education and training

The education and training market has developed more in the last 30 years than in the last 300. It has evolved from classroom to broadcast to distance learning. Current distance learning packages are becoming increasingly multimedia, and increasingly interactive. VR is the logical next step.

VR has been used in sport skill acquisition, training surgeons (see below), teaching school children (at West Denton High School in Newcastle), industrial training, and of course for flight and military simulations. Boeing Aircraft, in collaboration with the University of Washington's HIT Lab, have investigated the feasibility of using VR for the design of aircraft. Completed virtual designs are built to allow maintenance staff to virtually "climb all over" the concept, and assess potential problems with maintenance - before the financial commitment of "tooling up".

NEC have recently announced a VR ski training system as part of a project in sports computer-aided instruction. The novice wears a head-mounted display incorporating a position sensor and stands on two mobile steel plates driven by a "slope simulation machine" that induces tilt and vibration. The goal of the system is to teach the student how to shift weight to maintain balance and how to anticipate the need for corrective action.

Interestingly, for many types of training (for example fighter pilots) the key factor in training is to get effective collaboration and teamwork. Situational awareness is important: that is, the user needs to know what he or she was doing when the error was made. Consequently, image quality is less important, suggesting that this is an area that can be fully exploited now.

Medicine

Medical applications have been various. At the University of North Carolina, Chapel Hill, VR has been used to plan radiation therapy treatment. At the University of Leeds, VR has been applied to clinical psychology, especially in the field of anxiety related disorders such as phobias. Stanford Medical School have investigated the feasibility of a "virtual cadaver" for training surgeons.

At BT we are currently investigating the potential that this new technology offers for people with special needs. The main route for exploitation here is that VR offers new input and output devices that could enable those people with restricted mobility to meet and travel in a virtual world in ways that are not possible for them in the physical world. They could virtually shop, deal with their bank, work and play without the need to leave their home. They would be able to deal with able-bodied people without prejudice in this environment. In the longer term, the work aims to ensure that disabled people are not inadvertently excluded from using VR communication. VR technologies appear to offer further opportunities to assist people in participating more fully in the community. "Lost Citizens" are estimated to cost the US economy $175 billion per annum. Moreover, the recently passed Americans with Disabilities Act includes legislation designed to ensure that public buildings and spaces accommodate the needs of the physically disabled. This is an architecturally challenging task; but recently the Hines Rehabilitation and R&D Center have announced a VR tool that enables the physically disabled person to experience an architectural design and readjust cupboards, tables or other objects to better suit his or her needs.

Visualisation

VR provides enormous opportunities for analytic visualisation. There exist numerous demonstrations of visualising the very large (e.g. the Mars Navigator - a fly over the surface of Mars) and the very small (manipulating molecules); and VR is used in aircraft and driving simulators, architectural design, and to model economic, weather and financial data.

BT are currently looking at virtual environments to provide an interface to network management databases, enabling network managers to see patterns in complex information, and "fly through" the network. GEC are also investigating the potential of VR as an interface to telecommunications systems.

Shamrock Development, a UK based company, have recently described a VR tool that simulates the behaviour of groups of people in the presence of fires. Reports from survivors of fires show that they behaved in unusual but predictable ways. People do not immediately flee from the fire; some gather at a "safe" distance to look at the fire; mothers separated from children push against the flow. In one simulation, the company were able to demonstrate that simply increasing the width of one door by 20 cm doubled the speed at which people could evacuate the building. The company see this as a planning and training tool and not to be used for risk assessment.

High technology companies, including telecommunications companies, generate an enormous amount of data, most of which is stored and later archived but largely ignored because it cannot be visualised. This makes visualisation a promising area for virtual environments, especially since the user can "step into" the visualisation and manipulate it.

Networking

The real power of VR is in networking. Networked VR could ultimately steal market share from the travel industry as people choose to "travel by computer"; this is good news for the environment, and of course for the telephone company. However, at the moment, most suppliers are providing *systems* capable of being networked, but there are few networked *applications*. One of the best is Myron Krueger's VIDEODESK Teletutoring system (Krueger 1991). In this system, an image of the user's hands is superimposed upon whatever application is operating on the computer. The user's fingers can then be used as pointers: for example, to select from a menu, or to draw. The system has been networked over ISDN to allow a teacher at a remote site to communicate with a student.

Most information industry commentators agree that the future of databases lies in their global availability via broadband networks, the kinds of telecommunications links that will be widely available by the turn of the century.

Telepresence

Telepresence involves remote control of machines (usually robots) over a distance. Although this involves only one user, the application requires use of a network to transmit commands, and recently in the USA the telephone network was used by VPL Research Inc. (in California) to send control messages to paint-spraying robots at a construction plant in Japan. To overcome the transmission delay, predictive graphics were used to model the future state of the world, after the robot had acted. Future uses of telerobotics will be aimed at removing humans from hazardous environments, such as fires or nuclear accidents.

BT have developed a telepresence system called CAMNET. The heart of the system is a headset with earphones, a microphone and a miniature video camera. Information can be transmitted to a visual display anywhere in the world, allowing anyone, anywhere, to be the eyes of another person. The practical applications of this are endless: the hospital doctor can advise the paramedic at the crash scene; the designer can tell the engineer pitched on top of the satellite dish which wires to connect; specialist engineers could inspect a device without flying to the other side of the world.

Business applications

In 1989, Matsushita Electric started to participate in a major project sponsored by MITI called the "Housing Development Project for the 21st Century". Its purpose is to take a long-term strategic look at all aspects of housing design and construction. Matsushita decided to look at kitchen visualisation, and believed that VR was an appropriate solution. Consumers are able to experience many aspects of their kitchen before they commit to it - they can open cabinets, turn on taps, walk around, listen to the radio. They can also change the choice and layout of the units and appliances, and can experiment with colour schemes. The whole process is closely tied in with production which means once the customer is satisfied with the virtual kitchen and places an order, Matsushita can manufacture it within five days as a customised configuration. The system is now used daily by kitchen designers and consumers to experiment with kitchen layouts and facilities. It was seen by over 4000 people during 1991 and has proven to be highly successful. Matsushita have reported to us that before using the kitchen simulation, 32% of consultations resulted in a sale; now this figure has risen to 68% (personal communication). Interestingly, this is the only VR application so far designed that actually generates sales.

The key virtual environment for business applications will be a non-intrusive, 3-D interface for the desktop. BT have developed a demonstrator called Future Desk. Future Desk looks like a conventional desk, apart from a glass plate set into the desk top. When activated, images with a 3-D quality move around on top of the glass plate giving a sense of heightened reality to visual communications. The desk itself is active with an inductive working surface to allow battery charging and communication to cordless peripherals.

Summary

This section has summarised a number of current applications for virtual interface technology. The demonstrations are compelling, but need to be supported by extensive user testing. For each application, a major group of potential users must be defined and a formal task analysis carried out. Testable behavioural target goals should be set (see "Usability criteria" below) and follow-up studies should be made on people who are using these systems.

4.4 User performance criteria

Interacting with images - virtual or otherwise - has two key components. First, we must perceive (that is, see and process) the image: generally (but not exclusively) through our eyes. Second, we must manipulate the image: generally by using some pointing device such as a mouse or a glove. This paper addresses these areas using the framework of sensory psychology. In particular, we argue that one aim of future research should be to derive a set of performance characteristics that virtual interface technology can use as a benchmark. For more detailed information on this approach the reader is urged to consult the comprehensive volume edited by Ellis, Kaiser and Grunwald (1991).

Sensory filters

Our senses are merely detectors, albeit biological ones, and they have a restricted range of operation. This is seen elegantly in the case of human colour vision. Our sensitivity to spectral radiation is not constant through the electromagnetic spectrum; rather, we sample the electromagnetic spectrum through a pair of filters (see Figure 4.2). One filter, provided by the spectral sensitivity of the rod photoreceptors, has maximum sensitivity around 500 nm (Dartnall, Bowmaker, and Mollon 1983). A second, provided by the pooled responses of the three cone photoreceptors, has maximum sensitivity around 555 nm (Travis 1991). Below 400 nm and beyond 700 nm we are effectively blind. In vision, filtering occurs not just in the colour domain, but also in space (Blakemore and Campbell 1969) and in time (Hammett and Smith 1992). So there is a wide range of information that meets our eyes but which is ignored because it falls outside our "window of visibility" (Watson and Robson 1981). If we wanted to create the ultimate reality machine, sensory psychology would provide the key data in order to ensure that the world is not over designed. It would tell us exactly where we could make compromises and which information we could dispose.

Vision

Despite the obvious benefits, there have been few attempts to design visual displays based on a model of human vision. However, one oft-cited idea has been to design displays that exploit the declining sensitivity of the human eye with eccentricity. We are all aware of the fact that our vision is best in the centre of our field of view (the fovea): this is because the corresponding area of retina is subserved by a greater density of cone photoreceptors. In theory, if the direction of gaze could be accurately tracked, then the viewer could be provided with a high-resolution insert in the display. Within this area, processing power could be concentrated in order to provide the fovea with ample resolution; outside this area, resolution would be lower providing the visual system only with contextual information. In practice, this is not a simple task to achieve, partly because of display limitations, but mainly because the eye muscles are the fastest in the human body (Alpern 1982) - this makes tracking the fovea a very difficult task (for some flavour of the research in this area see Zangemeister 1991).

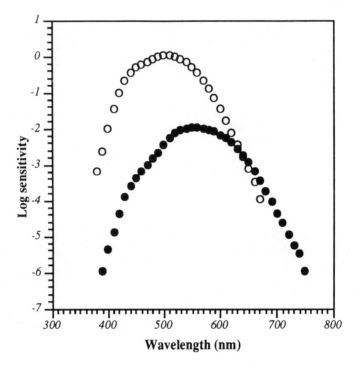

Figure 4.2. Photopic (filled circles) and scotopic (open circles) spectral sensitivities.

How much resolution is enough? The answer depends very much on the application. For some tasks resolution can be quite crude: for example, Cha, Horch and Normann (1992) report on the development of a visual prosthesis for partially restoring functional vision to the blind. Their work shows that a 25 x 25 array of pixels is sufficient to walk through a maze which included a series of obstacles. However, for some tasks - for example, surgery - a 1000 x 1000 array of pixels may not be enough. And of course, the issue is not simply the number of pixels but also their spacing and the distance at which the display is viewed.

Other senses

When considering perception of images we tend to think naturally about visual perception. But it is not necessary to look only at improving visual displays to make virtual environments more compelling. The reason for this is that our senses exhibit redundancy.

Imagine a helter-skelter ride at the seaside. On entering a sharp descent, I can see I am travelling at some speed towards the sea. Information from my other senses, although compelling, is largely redundant: they are not providing any great information that is not already being provided by my visual system. But now imagine the same ride in darkness - a trick frequently used by designers of helter-skelter rides to make it a more thrilling experience. As I enter the descent I am given this information from my vestibular sense. The wind on my skin confirms the fact that I am travelling at some speed. The noise of the tracks on the rails and the screams of other riders informs me that this is probably a ride at a fun fair. I know I am at the seaside, because I can smell the sea and taste the salt in the air. Robbed of the sense of vision I am still able to piece together a representation of the world which is just as compelling as the visual representation.

The point of this anecdote is that we should not concentrate on improving the visual image alone. Indeed, since current technology represents the visual world so poorly we have an opportunity to make virtual worlds more compelling by providing information to our other senses. Nor is this such a difficult task because our other senses are more easily fooled. Even a budget priced audio system can provide the illusion of being at a concert, so long as I close my eyes.

There is much work still to be done on the interaction between the senses in virtual environments. For example, despite user calibration of data gloves, there is still some decorrelation between the sensory information (the position of the virtual hand in space) and the kinaesthetic/tactual system (the position of the actual hand in space). Experiments with prismatic goggles that displace the visual environment have shown that users can adapt to these decorrelations by recalibrating their sensory-motor systems (Held, Efstathiou and Greene 1966; Welch and Cohen 1991). However, on removing the goggles, the sensory-motor system needs calibrating once more - and this could be unacceptable in certain conditions (for example, where users may be operating machinery soon after using the system).

Interaction

A virtual world with which we cannot interact is one in which we can affect limited useful work. Interaction affects perception. Without interaction our view of the world is predetermined by someone or something else: we are limited to a particular path through the world and a particular perspective. By perspective we mean a view, a set of filters, a way of dividing up the world. Perspective enables us to present information relevant to some goal or exploration while irrelevant information recedes into the background. We distinguish three types of information in virtual environments: space, the objects within in it and the people - other cybernauts.

When interacting with space it makes sense to use a real world metaphor. This restricts us to certain spatial constraints and to certain navigation rules (for instance, we seek the correct floor of a building before the appropriate place on the floor). We are used to being limited in this sense, and it reveals major axes of the information structure to us. For example, in a building various working groups are organised by floor, and the people on each floor have a closer relationship than with people on other floors. But we may choose in a virtual world to re-orient ourselves, to actually change the structure of the building in order to gain another significant perspective. For example, a personnel manager may wish to re-orient the structure in terms of years-of-service: we may then have a (virtual) building in which the new recruits are on one floor, longer-term employees on another and contractors on a third. Alternatively, we may choose to order the building and staff according to the projects that are currently active; and each time we receive the familiar building structure, but with a different projection of the database of people and tasks within the organisation.

When interacting with objects we are able to imbue the objects with properties they would never have in the real world. For example, at BT Labs research has been carried out into "Emotional icons". Emotional icons are objects that reveal some property about themselves by their behaviour. In terms of a conventional graphical-user interface, a "Save" button may grow in size (and hence urgency) to indicate time since the last storage operation. An icon representing a read-only database may put up a barrier of spikes as the user approaches. An environment in which users are actively encouraged to explore might use icons that importune, to request the user to follow.

But it is interacting with people that offers the most exciting opportunities in virtual environments. Of course, there is the ability to meet with people in a shared space, much as we do currently with the telephone, except that this space will be a visual one. But in addition, virtual environments facilitate interaction in a different time frame. Consider Table 4.1, which shows the ways two different users can communicate in space and time.

Table 4.1. Examples of communication in space-time.

Whereabouts in space	Whereabouts in time	
	Same time	*Different time*
Same space	Face-to-face	Post-it notes
Different space	Telephone	Answer machine, fax

For example, we may wish to chat with a colleague about some project details. If we are in the same office then we can interact face to face, in the same space and time. If we are in a different space (the colleague is in a different office) but the same time frame, then we can pick up the phone or turn to face the videophone. If we share an office but my colleague is absent, then I can leave a note, and get the reply in the future. Finally, I can leave a message on the colleague's answering machine or send a fax: this is communication in a different space and time.

When communicating in a different time frame, the opportunities for interaction are currently negligible. We are simply producing and consuming information at disparate times. With a virtual environment, we can leave any kind of note or message that we can imagine, and we can post it to our colleagues wherever they are in space to be consumed sometime in the future. We could leave a model of an engine and a *doppelgänger* to enact our movements as we repair the engine. My colleague is then free to play back my movements and view them from any perspective they choose. I could leave a script, a story for a virtual actor to animate.

Usability criteria

One final point concerns the usability criteria that we could use to evaluate different virtual environments. We are familiar with virtual worlds defined by their technological abilities: the number of polygons, MIPS, sensor lag etc. Although improvements in some of these areas may be related to improvements in usability, none of them guarantee that the virtual world will be usable. On the other hand, usability criteria list the required levels of usability of a system in a form that can be independently verified. For example, a system that is designed to enable non-technical users to build their own virtual worlds might have the following usability criteria:

20 experimental participants, familiar with computers but with no formal programming skills, will each receive two hours training on world creation using the target system. They will then perform five tasks. On task 1, 90% of the users must complete it successfully in 30 minutes, with no help from the experimenter. They may use all reference and help materials, but no help lines. Task 1 consists of two steps:

1. Design a bat and ball.
2. Enable the ball to be struck by the bat and travel at a velocity commensurate with the force exerted by the bat.
   (...and so on for tasks 2-5).

A specific application, such as the "virtual supermarket" described earlier, might have the following usability criteria:

Test participants, a random sample of persons using a shopping mall who are willing to participate in this experiment, must be able to visit three different virtual shops. In each shop, they must successfully complete at least one purchase using only the instructions contained in the manuals and on-line help. They should complete this task in 30 minutes.

Similarly, individual pieces of technology (such as a data glove or a 3-D mouse) can be evaluated by usability testing. The current unresolved issue is exactly what the criteria should be.

4.5 Conclusions

The design of virtual environments can be approached profitably from the point of view of behavioural science. A review of current applications suggests that an early and continual focus on users - although widely accepted as vital in the design of these applications - is being ignored in favour of a focus on the technology. One example of this can be found in the use of immersion as a defining characteristic of virtual environments: this defining characteristic ignores the tasks that the user may wish to solve. By adopting user performance criteria in the design of virtual environments, we can be sure that the focus is placed on the user and the user's capabilities.

Acknowledgements

We would like to thank the following colleagues who have generously allowed us to mention their work: Peter Cochrane, Gary Dalton, Kim Fisher, Andrew MacGrath, David McCartney, Paul Rea, Dennis Sheat and Steve Whalley.

References

Alpern M. (1982). Eye movements and strabismus. In H. B. Barlow & J. D. Mollon (Eds.), *The Senses* (pp. 201-211). Cambridge: CUP.

Blakemore C. & Campbell F.W. (1969). On the existence of neurons in the human visual system selectively sensitive to the orientation and size of retinal images. *Journal of Physiology*, **203**, 237-260.

Carmichael L., Hogan H.P. & Walter A.A. (1932). An experimental study of the effect of language on the reproduction of visually perceived forms. *Journal of Experimental Psychology*, **15**, 73-86.

Cha K., Horch K.W. & Normann R.A. (1992). Mobility performance with a pixelized vision system. *Vision Research*, **32**(7), 1367-1372.

Chapanis A. & Budurka W.J. (1990). Specifying human-computer interface requirements. *Behaviour and Information Technology*, **9**(6), 479-492.

Clarkson M. A. (1991, February). An easier interface. *BYTE*, p. 277-282.

Dartnall H. J.A., Bowmaker J.K. & Mollon J.D. (1983). Human visual pigments: microspectrophotometric results from the eyes of seven persons. *Proc. Roy. Soc. Lond. B*, **220**, 115-130.

Ellis S.R. (1991). Pictorial communication: pictures and the synthetic universe. In S. R. Ellis, M. K. Kaiser, & A. C. Grunwald (Eds.), *Pictorial Communication in Virtual and Real Environments* (pp. 22-40). London: Taylor and Francis.

Ellis S.R., Kaiser M.K. & Grunwald A.C. (Ed.). (1991). *Pictorial Communication in Virtual and Real Environments*. London: Taylor and Francis.

Gould J. (1988). How to design usable systems. In M. Helander (Eds.), *Handbook of Human-Computer Interaction* (pp. 757-789). North-Holland: Elsevier Science Publishers B.V.

Greenhouse D. S., Bailey I. L., Howarth P. A., & Berman S. M. (1989). Spatial adaptation to text on video display terminals. *Investigative Ophthalmology and Visual Science (Suppl.)*, **30**, 505.

Hammett S.T. & Smith A.T. (1992). Two temporal channels or three? A re-evaluation. *Vision Research*, **32**(2), 285-291.

Held R., Efstathiou A. & Greene M. (1966). Adaptation to displaced vision: a change in the central control of sensorimotor coordination. *Journal of Experimental Psychology*, **72**, 887-891.

Jaschinski-Kruza W. (1988). Visual strain during VDU work: the effects of viewing distance and dark focus. *Ergonomics*, **31**(10), 1449-1465.

Krueger M. (1991). *Artificial Reality II*. Reading, MA: Addison Wesley.

Lunn R. & Banks W.P. (1986). Visual fatigue and spatial frequency adaptation to video displays of text. *Human Factors*, **28**, 457-464.

McConathy D.A. & Doyle M. (1991). Interactive displays in medical art. In S. R. Ellis, M. K. Kaiser, & A. C. Grunwald (Eds.), *Pictorial Communication in Virtual and Real Environments* (pp. 97-110). London: Taylor and Francis.

McGreevy M.W. & Ellis S.R. (1986). The effects of perspective geometry on judged direction in spatial information instruments. *Human Factors*, **28**, 421-438.

McLellan H. (1992). Virtual reality design notes. *Virtual Reality Report*, **2**(5), 8-12.

Norman D.A. & Draper S.W. (1986). *User Centred System Design*. New Jersey: Lawrence Erlbaum.

Oman C.M. (1991). Sensory conflict in motion sickness: an Observer Theory approach. In S. R. Ellis, M. K. Kaiser, & A. C. Grunwald (Eds.), *Pictorial Communication in Virtual and Real Environments* (pp. 362-376). London: Taylor and Francis.

Shneiderman B. (1987). *Designing the User Interface*. Reading, MA: Addison-Wesley

Sheat D.E., Chamberlin G.R., Gentry P., Leggatt J.S. & McCartney D.J. (1992). 3-D imaging systems for telecommunications applications. In *Electronic Imaging Systems and Applications*, 1669 (pp. 186). San Jose, USA:

Travis D.S. (1991). *Effective Color Displays*. London: Academic Press.

Tversky B. (1991). Distortions in memory for visual displays. In S. R. Ellis, M. K. Kaiser, & A. C. Grunwald (Eds.), *Pictorial Communication in Virtual and Real Environments* (pp. 61-75). London: Taylor and Francis.

Watson A.B. & Robson J.G. (1981). Discrimination at threshold: labelled detectors in human vision. *Vision Research*, **21**, 1115-1122.

Welch R.B. & Cohen M.M. (1991). Adapting to variable prismatic displacement. In S. R. Ellis, M. K. Kaiser, & A. C. Grunwald (Eds.), *Pictorial Communication in Virtual and Real Environments* (pp. 295-304). London: Taylor and Francis.

Zangemeister W.H. (1991). Voluntary influences on the stabilization of gaze during fast head movements. In S. R. Ellis, M. K. Kaiser, & A. C. Grunwald (Eds.), *Pictorial Communication in Virtual and Real Environments* (pp. 404-416). London: Taylor and Francis.

5

Visualising Design Ideas

John Lansdown

5.1 Introduction

Besides the *appearance* of artefacts and their environments, designers also need to be able to visualise:

- *abstractions,* such as relationships and connections;
- *behaviour,* that is, performance and attributes of artefacts and systems;
- *movement,* both discrete and continuous.

Some of these elements lend themselves more readily to visualisation than others. Historically, however, designers have invariably used freehand drawing and sketching to help in visualisation - only occasionally might three-dimensional physical modelling also be employed. Contrary to the usual impression, sketching is needed not simply to illustrate completed ideas to others (a process we will call "presentation"). Its main purpose is to help designers to elicit, develop and evaluate the design ideas themselves.

This process of eliciting, developing and evaluating is not confined just to the early stages of design; it permeates designing from start to finish. Initially, sketches are used during discussions with clients when sketches help to more fully explicate needs and requirements. Later, they are used when design teams are discussing the implications of optional courses of action. Right through to the processes of production, sketches are used as the primary tool for interaction with all concerned (Schenk 1991). Visualisation via the act of freehand drawing and sketching then is part of the process of *externalisation* of ideas: something that is an essential feature of designing.

We know, for example, that good designers are better at externalising ideas than their less able colleagues. Good designers carry out externalisation sooner in the design process than poor designers. They also do it more frequently. However, we must not assume from this that the best designers are necessarily the best picture-makers. Jones (1984), in a

Interacting with Virtual Environments Edited by Lindsay MacDonald and John Vince

perceptive article, goes so far as to say that, ". . . many architects (and most engineers) can hardly draw in the picture-makers sense at all". The sketches I refer to here are different from artist's quickly-drawn views of scenes - freehand drawings that are often masterpieces of observation and technique. (See, for example, Marks 1972, who presents artist's sketchbooks from some of the earliest known, such as Adémar de Chabannes' work in the 11th century, through to mid-twentieth century work by artists like Henry Moore and Louise Nevelson).

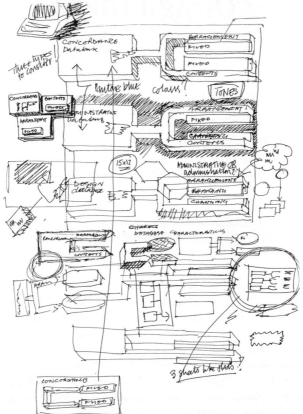

Figure 5.1. Showy sketch for a diagram (original in three colours).

As can be seen from the paper by Scrivener and Clark (1993) and Figures 5.1 and 5.2, design sketches are more akin to visual notes than illustrations. They comprise mixtures of words, diagrams, pictorial images, arrowed lines and so on aimed more at encapsulating ideas and aiding strategic thinking than depicting objects or scenes. In these sorts of sketches, masterful drawing ability is less important than clarity of organisation, well-developed mnemonic qualities and directness of communication. Of course, as in the case of Leonardo's notebooks (Drew 1989), sometimes these characteristics are combined with great drawing ability. This combination turns the results into artworks in their own right. Note though that Leonardo called his notebook drawings *"pensieri"*, that is, "thoughts". An interesting discussion on the relationships between design sketching and "seeing" is found in Schön and Wiggins (1992).

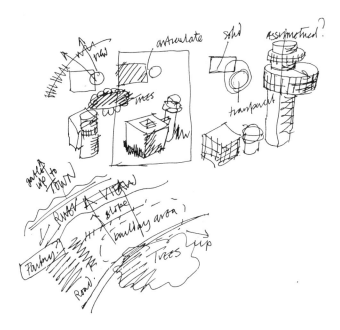

Figure 5.2. Design sketch for building.

5.2 Computer-aided design

Frequently commercial CAD system producers seem unaware that sketching is important to designing and they do not provide their systems with facilities for it to take place. Many so-called computer-aided design systems really expect designers to come to them with ideas already formed in considerable detail. But the amounts of information these systems require for proper working could not possibly be provided at an early design stage. Systems like these are therefore misnamed and should be thought of primarily as computer-aided presentation or production drawing systems.

It could be argued, of course, that computer-based systems will always be wholly inappropriate for the type of sketching I've referred to. Perhaps design sketching is too personally coded, too idiosyncratic, too wedded to pen and paper techniques, ever to be amenable to computer working. There is some force in this argument but I do not wholly accept it. (Although one has to agree with Schön and Wiggins, 1992, that there are design processes associated with sketching that "computers are unable - at least presently unable - to reproduce: the perception of figures or gestalts, the appreciation of qualities, the recognition of unintended consequences of moves". We will examine later whether this inability has any significance.) I believe that - properly configured - a CAD system is *exactly* what is needed in the early, formative stages of design. This is because, despite the ubiquity, necessity and usefulness of paper-based design sketching, it has serious limitations that cannot be overcome simply by improvements in representation, methodology or sketching technique.

5.3 The limitations of paper-based visualisation

We cannot overstate the role played in designing by imagination and intuition: they are elements central to a good designer's armoury. Externalisation can be seen as the way in which imagination and intuition are brought to bear on the design task in hand. In addition to these two things, a designer also needs knowledge and information: indeed, it is possible that knowledge and information are the essential prerequisites of creative imagination and intuition. We can put forward this possibility by referencing the work of those who have studied individual creativity (for example, Akin 1990; Gardner 1983; Guilford 1959; Roe 1952a, 1952b). It clear from this work - and much other - that one cannot be *consistently* creative in a subject unless one knows a great deal about it, and that very creative people have a profound, knowledge-based understanding of those areas in which they create. (The child Mozart is often used as a counter-example to this thesis. As young as five years old, Mozart was able to compose pieces and, by the age of 15, had already created more than 100 works, some of them quite significant. How could someone so young have known a "great deal" about composition? Many myths have grown up about Mozart's genius but we know that his father drilled the infant in the techniques of harmony and composition from the beginning - to an extent that we would now regard as unnatural and perhaps cruel.)

However, designers often forget the relationship between creativity and knowledge. Frequently they think that everything important to a design springs from some inner well of intuition that somehow exists independently of knowledge, reason or information. The artist Kandinsky (1931), who taught designers at the Bauhaus from 1922 to 1933, puts matters in a way that many would support:

"Woe to him who gives himself up to mathematics or reason. . . The works of an artist come from the commonest source of all, intuition. Reason plays a part. It helps, but always as a factor of secondary importance. The intellectual approach by itself, when there is no element of intuition, has never given birth to works of vital quality."

Thus we often find that, in the early formative stages of designing, designers come to important decisions using subjective judgments unsupported by explicit knowledge or information. Some of us would suggest that this was using "guesswork", and not surprisingly this strategy can often lead to problems. We know, for example, that most design failures occur not because those involved are working at the frontiers of human knowledge. On the contrary, most failures, trivial or serious, arise because readily available information has not been properly taken into account. This important point is discussed in more detail in Lansdown (1989).

Of course, if one is an experienced designer, one's intuition is supported by much implicit and explicit knowledge gained simply by exposure to previous design situations. (Downing 1992, is especially relevant to this point, although we should not ignore the negative effects that previous experience has on imaginative thinking - see Birch and Rabinowitz 1951).

When similar situations to those previously experienced arise and are readily coped with, it is natural to assume that it is intuition at work rather than knowledge or systematic thinking - intuition indeed is often defined as "making judgments without explicit or conscious processes of reasoned thinking". But we know that, whilst people are reasonably good at making judgments about situations lying within their experience, they are not good at extrapolating these judgments into previously unencountered situations. Nor are they good at making unaided judgments in multi-attribute cases, that is, ones where many conflicting factors need to be considered. Russo and Dosher (1976), for instance, suggest that systematic errors occur when human beings are asked to choose between five to seven options based on just three criteria. Shepherd (1964) shows that, faced with what appear to be simple choices between geometrical figures possessing as few as *two* attributes (size and orientation), people are unable to make rational and consistent decisions. (To be fair, there are some significant counter-examples: see, for instance, Phelps and Shanteau 1978, as well as Ebbesen and Vonevcni 1980, who take a critical view of some of the research in this area). Generally though, people are not at their best when faced with new situations where choices have to be made while considering many different factors. Designing, however, is characterised by its tendency towards previously unencountered, multi-attribute situations. It is not surprising then that errors occur. What is surprising is that they do not occur more often.

Thus, although designers are conscious of the need to externalise their ideas to expose them to a critical light, they often feel that both the creation and the critical assessment of the ideas can be done entirely intuitively. Even if they do not take this view, the process of external visualisation is so engaging and central to creative design that designers are often unwilling to interrupt the activity to obtain information that might be relevant to the task in hand. In order to continue with the more congenial job of "designing" rather than the less rewarding one of finding necessary information, they use a technique of "deferral". In this they put off consideration of some elements of the task on the (sometimes correct) assumption that these can be dealt with later. This is not to suggest that a hierarchical approach to designing is adopted: there is no sense of "top-down" in this. What is deferred may not be lower down a tree of decisions than something that is examined in detail. Thus, during the process of externalisation, decisions on some important elements may be deferred whilst less important ones are dealt with in depth.

An example of this occurs at the early stages of architectural design when the form of a building is chosen. The shape of a building is an important (and sometimes the major) determinant of the building's life-time cost. A convoluted shape, for example, is likely to be more costly to build than a simple one and, because it has more surface area, will probably cost more to heat. On the other hand, the larger surface area gives opportunity for more window space. This will reduce daylight lighting costs and improve sunlight penetration. It will also bring usually welcome glimpses of the outside to the building's inhabitants. Furthermore, the right shape could minimise the need for air-conditioning even in hot climates. Unfortunately, though, the relationship between shape and cost is not a simple one that might lend itself to easily-applied empirical design "rules". The relationship is both complex and multi-attribute and needs to be examined in detail for each case - often with recourse to extensive calculations and information search. Frequently, though, an architect will develop the form of the building intuitively using sketching, and defer examination of energy and cost implications until later. Unfortunately, when these important items are examined in detail, other major and perhaps irrevocable decisions dependent on the original choice of shape will have been made. Thus the design becomes locked in place, probably making it necessary to take other measures to minimise the problems arising. (I do not wish to suggest by this that, necessarily, cost or energy consumption *are* the most important features of a building design. The important items will differ from case to case and there are many cogent reasons why one would want to choose the shape of a building independently of implications on cost and so on.)

Externalisation by means of conventional sketching then is a strategy that works for those with expert design knowledge who can apply their experience to a well-understood situation. It does not work well:

- when designers are inexperienced;
- when designers (even experienced ones) are faced with unfamiliar situations;
- if the outcome depends crucially on unfamiliar materials, forms or techniques, or is heavily dependent on technology.

5.4 Computing as an aid to visualisation

What is needed in these cases is a system that will help supplement lack of knowledge and experience. Brady (1986) writes about such a system applied to the special case of VLSI design. He found that considerable advantages came from the use of a system that delivered relevant information to designers exactly when it was needed without their having to interrupt the "creative flow". The evidence of his experiments suggests that, given the right sort of system, designers can be much more productive and "creative" than they are when they use conventional methods.

It might be suggested that certain cases - like VLSI designing - would especially lend themselves to this sort of treatment. Arrangement, placement and choice of elements in VLSI designs are highly dependent on factors that require calculation and the sort of manipulations that computer programs are good at (Mead and Conway 1980). In addition, future performance of the designed artefacts can be tested in a comparatively straightforward way using well-understood methods. I would have to concede this point. Clearly some forms of designing rely more on imaginative flair and less on calculation than others. Fashion design, for example, is not like bridge design. Nonetheless, there are general lessons to be learnt. Designing, whatever its outcome, requires information: it is a knowledge-based activity. The information needed is of three forms:

- Global
- Domain
- Task

Global information

This information is that which designers need about the world: the sort of information that is the stock-in-trade of educated people. It is acquired through the process of living via general education, reading, listening and so on. Despite the current growth in provision of multimedia databases of encyclopaedic proportions, it is unlikely that more than a small subset of global information will ever be available in computer-based form. Designers need global information, however, not only to increase their general understanding of the world. They need it too to help trigger imaginative leaps.

Taking just one example more or less at random: that of nanotechnology (Peterson 1992). Nanotechnology is a subject of growing interest to the scientific community. It deals with the manufacture of artefacts at the molecular, atomic and even sub-atomic levels. Based on the rubric propounded by Richard Feynman in one of his Christmas talks that, "there is plenty of room at the bottom", the creation of objects at these minute sizes offers new and exciting challenges undreamed of even ten years ago. The possibilities that nanotechnology - and its related subject, nanobiology - opens up are leading some scientists to rethink, for example, the way in which space exploration will proceed. Rather that send conventional rockets weighing tens of tonnes into space there is an idea gaining ground that quite small "intelligent" quasi-living devices weighing a few kilograms will be better. These devices will be constructed partly from living matter assembled at the atomic level (see, for instance, Hansson 1992). Freeman Dyson's *astrochicken* will become a reality.

The astrochicken, Dyson (1988 p197) tells us, "will not be built, it will be grown. It will be organised biologically and its blueprints will be written in the convenient digital language of DNA. It will be a symbiosis of plant and animal and electronic components".

It is clear that the idea of being able to create "intelligent" objects of surpassingly small size will have a profound influence on design thinking. Already many designed artefacts - refrigerators, toasters, motor vehicles and so on - include microtechnological devices. The presence of these devices has allowed new ideas and new forms of control to flourish. Nanotechnological devices could be incorporated in virtually anything. If nothing else these would allow designers to monitor the way in which their artefacts are used, providing much needed feedback on the assumptions, faults, limitations and successes of their designs. These devices could, for example, check whether and exactly how and where cups of hot coffee are picked up and held. They could ascertain how often and in what circumstances people clean their spectacles, and if and when they try to make adjustments to the frames. They could monitor which house windows are most frequently opened and which not at all, or which door handles are pulled and which push plates are pushed and with what outcomes. The possibilities are endless. They point the way to providing us with essential information for analysing and improving designs. But we do not have to wait for the establishment of nanotechnology to be able to benefit from these ideas: microtechnology could do more for us than it does. Nanotechnology here simply suggests imaginative lines of attack. It acts as a catalyst for new approaches.

However, most information on subjects like nanotechnology is published in specialist journals normally unread by designers. The information, though, is there. Because it is needed by specialists in their own domains, it is often in machine readable form - one person's global information is another's domain information. In some ways, therefore we can think of global information as the sum of all the separate sets of domain information and that which can be deduced from it. What is needed by designers is a system to browse the domain information of other disciplines and report any "items of interest".

The work of de Jong (1979) on FRUMP (Fast Reading Understanding and Memory Program) is relevant in this respect. This system looked at news reports coming over the AP wire service and made a special note of those dealing with earthquakes. It paraphrased these reports in a standard form building up a knowledge base of earthquake details in the process. The paraphrasing was achieved via a script-based program having a vocabulary of about 1200 words and 48 scripts. One can imagine similar programs looking through online publications of all sorts, searching specially for items of interest to particular groups or individuals. What comprised "items of interest" would be tailorable to individual needs.

Domain information

This information is the sort that designers learn about the area of their particular concerns (architecture, fashion, products, VLSI and so on) during their training and practice. In some forms of designing aspects of domain information flow from the exercising of skills: for example, how particular materials - like china clay, or silk, or glass - behave while being worked. This sort of information can only be properly acquired by doing. Nevertheless, a large subset of domain information could be recorded in a design computer system, ready to be retrieved on demand as circumstances arise.

Clearly, systems for different types of designers require different sorts of domain information. However, a major need in almost all design systems is for a store-house of "precedents": images of, and other information about, relevant designs of the past. The role that precedent plays in some forms of designing cannot be over-emphasised and much designing proceeds by progressive refinement of these precedents (Darke 1979; Oxman 1990; Oxman and Oxman 1992). Sometimes this is done overtly with the new design being in some sense a "homage" to the precedent. More frequently the precedent is used as a "prototype" from which new designs are evolved (Figure 5.3).

Perhaps the most successful design prototype is that of the London Underground map designed by HC Beck in 1933. The basic topological form - showing relationships between stations and lines rather than their precise locations - has been in use in London for sixty years. All over the world this form of map, derived from Beck's prototype, has now become the primary means of depicting rail transport systems (see Herdeg 1976, Chapter 5 for a selection of these).

But not only successful precedents need to be recorded. Petroski (1989) explicitly warns us of the dangers of only trying to emulate success and provides cogent examples from bridge design, where trying to do this without also examining failure has led to disaster.

It would be perfectly possible for multimedia systems to store immense numbers of the sort of domain precedents particular designers might need. (We must guard against assuming though that architects, for example, would only require architectural precedents or that product designers would only require product design precedents. The requirements are more subtle than this.) Besides images, plans and sections of precedents, other domain information would be needed. This would be about materials, regulations, manufacturing processes and so on.

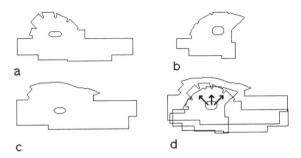

Figure 5.3. (After Ching, Architecture: Form, Space and Order) showing three library plans (a, b, c) by Alvar Aalto which all share the same basic prototype of a fan-shaped book storage space under the control of a central desk (d).

Task information

Domain information is distinguished from task information because it is possible (in theory, at least) to store and retrieve it. Task information is too closely integrated with the particular task in hand to be retrievable: it requires in some sense to be synthesised in each case. For example, it is inconceivable that any system could store details of every staircase that an architect might need. The multiplicity of possible floor-to-floor heights alone would make this impractical. In this case what is required is that, given a floor-to-floor height, the system works out a possible staircase design to suit. It can do this either by creating a finished design or, more likely, by providing the designer with information such as the numbers of treads and risers and their dimensions, whether intermediate landings are needed, whether handrails are required on both sides or just one and so on. To do this the system would need to know the empirical "rules" of staircase design as well as any regulations that apply and how to apply them.

In another domain, graphic design of newspapers or magazines requires setting text and images within a pre-designed grid (Figure 5.4). The grid or grids can be stored and retrieved as necessary but the fitting of the text requires working out in each case. Sometimes, in order to accommodate a particular piece, it becomes necessary to cut or add to the text or to crop an image. Until the advent of computer-based page-setting systems much time was devoted to the process of "copyfitting" - manually calculating the number of characters in a piece of text to ensure that sufficient space was available to accommodate it. Nowadays, this can be done visually by means of WYSIWYG systems but, nonetheless, design skill and judgment are needed. We can look forward, though, to a time when knowledge-based "design assistants" will be available to help in the process of copyfitting and layout. Biles *et al.* (1987) outline some of the possibilities and problems in providing these for non-professional designers.

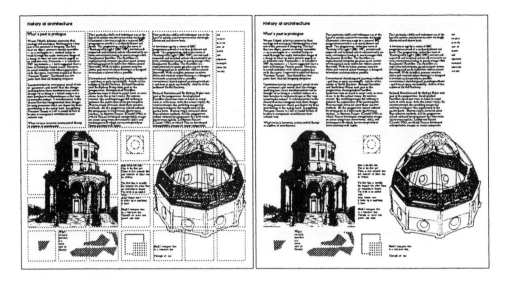

Figure 5.4. A page layout with and without its design grid.

5.5 A description of a possible system

With these points in mind we can suggest the characteristics of a system to help the process of design visualisation.

1. It would be receptive to sketching and handwritten annotations as input. It would not necessarily need to be able to interpret the sketches in the way that Negroponte *et al.* (1972) once hoped might be possible (although this would be desirable). There are considerable pattern recognition problems that arise in sketch interpretation. It is not just that the machine would need to understand what is drawn. It would have to deduce what is *meant*. Further, it would need to be able to do something that people are very good at but that, as yet, computer programs cannot do. This is to be able to recognise what designers call "emergent forms". These are shapes which accidentally arise from the intersection of two or more other shapes and give rise to another level of interest and exploration. Thus, in Figure 5.5, two triangles overlap to produce not only the butterfly shape but four triangles and a square. In the process of designing, such figures continually arise and suggest further developments and lines of progress. Sometimes because, for example, an emergent form on a designed page becomes too eye-catching and insistent, it is necessary to alter a layout to prevent the form emerging.

   As with pen and paper working, the interpretation of the drawings would then be in the hands of designers. The system would however be able to work interactively with the sketched information as well as to rectify it. Thus it would thus be able to do such things as straighten lines that are meant to be straight and turn roughly-drawn circles or freehand curves into geometrical ones and so on. This facility existed in the original Sketchpad system (Sutherland 1963) and, according to the pre-publicity, will be a feature in the forthcoming Apple Newton hand-held computer (Bajarin 1992). The newly-announced Amstrad pen computer apparently can store and display hand-drawn images but seems to have no facilities for working with them.

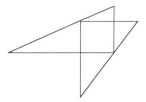

Figure 5.5. Emergent forms: two triangles intersect to produce four triangles and a square.

Although a design system having the qualities described might not be able to "understand" the sketches it receives, it must be able to manipulate the drawings in an object-orientated way once they have been rectified. That is to say, it must be possible to make it group together elements which form meaningful entities and to work with these as a whole. Thus a product designer might want to identify a group of lines that represent say, the handle of an artefact and give a set of attributes to this. Bier and Stone (1986) outline the sort of additional facilities that would benefit the system. These include aligning elements to arbitrary setup lines; automatically closing open figures; allowing lines to be accurately offset from others and so on. De Vries and Wagter (1992) claim rather grandly (or perhaps with tongue-in-cheek) to have designed the "first computer-aided architectural design (sketch-based CAD)" system. What they have in fact done is to suggest a way in which some aspects of sketch understanding might occur and their work is worth examining from that point of view.

2.   The system would have a substantial store of visual precedents: photographs, drawings and similar visual material. These precedents would need to be retrievable by visual means as well as by conventional textual ones. Two possible methods of visual retrieval that suggest themselves are:

   •   Providing pages of thumbnail-size but recognisable pictures of images something in the manner of the VPL Data Browser (Davison, Otto and Lau-Kee 1993) or the VIPS/ip interface (Cupitt and Martinez 1993). These images could be displayed in groups of perhaps 50 or so at a time for search purposes. Thus a search of a CD ROM having about 1000 compressed images could be achieved by glancing at just 20 frames. However, a single videodisc can hold 54000 still images! Searching one of these, even with thumbnail groupings, would present a quite different problem. Browsing this information (when one is stuck for ideas and one needs to seek prototypes to spark off new trains of thought) would be different again. Lansdown (1992) has some remarks about the scale of visual search and browse problems arising when vast amounts of data are available.

- When one is seeking a half-remembered image, a quick sketch of the disposition of parts might be sufficient for a retrieval system to recover at least a selection of possible candidates (Figure 5.6). In Lansdown (1979) I suggested that a similar approach could be tried using the visual mechanism of saccades and fixations as a way of image retrieval. The idea is to store with each image a record of the eye-tracked scan pattern obtained when viewing it. When one wishes to retrieve a particular image one would imagine its appearance on a blank screen and track the saccades and fixations resulting from this visualisation. The pattern arising would then be compared with stored patterns. Obviously the remembered and visualised image would only approximate the desired pattern but, once again, the computer could present the user with 20 or so images whose patterns were a close match (Figure 5.7).

More research will be needed into appropriate methods of visual search before this aspect of the system can be fully realised. Promising routes are suggested by Baron (1985) who proposes a neural network model based on the use of saccades and fixations. This differs from the model that I propose in Lansdown (1979). Bordogna *et al.* (1990) look at documents which contain both text and pictures. Charles and Scrivener (1991); Koons and McCormick (1987); Scrivener and Schappo (1988); and Takahashi *et al.* (1991) all propose interesting possibilities. The analysis by Garber and Grunes (1992) of advertising art directors' picture search protocols is also of relevance.

We should not ignore, too, the 40 years of work that has gone into the Iconclass system of picture classification. This was devised primarily for art historians and museum curators and is essentially a way of describing the contents of art images by means of a comprehensive set of more than 23000 hierarchically arranged and numbered keywords. (The Iconclass descriptions, indeed, run to 17 volumes). Brandorst and Huisstede (1991) and Pountain (1992) describe the Iconclass Browser, a computer program that allows one to examine in hypertext-like fashion connections between and among images that have been classified by Iconclass.

3. The system and its interface should have the facility to be tailored to suit the needs of individual designers or groups of designers - although this facility might not be used as much as might be supposed. Research on the possible extent of idiosyncratic tailoring, for example, is inconclusive: Mackay (1991) suggests that most users will not want to interfere with a standard interface. Gantt and Nardi (1992) found otherwise. They suggest that "gurus" grow up local to a user community. They are entrusted by the community with modifying the interface to suit local needs.

Yet one of the commonest complaints among designers who want to use computers is that these seem to require fixed patterns of work that are alien to them. Especially in the early stages of designing, actual work patterns are necessarily idiosyncratic, unstructured and personal. It is therefore likely that any system that requires designers to conform to some standard set of activities or approaches will not be fully used unless there are

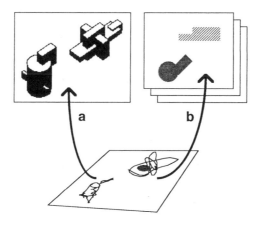

Figure 5.6. How a sketch might be used to retrieve a desired set of images.

substantial benefits from so doing.

Progress has been made on providing congenial tool kits for system designers to create new interfaces simply and quickly. Not much progress, however, has been made in allowing users radically to modify existing interfaces. Similarly there has been little work in providing users with facilities for altering the functionality of existing CAD programs. The experimental program, TelePICTIVE (Miller, Smith and Muller, 1992), is one that allows end users to become involved in the design of an interface but it is still assumed that specialists will do the actual modification or implementation.

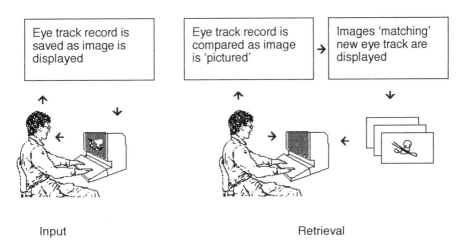

Input   Retrieval

Figure 5.7. How saccades and fixations might be used to retrieve images. The eye track record of viewing the image is recorded on input. When wishing to retrieve the image, the user pictures it on the screen and the eye track of this picturing is compared with the stored tracks and "matching" images are displayed.

4. It must not be forgotten that most artefacts are designed by teams rather than individuals. Most CAD systems do not recognise this fact. Again more research is needed to find the best form for a system to support team working particularly at the early design stage. In broad terms this is a burgeoning area of research that is already beginning to produce experimental results. Shu and Flowers (1992) look at the way in which designers can cooperate to design a three-dimensional object by means of a process of simultaneous editing. Takemura and Kishino (1992) propose the "virtual manipulation concept" which seems to work successfully in tasks involving pairs of workers involved in object arrangement tasks. Luff, Heath and Greatbatch (1992) report on the way in which paper-based systems are being used in parallel with screen-based ones in a design office. Other relevant work is that of Grudin (1991); Ishii (1990); Ishii and Arita (1991); Lowe (1985); Mantei *et al.* (1991); Minneman and Bly (1991); and Tang and Minneman (1991).

5.6 Conclusions

Given a system that has the properties I have suggested, we could look forward to design teams being able to work largely in their present, time-honoured manner but with substantial computer assistance. This assistance will be in the form of:

- more direct translation of sketches to finished drawings;
- provision of large amounts of pictorial and diagrammatic information;
- facility to alter the order and manner of working;
- support for group-based designing.

All this would allow designers to move seamlessly from initial, formative design work through to the making of presentation and production drawings. All members of the design team would hence share common data and models for the purposes of decision making, testing and evaluation. With such an integrated and integrative system, designing could proceed largely as it does now - but with marked improvements arising from what might be called, the "Brady" effect (Brady 1986).

But there is another option. This is to accept that designing by computer *ought to be different* from designing by manual means. This would imply seeking ways of designing that are more appropriate to computer working than designing through the medium of sketching and via the application of intuition. To be of value, these methods would have to produce better outcomes too. This is perhaps not the place to discuss modes of designing that are different from the one that currently holds sway. It is sufficient to flag that other options exist. In the future they will need to be explored. They will give rise to new needs and new opportunities for visualisation.

References

Akin O. (1990). Necessary conditions for design expertise and creativity, *Design Studies* (11) 2 pp107-113

Bajarin T. (1992). Apple Newton, *Personal Computer World*, (15) pp218-221

Baron R.J. (1985). Visual memories and mental images, *International Journal of Man-Machine Studies* (23) 3 pp275-311

Bier E.A. & Stone M.C. (1986). Snap-Dragging, ACM Computer Graphics (20) 4 pp233-240

Biles A., Cort F., Johnson G. & Reek K. (1987). Using expert systems in typographic design, *IEEE Transactions on Professional Communications* (PC-30) 2 pp102-111

Birch H.G. & Rabinowitz H.S. (1951). The negative effects of previous experience on productive thinking, *Journal of Experimental Psychology* (41) pp121-125

Bordogna G., Carrara P., Gagliardi I., Merelli D., Mussio P., Naldi F. & Padula M. (1990). Pictorial indexing for an integrated pictorial and textual IR environment, *Journal of Information Science* (16) pp165-173

Brady J.T. (1986). A theory of productivity in the creative process, *IEEE Computer Graphics and Applications* (6) 5 pp25-34

Brandhorst H. & van Huisstede P. (1991). The iconclass connection: Iconclass and pictorial information systems, *Computers and the History of Art* (2) 1 pp1-20

Charles S. & Scrivener S.A.R. (1991). Searching pictorial databases by means of depictions, *Interactive Multimedia* (2) 2 pp5-16

Cupitt J. & Martinez K. (1993). Image processing for the visual arts, this volume

Darke J. (1979). The primary generator and the design process, *Design Studies* (1) 1 pp36-44

Davison A., Otto P. & Lau-Kee D. (1993). Visual programming language, this volume

de Jong G. (1979). Prediction and substantiation: A new approach to natural language processing, Cognitive Science (3) 3 pp251-273

de Vries M. & Wagter H. (1992). The first CAAD package (sketch based CAD), In Schmitt G.N. (ed) *CAAD Futures '91*, Vieweg, Wiesbaden pp497-510

Downing F. (1992). Conversations in imagery, *Design Studies* (13) 3 pp291-319

Drew J. (1989). *Leonardo da Vinci*, Catalogue of exhibition at South Bank Centre, London

Dyson F. (1988). *Infinite in all Directions*, Penguin, London

Ebbesen E.B. & Konevcni V.J. (1980). On the external validity of decision making research: What do we know about decisions in the real world?, In Wallsten T .(ed) *Cognitive Processes in Choice and Decision Behaviour*, Erlbaum Associates, Englewood N.J., pp21-45

Gantt M. & Nardi B.A. (1992). Gardeners and gurus: Patterns of cooperation among CAD users, In Bauersfeld P., Bennett J. and Lynch G. (eds) *Striking a Balance*, ACM, New York, pp107-117

Garber S.R. & Grunes M.B. (1992). The art of search: A study of art directors, In Bauersfeld P., Bennett J. and Lynch G. (eds) *Striking a Balance*, ACM, New York, pp157-163

Gardner H. (1983). *Frames of Mind: The Theory of Multiple Intelligences*, Heinemann, London

Guilford J.P. (1959). Traits of Creativity, In Anderson H.H. (ed) *Creativity and its Cultivation*, Harper, New York, pp142-161

Grudin J. (1991). CSCW: The convergence of two development contexts, In Robertson S.P., Olson G.M. and Olson J.S. (eds) *Reaching Through Technology*, ACM, New York, pp91-97Kandinsky W (1931) Reflections on abstract art, *Cahiers d'Art* (1) pp7-8

Hansson P.A. (1992). To the stars with the cytoskeleton?, *Journal of the British Interplanetary Society* (45) 10 pp415-420

Herdeg W. (1976). *Diagrams: The Graphic Visualisation of Abstract Data*, Graphis, Zurich

Ishii H. (1990). TeamWorkStation: Towards a seamless shared workspace, In *Proceedings CSCW90*, ACM, New York, pp13-26

Ishii H. & Arita K. (1991). Clearface: Translucent multi-user interface for teamworkstation, *ACM/SIGCHI Bulletin* (23) 4 pp67-68

Jones P.L. (1984). Drawing for designing, *Leonardo* (17) 4 pp269-276

Koons D.B. & McCormick B.H. (1987). A model of visual knowledge representation, In Brady J.M. and Rosenfeld A. (eds) *Proc 1st International Conference on Computer Vision*, IEEE Computer Society, Washington DC, pp365-372

Lansdown J. (1979). Visual databases in the Designers Information Environment, Working Paper, Group Interface Ltd, London

Lansdown J. (1989). The Designers' Information Environment: Tools for design knowledge manipulation, *Civil Engineering Systems* (6) 1-2 pp5-10

Lansdown J. (1992). Mnemotechnics and the challenge of hypermedia, In Cunningham S. and Hubbold R.J. (eds), *Interactive Learning through Visualisation*, Springer, Berlin pp37-47

Lowe D.G. (1985). Co-operative structuring of information: the representation of reasoning and debate, *International Journal of Man-Machine Studies* (23) 2 pp97-111

Luff P., Heath C. & Greatbatch D. (1992) Tasks-in-interaction: Paper and screen-based documentation in collaborative activity, In Mantei M. and Baecker R. (eds) *Sharing Perspectives*, ACM, New York pp163-170

Mackay W.E. (1991). Triggers and barriers to customising software, In Robertson S.P., Olson G.M. and Olson J.S., *Reaching Through Technology*, ACM/SIGCHI, New York pp153-160

Mantei M.M., Baecker R.M., Sellen A.J., Buxton W.A.S. & Milligan T. (1991). Experiences in the use of a media space, In Robertson S.P., Olson G.M. and Olson J.S. (eds) *Reaching Through Technology*, ACM, New York, pp167-172

Marks C. (1972). *From Sketchbooks of the Great Artists*, Hart-Davis MacGibbon, London

Mead C. & Conway L. (1980). *Introduction to VLSI Systems*, Addison Wesley, Reading, Mass

Miller D.S., Smith J.G. and Muller M.J. (1992). TelePICTIVE: Computer-supported collaborative GUI design for designers with diverse expertise, Proceedings of UIST92, ACM, New York pp151-160

Minneman S.L. and Bly S.A. (1991). Managing à trois: a study of a multi-user drawing tool in distributed design work, In Robertson S.P., Olson G.M. and Olson J.S. (eds) *Reaching Through Technology*, ACM, New York, pp217-224

Negroponte N., Groisser L.B. and Taggart J. (1972). HUNCH: An experiment in sketch recognition, In Mitchell W.J. (ed), *Environmental Design: Research and Practice*, UCLA, Los Angeles

Oxman R. (1990). Prior knowledge in design: a dynamic knowledge-based model of design and creativity, *Design Studies* (11) 1 pp17-28

Oxman R.E. & Oxman R.M. (1992). Refinement and adaptation in design cognition, *Design Studies* (13) 2 pp117-134

Peterson C. (1992). Nanotechnology: evolution of the concept, *Journal of the British Interplanetary Society* (45) 10 pp395-400

Petroski H. (1989). Failure as a unifying theme in design, *Design Studies* (10) 4 pp214-218

Phelps R.H. & Shanteau J. (1978). Livestock judges: how much information can an expert use., *Organisational Behaviour and Human Performance* (21) pp209-219

Pountain D. (1992). Browsing art the windows way, *Byte* (17) 4 pp821

Roe A. (1952a). *The Making of a Scientist*, Dodd Mead, New York

Roe A. (1952b). A psychologist examines 64 eminent scientists, *Scientific American* (187) 5 pp21-25

Russo I.E. & Dosher B.A. (1976). *An Information Processing Analysis of Binary Choice*, Technical Report, Carnegie-Mellon University, Pittsburgh

Schenk P. (1991). The role of drawing in the graphic design process, *Design Studies* (12) 3 pp168-181

Schön D.A. & Wiggins G. (1992). Kinds of seeing and their functions in designing, *Design Studies* (13) 2 pp135-156

Scrivener S.A.R. & Clark S. (1993). How interaction with sketches aids creative design, this volume

Scrivener S.A.R. & Schappo A. (1988). Perceptual approach to picture interpretation, *Knowledge-Based Systems* (1) 2 pp105-113

Shepherd R.N. (1964). On subjectively optimum selections from multi-attribute alternatives, In Shelley M.W. and Bryan G.L., *Human Judgments and Optimality*, Wiley, New York

Shu L. & Flowers W. (1992). Groupware experiences in three-dimensional computer aided design, In Mantei M. and Baecker R. (eds) *Sharing Perspectives*, ACM, New York pp179-186

Sutherland I.E. (1963). Sketchpad: A man-machine graphical communication system, *SJCC*, Spartan Books, Baltimore (reprinted in Freeman H. (ed) (1984), *Tutorial and Selected Readings in Interactive Computer Graphics*, IEEE Computer Society, Silver Spring pp2-19)

Takahashi S., Matsuoka S., Yonezawa A. & Kamada T. (1991). A general framework for bi-directional translation between abstract and pictorial data, In *Proceedings UIST 91*, ACM SIGGRAPH and ACM SIGCHI, New York, pp165-174

Takemura H. & Kishino F. (1992) Cooperative work environment using virtual workspace, In Mantei M. and Baecker R. (eds) *Sharing Perspectives*, ACM, New York pp226-232

Tang J.C. & Minneman S.L. (1991). Videowhiteboard: Video shadows to support remote collaboration, In Robertson S.P., Olson G.M. and Olson J.S. (eds)*Reaching Through Technology*, ACM, New York, pp315-322

6

The Art of Interaction

Gillian Crampton Smith

6.1 Introduction

Awesome effort has been applied to representing the real world in digital form. Much less effort has been spent on translating digital information back to the real world, to the user. Thirty years after SketchPad, what have we got? Only the Desktop.

To be fair, the Desktop was an imaginative response to two new developments. First, computers began to be used not just by technological professionals, but by ordinary people, who were not interested in computers, just the job in hand. Second, high resolution graphic displays appeared with enough computing power to drive them. This allowed graphic images and representations to be generated which were dramatically more rich and complex than had been possible on alphanumeric screens. From being a specialist tool for professionals the computer has now become part of everyday life, like buildings.

A building's basic purpose is to keep the rain off. But a good building must do much more. We must be able to "read" it: know where the entrance is, what kind of building it is. It must appear appropriate to its function and suit the activities and the social relationships of its users. So why should we not expect expect the electronic environments in which we now work and play to serve us as well as good architecture?

The Roman architect Vitruvius said buildings should have firmness, commodity and delight. By this principle human-computer interfaces should be robust, useful and pleasurable. Their design should be as much an art as a science.

The study of human-computer interface grew out of the needs of safety-critical systems such as fighter cockpits and nuclear reactors where the concerns of art have been thought irrelevant, if not dangerous. But one need not have the creation of an artwork as one's primary goal in order to use the techniques of art. Far from being opposed to function, the aesthetic is *part* of function. A well-designed artefact is by definition a pleasure to use, an ill-designed one awkward and annoying, a cognitive pea under the mattress, diluting our concentration. Aesthetic connotations, moreover, are inevitable: there is no such thing as "neutral" design.

Interacting with Virtual Environments Edited by Lindsay MacDonald and John Vince
© 1994 John Wiley & Sons Ltd

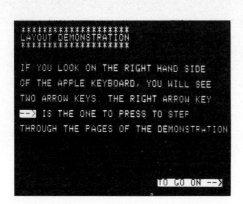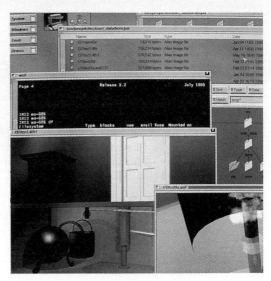

Figure 6.1. The increasing complexity of computer interfaces, 1981-1991.

Stroll down any city street, switch on the TV, read a magazine, visit a museum, and you will see images - complex, subtle, expressive, moving, beautiful, witty. Although bit-mapped displays have been affordable for a decade or more, computer systems, however, show none of these qualities.

Ten years ago a designer of computer interfaces, with only a text-based display, had few variables to manipulate: position on the screen, normal type, reverse type and flashing type. There was little potential for visual design, and in any case few of the designers involved had been trained in the visual arts (Figure 6.1). But modern bit-mapped colour displays allow the designer to use the techniques of typography and graphic information design to express qualities beyond the simple content of the words. He can combine symbolic communication (where the relation to the referent is arbitrary, as in words) with the rather more direct iconic form (which has some correspondence to the object represented). Full-colour digital images also allow him to use the allusive and suggestive qualities of images, offering an almost unlimited range of representations.

The design problem now becomes far more subtle, however. Interface design has grown from the equivalent to laying out a typewritten page to the design of a cross between a complex book and a televison programme. To exploit its potential needs skills not usually in the software designer's repertoire. The interface designer needs to be someone who knows how to manipulate the power of graphic representation.

6.2 The power of images

Walking through an art museum like London's National Gallery one is struck by the fact that paintings made five hundred years ago or more, in a social and technological setting vastly different from our own, still speak to us. Indeed, the line of Western European visual representation, starting from the Classical era through early Christianity to our own day, appears unbroken, though undoubtedly disturbed, by the great social and technological upheavals of the past two and a half millennia.

This is a deep tradition, although it tends to be taken for granted. (It is also powerful: some religions forbid images, for example, judging them a usurpation of God's creativity.) Many people find it a source of rich meaning and great pleasure. So for these reasons the design of computer systems needs to tap this long tradition, which can build for the ordinary user a bridge from the familiar world to the less familiar one of the computer.

Many paintings in the National Gallery have their roots in societies where, because literacy was uncommon, images were the main transmitters of society's shared meanings. Painting, sculpture and architecture were in this situation strong and dense carriers of meaning and myth, becoming in many cases (paintings of saints for instance) as revered as those whom they represented. After the Renaissance, painting began to lose this mythic quality and refer, not only to the scene depicted, but also to the art of painting itself. The unexpected and novel - daring foreshortening, perhaps, or deliberate flouting of well-understood conventions - gave viewers a visual and intellectual frisson.

Until the invention of photography the main challenge was to see and then represent what one sees. Later, when some of the key problems of representation had been solved, particularly by the invention of linear perspective, artists looked to express more intangible qualities of experience and mood, experience that could only be *implied*, not described.

6.3 Types of ambiguity

Some notations, notably mathematics, are very precise. Words, *pace* Jacques Derrida, can also be used precisely but, because the meaning they transmit depends on both speaker and audience, they are usually alarmingly open to multiple or false interpretation. Poetry, on the other hand, defined by Anthony Burgess as "conventional language trying to be iconic", actually exploits this ambiguity to weave a dense web of allusion and evocation which depends on the reader's knowledge external to the poem.

Take for instance Edward Thomas's "Cock-Crow", which evokes startlingly brilliant visual images:

> *Out of the wood of thoughts that grows by night*
> *To be cut down by the sharp axe of light, -*
> *Out of the night, two cocks together crow,*
> *Cleaving the darkness with a silver blow:*
> *And bright before my eyes twin trumpeters stand,*
> *Heralds of splendour, one at either hand,*
> *Each facing each as in a coat of arms:*
> *The milkers lace their boots up at the farms.*

The metaphor of each couplet contains a different semantic turn. We are carried along a rhythmic chain of associated meanings: wood, axe; cleave, blow (to strike, to trumpet);

heralds, coat of arms. Then, in the last line, we are brought down to earth with a thud of both rhythm and meaning: "The milkers lace their boots up at the farms".

A second level of ambiguity is that of allusions to knowledge outside the poem itself: cocks crowed at dawn to remind Peter he had denied Christ, trumpeters sound at the day of judgement, buglers sound reveille. And, when we recall that Thomas, a war poet, died in 1917, "The sharp axe of light" begins to resonate differently, as does "the wood of thoughts that grows by night".

Poetry's analogue, the visual image, can also suggest the non-visual, and allude to knowledge of the world outside itself. Allusion depends on the viewer, so its effect is difficult to predict, but the fact that it is not overt is what makes great art continue to move us.

In computing, the shift to the iconic allowed by improved graphic technology has expanded the possible range and power of expression of computer systems. The potential for implicit communication lends images a density of meaning invaluable at the interface. In contrast with words, not everything has to be spelled out or demands the user's conscious attention. And graphic representation, having no syntax or well-understood, repeatable building blocks, is splendidly open to multiple interpretation. An image can be scanned in any order, gathered in a glance, or perused for hours. It does not have to be complete, just suggestive enough for viewers to complete it in their imaginaton. This imprecision of course precludes any invariable rules of design, because every interplay of form and meaning has a different effect.

6.4 Layers of meaning

Many paintings, perhaps most, are conceived as contemplative objects, designed not to surrender all their meaning at a single glance, but to keep the viewer's attention, providing a profundity of experience for possibly a lifetime of viewing. Classical compositional techniques lead the eye through the picture, in depth and in the plane, giving a cognitive transparency to an otherwise opaque complexity (Figure 6.2).

The role of the single, multi-layered, multi-meaning image, such as the painting, has steadily declined as a conduit for society's values and myths; its only dominant use outside fine art today is in advertising. But interactive media could restore its former importance. The computer interface can allow users to concentrate on performing their work without needing to think consciously level about how they are doing it. For, since our minds can process images in parallel, much implicit information can be absorbed subliminally while other tasks are tackled consciously.

Recent typographic design has been exploring aspects of layering, ways of differentiating parts of information in a single image by implying three-dimensional relationships, not necessarily consistent, between elements (Plate 5). This is not yet much exploited in interface design because the emphasis has been on precision rather than impression and suggestion. But the density of meaning which images can accommodate is a particular virtue. For one thing, screen real estate is at a premium. For another, users grasp information better the more rapidly they can shift mental attention between layers of meaning without having to shift their visual attention (Plate 4).

6.5 The language of images

Pictures work on four levels:

1. Narrative: the story being told, the scene being described
2. Symbolism and allusion: references to things outside the painting itself
3. The visual representation: how narrative is given form.
4. The surface appearance of the picture: does it interfere with the narrative?

Narrative

The "narrative" in interface design is how designers represent the system to the user, the story they want the user to believe. Early interfaces were conceived as control panels to a machine.

But the graphically sophisticated screen representations now possible allow a different relationship between the system and its represention to the user: we can depict it however we wish. So the central element of the design of information tools, "tools for the mind", is the design of their representation.

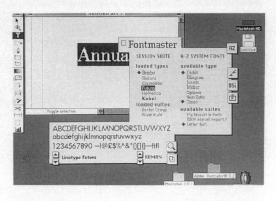
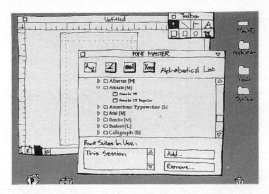
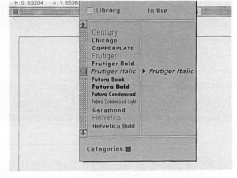

Figure 6.3. Narrative in interface design: Suitcase desk accessory; alternative versions by RCA CRD Department, 1993: Colin Burns, Sally Grisedale, Martin Locker. A text-based interface offers few clues about what a system does and how to use it, without literally spelling it out. The alternatives tried to express what was happening graphically.

The workings of mechanical machines are obvious - pull a lever here, press another there, fill up the boiler, adjust the pressure. Actions have an overt relationship to what happens. Electro-mechanical machines operate more opaquely, but the actions needed to control them bear some relation to the physical changes necessary for its operation: a contact here, varying resistors there.

A computer, on the other hand, offers few external clues to its operation and no necessary correspondence between the controls and their feedback. We can program the feedback to appear however we like. So how the virtual machine is represented to users determines their ability to use it. In a sense, the interface *is* the tool.

Some representations of information allow us to grasp its import more or less effortlessly. Others impede our understanding. The interface of the otherwise very useful desk accessory *Suitcase*, for instance, constrained perhaps by the conventions of the Macintosh interface guidelines to a textual approach, offers few clues as to what the program does and how you use it; it lacks narrative. (Figure 6.3). A student project to design alternative versions of the desk accessory (which sets up pointers to fonts anywhere on the system) centred on ways of showing which fonts are merely accessible and which are actually loaded. Some solutions labelled the lists of fonts "library" or "active"; others, more successfully, implied the relationship by making the connection visually, showing the movement of the fonts from the library to the font menu.

As allegory is to story-telling, so metaphor is to the interface narrative: the Desktop or humanoid agents are obvious examples. Metaphor allows the user to infer a great deal of information about what to expect from a system without having it tediously spelt out. It also implies a logic which enables the user to reason about the system when things do not go as expected.

Metaphors have their dangers. They rarely map completely onto the actions the system allows, leading users to make mistaken inferences about the way the system works. And if systems must behave like objects in the real world, they may be prevented from following their own logic, particularly if the representation depicts things that did not exist before the computer and have no real-world equivalent, like the spreadsheet, for instance.

Metaphors do not need to be literal, however. They can be abstract. Lakoff and Johnson, who consider thought to be almost impossible without metaphor, distinguish a range of abstract metaphors about movement, direction, and the way we act in the world which are not specific to particular objects or conventions in society.

It is often more useful to the user, incidentally, to represent the system in a way that masks its real operation. The Desktop trashcan, for example, implies that the data is being discarded rather than simply dereferenced. This is a lie but, to the user, a mercifully simplifying one.

Symbolism and allusion

Paintings of the past were rich in symbolic code (Figure 6.4). Saints, for instance, were depicted carrying the instrument of their martyrdom in order to identify them without a verbal label. As we have seen, symbolism and allusion is cultural. They depend on, and add to, society's shared meanings and implicit knowledge, the world outside the representation itself.

The symbolic world varies according to social groupings and changes over time. The phrase "Covent Garden" once meant a convent garden, later a vegetable market; now it means either an opera house or a tourist shopping mall. Most people, asked recently in a survey what they associated with the word "Madonna", replied sex, not the Virgin Mary.

Connotations are powerful because they set up expectations in the user about the system at both rational and emotional levels. People identify powerfully with things that support their view of themselves: *Guardian* readers would not be seen dead reading the *Sun*, for instance - or the *Daily Telegraph*. Marketeers exploit this by designing products to appeal to very specific groups of people. The graphic design of the database we designed at the Royal College of Art for fashion designers made them feel it was visual and stylish, appropriate for them - and they liked it. (Plate 1). Connotation cannot be avoided: even apparent neutrality is a style .

Figure 6.4. Symbolism and allusion: *Venus, Cupid, Folly and Time* by Bronzino (1503-72). Pictorial representation allows complex symbolism whose interpretation can change over time. Michael Wilson explains what this painting meant in Renaissance Florence: "An adolescent Cupid embraces Venus who, removing an arrow from his quiver, disarms him. Above, winged Time attempts to expose the hollow mask of Fraud, while (below) Jealousy tears her hair in distraction and Childish Folly comes to shower the couple with roses. Behind him, Pleasure, offering a honeycomb in one hand, holds in the other her reptilian tail bearing a sting. While apparently demonstrating the snares of physical lust and vanity, the teasing symbolism of these figures and devices serves only as a foil to the erotic imagery." (Reproduced by courtesy of the Trustees, National Gallery, London.)

The representation of space

The main focus of a painter's interest has changed over history. It has been in turn the painting's subject (in the work of Giotto and Fra Angelico for instance), the decorative surface of the painting (Pisanello), perspectival representation (Crivelli, Michelangelo, Vermeer), and the sensation of visual reality (Turner, the Impressionists).

In the late nineteenth and early twentieth century, especially in Cubism, interest focused on the tension between the picture's surface and the illusion of depth. A painting's frame, traditionally but fairly arbitrarily a rectangle, marks the boundary of the canvas surface. It is also a metaphor for a window, an aperture through which we apparently see space in three dimensions (Figure 6.5).

Figure 6.5. The frame in pictorial composition: *Boy Bitten by a Lizard* by Caravaggio (1573-1610), The frame controls the turbulent play of forces in this painting. The composition, the boy's torso, defined by areas of bright light, cuts into the background diagonal and seems compressed by the frame. The picture is also riven by other competing diagonals. Composition and meaning are interwoven. Our eyes are drawn to the vase, partly because it gleams in the foreground, but also to seek the source of the boy's horror. (Reproduced by courtesy of the Trustees, National Gallery, London.)

The monitor screen is also a rectangle, imitating the painting, and is both a plane and a window. But the window metaphor is stronger here than in a painting because the screen emits light and its images can move.

What we "see" through that virtual window is necessarily convention-based. When Picasso was painting a woman, her husband complained that the portrait did not look like her. Asked by Picasso to describe what she did look like, the husband took a photo from his wallet and showed him. Picasso looked at the photograph and commented, "Rather small, isn't she?" The moral is that, however realistic an image appears, our ability to understand it depends on our knowledge of the conventions by which it is represented.

Ernst Gombrich describes the many conventions, from Ancient Egyptian murals to the photograph, used to represent visual phenomena; even the camera, it appears, is a device for making images which imitate the perspectival conventions of Renaissance painting. We may not respond equally readily to every convention, but all are available to the designer, and it would be wrong to imagine that any was inherently "more realistic" than another.

How then do we choose between them? I'm afraid, once again, it depends - this time on what aspects of reality we want to represent. After all, we cannot represent them all, and sometimes only one aspect will imply the rest. A Matisse drawing, for example, a few quick lines, sums up the form of a woman's body sufficiently for us to "complete the picture" and summon up her presence in our imagination. By forcing the viewer to work, the drawing makes the illusion more vivid.

In interface design, similarly, representational conventions must make the user focus on the ideas that sustain the overall story we want to communicate. Software designers, for instance, sometimes appear to believe that the illusion of three dimensions is always a good thing: two dimensions good, so three dimensions better. Yet it depends what the interface is trying to do. A GUI with widgets in aggressive relief, unless this supports its metaphor, is just a showy distraction from the job in hand.

Abstraction

Visual representation, as we have seen, the clothing of narrative with form, can support the literal depiction of the narrative, in the representation of space for instance. But it can also have abstract elements, communicating more than just a story to the viewer. In the first half of this century artists became interested in how the abstract qualities of a painting - colour, form, composition, and so on - could be made to affect the viewer independently of the painting's subject.

The artists at the Bauhaus investigated these abstract qualities in their teaching. Wassily Kandinsky's *Point and Line to Plane* (1979), Paul Klee's *Pedagogical Notebooks,* and Johannes Itten's *Art of Colour* (1961) later formed the basis of foundation courses followed by generations of British and American graphic designers, who used what they had learnt to manipulate viewers' attention as they read a book, scan an advertisement or choose which soap powder to buy. Other seminal books published in English included Gyorgy Kepes' *Language of Vision* (1944), influenced by gestalt psychology, Emil Ruder's *Typographie* (1967) and Jan Tschichold's *Asymmetric Typography* (1967). Studio Vista also published in the 1960s a series of small but influential paperback guides, many by tutors at the Royal College of Art.

Composition and the picture surface

The visual arts succeed by making works that balance order with complexity, predictability with surprise. Too much order bores, too much complexity worries and annoys.

Unfortunately, there is no definition of "too much". A matter of judgement, it varies with the purpose of the work, its audience, and fashion.

The techniques of composition can invest complexity with hierarchy and order by indicating which things are important, which should be looked at first, which are similar, and which different. Here are some compositional tools and topics:

Symmetry and asymmetry

Before the Modern Movement, mirror symmetry was the most common organising principle for the design of artefacts from books to buildings. Now, however, a symmetrical poster or magazine layout is rare: it is too tame for today's taste and carries "old world" connotations. A satisfying asymmetric composition is balanced but in tension, with strong directional forces opposed by counterforces. No element can be removed or altered without imperilling the balance, which is why a change in content usually necessitates some degree of redesign.

The frame

Pictorial composition cannot ignore the frame - of the page, the painting, the computer monitor. It is one of the strongest forces in the composition, and all elements appear in relation to it. It has the apparent effect of a visual magnet, attracting elements that get too close and setting up an uncomfortable tension. It also defines the dynamic angles of the composition, the directions of force that lead the viewer's eye through it. A unified composition interweaves these forces, never letting the viewer's eye wander out of the frame.

The impression of space

A blank sheet is a space. A single black line will be read as lying "on" the sheet; add two different coloured rectangles and they will be seen in a spatial relationship with each another. Our urge to interpret images in spatial terms is almost irresistible. Frank Mulvey lists some of the mechanisms behind these illusions:

- Size: perspectival geometry means that, if there are no other clues, larger things appear nearer

- Tone: atmospheric perspective makes distant things appear misty. So greys and pastel colours appear further away than objects of a bright, saturated colour

- Position: objects at the bottom of the frame appear closer, as if they were below the horizon

- Edge: a soft-edged object appears further away than one with a crisp edge

- Overlap: an object that overlaps others appears closer than them to us, as do transparent objects through which we appear to see other objects

- Format: objects large in comparison to the frame appear closer than objects small in the frame.

It is also well-known that colours can encourage the illusion of space. Red and yellow appear to come towards us, cool colours to recede. This is both a retinal effect, particularly extreme when looking at a slide in a slide viewer for instance, and a product of atmospheric perspective, which turns distant mountains blue. A depicted shadow - behind type, say, or a GUI "button" - also implies depth.

Importance

Such techniqes can be used to indicate the relative importance of elements in the composition, things near being interpreted as more important than things far. We can emphasise things by making them brighter, or more saturated in colour. On the other hand, it is also possible to emphasise things by making them smaller, darker, or less saturated. The effect is not absolute; it depends on the relationship between the elements.

Similarity

Composition can be used to indicate similarity, to "chunk" elements. Tschichold (1967) observed that printed "matter set in different sizes of type must, to look well, be grouped. Too many units cannot be comprehended easily and are like ungrouped matter set in a solid mass. Groups defeat their purpose if they cannot be absorbed at a glance but have to be counted." Things near each other are interpreted as a group, as are things of similar colour, or weight (such as typefaces), or perceived as being in the same plane. Things can be seen as similar if they have the effect of closing a form and completing a gestalt, the stars in the European flag, say.

Contrast

The opposite of similarity is contrast. Frequently a composition must distinguish elements from each other, to make clear for instance which elements of the screen belong to the environment, which to the user's work, or which areas are active, which not. Carl Dair (1967) distinguishes seven types of contrast: size, weight, structure, form, colour, direction, and texture. Emil Ruder's (1967) more diverse taxonomy of contrasts includes light-dark, thick-thin, line-surface, vertical-horizontal, active-passive, static-dynamic, geometric-organic, agitated-restful, asymmetric-symmetric, round-straight, hard-soft, stable-unstable, wide-narrow, eccentric-concentric, and closed-open.

All the compositional tools in this by no means exhaustive list are means which artists and designers use to suggest rather than spell out significance. They contribute to the density of meaning carried by images, because viewers interpret them without conscious attention. But they are not a set of rules that can be used to transform requirements into a design. They are instead a way of making sense of how art seems to work, and they derive from practice and reflection, considering the designs one has made in relation to the principles. Every instance is different and depends on the interplay between each element of the composition - and their meanings.

George Steiner (1990) has pointed out that aesthetic theories are not like scientific theories: they cannot be proved or disproved, nor can they be predictive. Critical theories, on the other hand, of which those listed above might be fragments, are taxonomies, allowing us to reflect on what exists.

6.6 The artist-designer's approach

What we might call "artist-designers" need increasingly to be involved in interaction design. We at the Royal College of Art's Computer Related Design department, recognising this need, are preparing them for this role.

Artist designers are distinct from both fine artists and "engineer-designers". Fine artists set their own agenda in terms of aim and process, while engineer-designers are more concerned with *how* to make things work, than *what* is made to work. But artist-designers, while working to the agenda of others, use the approaches of painting and sculpture, and people's understanding of those languages, to design things which are both satisfying and useful - reconciling, as David Pye neatly puts it, the requirements of use, economy and appearance.

Artist-designers need to feed their imaginations, both with outside influences and by making and reflecting on their own work. The product designer Bill Moggridge, a founder of IDEO, calls this brainfood "creative soup". The recipe is typically unpredictable. For artist-designers are divergent rather than convergent thinkers, working not by narrowing in to derive a solution, but by broadening out, constantly generating alternative ideas which in turn spark further alternatives. To work with this intentional uncertainty can feel vertiginous for designers from engineering disciplines, who have to think convergently to get results. If they can learn tolerate each other, however, artist-designers and engineer-designers together make a powerful team.

It is often assumed that artist-designers only do visual design, the gift wrapping tied on after the system has been designed. This is a wasteful mistake. It does not exploit the artist-designer's skill which, as well as crafting the final artefact, includes analysing the needs of users and inventing ways of suiting them.

The design of the representation of a system, moreover, is central to the design of the whole software, not the final touch. The interface is all the user knows about the tool; its success or failure distinguishes a good tool from a bad. But an initial decision for representing the system, made before the interface designer is consulted, may turn out incapable of adequate represention on screen. This either prevents him or her from maximizing the effectiveness of the system as a whole, or necessitates its costly redesign.

In the Royal College of Art's prototype for a fashion designer's database, for instance, we had hoped to use a direct manipulation paradigm, with the elements represented iconically (Plates 2, 3). When we came to representing it on screen, however, we found we could not display all the information needed while keeping the icons legible. So we decided to use a more abstract, typographic representation. Had the interface design only been considered at the end, the structural changes necessary would have wrecked our timetable and our budget.

The first stage of interaction design is user-observation and research. Artist-designers use this stage to clarify the user's needs and kick-start their imagination. Their solutions build on both the intellectual analysis of the tasks to be done and a trained creative intuition.

The second stage is to invent and evaluate alternative concepts for the interface's central organising idea. This might be metaphor based on real-world objects, as in the Desktop interface, or more symbolic, like the control panel of a VCR. The organising idea is vital to the interface's success; without it a potent representation of the system to the user is precluded. It also helps guide otherwise arbitrary choices about the interface and makes them cohere. The organising idea synthesizes what would otherwise be a ragbag of unrelated functions.

At this stage, before designing screens in detail, interaction designers simulate alternative solutions, using sketches scanned in and roughly animated, to test if they can be made to work.

Though concept and surface design are distinct, they must be worked on in parallel. The designer switches between the two, having an idea and immediately making a sketch to see how it could be represented visually; seeing the sketch may generate new ideas which are fed back into the concept. When a concept evolves which both meets the requirements and seems visually representable, the designer starts to design the screens in more detail and consider other qualities of the interface: movement, pace, sound, and so on.

A constant round follows of simulations and adaptations. Designers can proceed only so far in their heads before needing to test a solution informally, first on themselves, later on colleagues, then on final users. When a solution seems relatively promising it is tested more formally on a new set of users. Only then is it sensible to go to a prototype, to test with real data.

The process is not linear but raggedly cyclical. One seldom gets it right first off, however careful or experienced the designer - and few people can as yet be very experienced in interaction design. So at each stage we need ways to test ideas quickly at an appropriate level of detail. Working from the interface back to the system, rather than the other way around, makes designers concentrate on the user's needs rather than the system's.

6.7 A new medium

Marshall McLuhan described memorably how the invention of printing radically changed society. He then showed the effect of new media such as radio, film and television on our own society, whose cultural, intellectual and technological development had been determined by the printed word for more than five hundred years.

For the past half-millennium ideas have been reproduced mainly through words. During this period visual imagery as a driving force in culture has waned in favour of the verbal and, particularly in our own century, the numerical. In the alphabetic tradition, as opposed to the ideographic, images were costlier to reproduce than words and so rarer. It is only in my own lifetime, for example, that the development of photo-lithographic printing has made economic the mass production of generously illustrated books or full-colour posters. Before then every illustration was engraved, originally by hand and more recently photographically, an expensive process. Litho printing and photo-reproduction also gave birth to a new type of artist-designer: the graphic designer, as opposed to typographer, who communicates messages by combining words and images.

The invention of printing radically changed ways of thinking, not just how things are communicated but what can be thought. As it became possible to own books it became less necessary to memorise knowledge, so the codified arts of memory atrophied. Similarly the arts of the spoken word - rhetoric, poetry, drama - took second place to those of the book.

McLuhan realised that every medium enables some types of thought and expression and inhibits others. Serious and sustained debate, for instance, as Neil Postman points out, cannot be developed on television. Good TV allows no gaps, the action must flow fast to keep the viewers' attention; pauses for thought, essential in a complex argument, are just not entertaining.

Interactive computer graphics is a dauntingly new medium, potentially as radical as the invention of printing or television, and likely to change not only what is transmitted but also the cognitive skills needed to receive it. It will revolutionise how and by whom information is authored, compiled, authored, sold, bought, understood and exploited. But in what way it is too early to say.

Similarly, we cannot yet predict the cultural effects of interaction design. But we can be sure it will draw on existing families of aesthetic languages:

- Haptic: three-dimensional form and touch (product semantics)
- Auditory: sound, music
- Filmic: narrative, cutting, animation
- Literary: prose, dialogue
- Visual: graphic composition, iconic representation, pictorial space.

We certainly seem to see a change in the balance of culture, from the symbolic, the verbal, to the iconic, the image-based. Western culture is already strongly oriented towards film and television. Interactive media will tip the balance further: colour pictures and animation can be displayed at little extra cost and text on screen appears destined to remain for some time less legible than on paper. Interactive media have the potential to be powerfully engaging, but only when we have developed the aesthetic languages to exploit their advantages. People will "read" displays in the same way as they read other complex visual images - posters, record sleeves, paintings - and will invest them with cultural meaning. Displays will also be judged by the same exacting standards: whether we intend it or not, they will become part of culture. Since the aesthetic dimension is inevitable it must be exploited with sensitivity and skill.

Our challenge today is to discover, drawing on the tradition and techniques of the visual arts, how to forge a new language of interaction design. It is to incorporate in the design of software the judgement and skill of artist-designers to make user interfaces that are powerful, subtle and pleasurable.

I have not tried to offer recipes for interaction design. It is an art, for which there is no quick fix. I have not even attempted to cobble together a theory. The practice of our art is in its infancy and, as Kandinsky wrote in 1914, "in real art, theory does not precede practice, but follows her". But I have tried to show that, far from starting from scratch, we can draw practical and philosophical sustenance from two and a half thousand years of patient and passionate visual research. We see further and go faster if we ride on the shoulders of the past.

Acknowledgements

I am indebted to Dr Philip Tabor of University College London for our numerous discussions during the development of this paper.

References

A Mouthful of Air; *Anthony Burgess;* London 1992
Design with Type; *Carl Dair*; Toronto 1967 (1952)
Art and Illusion; *Ernst Gombrich;* London 1960
Concerning the Spiritual in Art: *Wassily Kandinsky;* New York 1977 (1914)
Point and Line to Plane; *Wassily Kandinsky;* New York 1979 (1926)
Language of Vision; *Gyorgy Kepes;* Chicago 1944
Pedagogical Sketchbook; *Paul Klee;* London 1953 (1926)
The Art of Colour; *Johannes Itten;* London 1961
Understanding Media; *Marshall McLuhan;* London 1964
Applying Visual Design: Trade Secrets for Elegant Interfaces; *Kevin Mullet and Darrell Sano;* Sunsoft CHI Tutorial 1993
Amusing Ourselves to Death; *Neil Postman;* London 1986
Typographie; *Emil Ruder;* Basle 1967
Real Presences; *George Steiner;* London 1990
Principles, Techniques and Ethics of Stage Magic and their Application to Human Interface Design; *Bruce Togazzini;* Proceedings of Interchi 1993
Asymmetric Typography; *Jan Tschichold;* London 1967 (1935)
The National Gallery, London; *Michael Wilson;* London 1977
Studio Vista Books, London:
   Basic Design: the Dynamics of Visual Form; *Maurice de Sausmarez;* 1964
   The Graphic Perception of Space; *Frank Mulvey;* New York 1969
   The Nature of Design; *David Pye;* 1968

7

Sketching in Collaborative Design

Stephen A.R. Scrivener and Sean M. Clark

7.1 Introduction

> Of all the creative acts performed by the artist, the most directly legible is drawing. Drawing is also the first to which the artist resorts when he sketches the future form of what is still a mere feeling within himself. Finally, it is the act most directly and spontaneously governed by his nervous and muscular system. It is a gesture even when it wants to be a thought. As gesture, it is inseparable from, and hence expressive of the organism that made it, both in its physical and its psychological structure.
>
> Rene Huyghe

High resolution, full-colour, easily modified computer-displayed images of real or imagined worlds are commonplace - almost ubiquitous. It is to be hoped, therefore, that the reader of this paper will not be disappointed to discover that the primary subject of discussion here is a more ancient and visually impoverished form of image still widely created using low-technology pen and paper. The subject of this paper is the humble and truly ubiquitous sketch.

A sketch is a special kind of sparse drawing, usually produced quickly and in a manner peculiar to its creator. Sketches are usually of objects visible to the sketcher at the moment of sketching, or objects recalled from memory, or non-experienced objects constructed by the imagination. It is this latter type of sketch, conjured from the mind onto paper, that we focus on here. Furthermore, we are only concerned with how sketching is used in design.

Why should we be so interested in the sketch and sketching? Isn't this kind of image

Interacting with Virtual Environments Edited by Lindsay MacDonald and John Vince
© 1994 John Wiley & Sons Ltd

making anachronistic, an activity constrained by a technology out-performed and perhaps about to superseded by computer-based imaging technology? We will argue quite the reverse. We hope to show that neither the sketch or the activity of sketching is simply a product of pen and paper technology. To the contrary, in our view, the particular visual characteristics of the sketch are ones that support and facilitate the kind of visual reasoning engaged in the early stages of design, as does the actual activity of sketching. Whilst the technology of pen and paper may be substituted by the computer without loss, a loss of sketching functionality would have a significant impact on designers' ability to innovate.

Furthermore we will postulate that object-oriented approaches to two-dimensional image making impede rather than augment conceptual design because the interaction required by these systems interferes with the free flow and development of design ideas, and the repertoire of geometric shapes and solids is inadequate for representing imagined objects. If we are to develop computer-based tools that augment early design, tools that go beyond sketching, we need to understand the cognitive processes underlying creation and how and why they are supported by sketching. In this paper we attempt an initial step in this direction.

7.2 Sketching and technology

Whilst many may regard themselves as poor draughtpersons, few people could fail to acknowledge that from time to time the ability to make meaningful marks with a pen on paper is a most useful skill. For example, we may need to represent the shelving unit we propose to build as a preliminary to calculating the wood required, or we may want to show friends how to get to our home for the New Year's Eve party we are holding, or as a joke we may simple want to illustrate how Tom appeared the day after the night before.

Since around 30000 BC mankind has been using simple mark making implements to scratch, score, and disfigure surfaces with marks intended to represent the real or the imagined. Indeed, a pencil, crayon, or brush is one of the first tools manipulated by many a child, in the first instance to simply make marks and later more deliberately to represent the dog, the home, mother, or whatever.

These pleasures of childhood we owe to the simple technology of pencil, or mark maker, and paper, commodities that became available in the late fifteenth century, and ubiquitous in the twentieth. Since the Renaissance, artists, architects, and designers have elevated the use of this technology to an art, producing dazzling images of huge variety and invention. In comparison to such works of art most people find their own scribblings rather inadequate and even embarrassing, relegating drawing to a competence only exercised by necessity. Notwithstanding the skill with which artists exploit pen and pencil it is tempting to view this technology as a constraint on visualisation. Indeed, a sketch is visually impoverished in comparison to a painting, lacking colour for example.

Computer-based imaging technology has developed to the point where a massive image making and manipulation capability can be placed in the hands of all who can afford it. Today, high quality colour images can be generated with low cost computers and manipulated with some ease We might speculate on a future in which the infant reaches not for a pencil to visualise but for the stylus of a digitising tablet. In the face of this technology, drawing with a pencil on paper may seem not only visually impoverished but difficult - somewhat anachronistic in other words.

But is this really the case? Is sketching outmoded? If full colour, high resolution digital image making commodities were as readily available, accessible, portable, and affordable as pen and paper would sketching and the sketch simply become redundant, disappearing from shop and home? Or are there properties of the sketch and the process of sketching that add value to pen and paper that has nothing to do with its limitations as an image making technology?

7.3 Sketching and visual thinking

The origins of sketching

Gombrich (1966) argues that Leonardo Da Vinci was probably responsible for the invention of the sketch. Just prior to Leonardo, drawings were working material for paintings. In the case of the "cartoon" quite literally a template for a painting. The cartoon was drawn at the intended scale of the painting and the drawn lines were then pricked out with a needle. The cartoon was copied onto the painting surface by blowing pigment through the pin pricks. Other drawings were produced in order to work out the details of a picture or to record objects that might be used in a future painting. Typically these drawings were realistic and highly finished (see for example the drawings of Pisanello).

Leonardo's sketches were quite different, being characterised by "pentimenti", multiple alternative contour lines that shatter the integrity of the perceived image, and "sfumati", mysterious dark shadows. The sketches produced by Leonardo using these techniques are visually indeterminate. Gombrich also argues that Leonardo allowed the indeterminate to rule the sketch as a means to stimulate the mind to invention. Viewed in this way, the sketch is not simply a representation of some external object used as model for an artifact yet to be produced, such as a painting. Instead, it functions as an external support for images in the mind of the creator; a framework for the imagination. In this sense, the sketch can only be properly comprehended by the sketcher since it is the external part of a construct that is largely in the mind of its creator.

The properties of sketches and visual cognition

If this is the case, why is it that sketches are able to support the mental processes of imagination? To answer this question we need to consider the attributes of the sketch and how these attributes contribute to, and amplify, visual cognition. Fish and Scrivener (1990) identify three primary attributes of the sketch. First, a sketch is composed of abbreviated two-dimensional sign systems used to represent three-dimensional visual experience. These marks operate in two ways: first they have a variety of descriptive meanings that are (partly at least) culturally acquired (e.g. a line can stand for an object boundary) and frequently such systems are supported by handwritten notes; second, they are depictive in the sense that they provoke visual experience resembling that associated with the objects they represent (e.g. a line might be shaped like a facial profile). The second attribute of the sketch is that it contains selective and fragmentary information. The final attribute of the sketch is that it contains deliberate or accidental indeterminacies. Amongst the indeterminacies commonly found in sketches are incomplete contours, pentimenti, sfumati, wobbly lines, suggestive scribbles and accidental smudges, energetic cross-hatchings, blots, and scratch marks.

Fish and Scrivener argue that the sketch provides an incomplete structure that amplifies the inventive and problem-solving uses of mental imagery by three mechanisms. First, the sketch provides a framework to facilitate and refresh spatially superimposed mental image manipulation, in a percept-image hybrid. Faint or vague marks may become assimilated into the mental image, and the image may modify the percept (arising from the sketch).

Second, the ambiguous and indeterminate signs of the sketch provoke innate, unconscious recognition mechanisms to generate a stream of mental imagery. Fish and Scrivener note that the theory of recognition by completion (Biederman 1987) fits this hypothesis, and evidence suggests that novel or problematic stimuli elicit the most vivid imagery (Sheehan 1972). Finally, sketches facilitate translation between different modes of visual representation. The act of drawing usually involves translating from a categorical description (in memory) to one of many possible spatial depictions. In addition sketches use sign systems and often written notes that access long-term memory and stimulate the mental translation of descriptive information to spatially depictive imagery. The reverse translation, from depictive image to many possible categorical descriptions, may be stimulated by incomplete recognition cues of the kind provided by Leonardo-like indeterminacies.

According to Fish and Scrivener the sketch supports and stimulates the construction and manipulation of depictive images and descriptive categorical structures in the mind, because the sign systems employed are both descriptive and depictive in character, abbreviated and incomplete, and ambiguous and indeterminate. There is an intimate and fragile connection between the sketch and mental processes it supports. Intimate, because without the sketch mental constructs would be more difficult to construct, manipulate, and alter. They would be less vivid, less coherent and less memorable. Fragile, because too much completeness and realism of representation in the sketch may overpower these imagined mental structures.

Sketching as a conversation with self

Of course, although a sketch may be retained after a problem has been solved or a artifact designed, it is not in essence a static thing, and often in stasis what it represents is unclear, sometimes completely unintelligible to anyone other than its creator. Usually a sketch is developed over time as problem-solving or design activity is progressed: in other words the sketch contributes to mental structures that are elements in a reasoning process. Hence it is not just the characteristics of the sketch that are of interest, but also how the sketch and the process of sketching supports such reasoning.

Goldschmidt (1991) has investigated the role of sketching in design reasoning. She observes that whilst sketches have been studied as steps leading to finished works of art or design, the process of sketching has commanded little attention. Like Fish and Scrivener (1990), she sees mental imagery as central to visual thinking and sketches as an essential support for a flow of images. She makes the important point that an entity being designed does not yet exist and therefore has not been perceived and must be constructed in parts using memory of previously seen objects. Sketches provide a means of support and visual stimulation for the visual reasoning that operates on this visual imagery.

Given the unresolved debates as to the nature of visual mental imagery (i.e. whether it is depictive, descriptive, or both), she distinguishes two modalities of visual reasoning during sketching - "seeing as", and "seeing that". Goldschmidt postulates that "seeing as" reasoning references figural mental imagery, whereas "seeing that" involves non-figural mental constructs relating to the thing being designed. To investigate this proposition she studied the design behaviour of experienced architects by analysing the cross-referenced verbal protocols and sketches produced by them when working on a prescribed design task.

Using this data, she shows that the visual reasoning supported by sketching involves regular switches of mode between "seeing as" and "seeing that". She concludes that the process of sketching is a systematic dialectic between "seeing as" and "seeing that" reasoning modalities. The creation of a new and therefore unperceived entity (design) is aided by this dialectic in "a back and forth swaying movement which helps translate particulars of form into generic qualities, and generic rules into specific appearances" (Goldschmidt 1991, page 132).

A marriage of mind and material

From the above we conclude that sketching is not an anachronistic activity bound by the peculiar properties of an ancient technology. Sketches are not neat thoughts drawn untidily, nor are they inadequate, impoverished representations of richer imaginings. Sketches, by virtue of their sparseness and imperfection, provide a perceptual stimulus that supports, stimulates and facilitates the formulation of novel unperceived mental objects without overpowering the imagination with the here and now of the concrete visual world. Furthermore, sketches support the movement of visual reasoning as it searches for a resolution to both the generic qualities of the imagined artifact and its particular formal properties.

Of great importance in this latter respect is the speed and lack of effort with which meaningful sketch marks can be produced: in the hands of the skilled, pen and pencil can be used with great speed and dexterity. Clearly, the dynamics of visualisation will be determined by the short duration and limited capacity of working memory: the process of visualisation should support rather than compete for working memory and attention. The act of mark making by hand requires little preparation and can be completed without obliterating the mental image represented: in other words an entity can be held in the mind whilst it is being drawn.

7.4 Designing computer supports for sketchers

To date, computer graphics and computer-aided design researchers and developers have largely ignored sketching to focus on the problems of three-dimensional modelling and visualisation. This choice was appropriate since the new technology had most potential in this area and the results have been beneficial. With such technology it is a relatively straightforward matter to construct, manipulate and verify properties of complex artifacts, before they are constructed, using computer models that can display with great realism. Such systems have taken design beyond the limitations of paper-based media. More recently, improvements in digital media have made it possible to perform similar operations on essentially two-dimensional designs, such as those for magazines and fabrics. A characteristic of such systems is that, in general, they are object-oriented, the visible display being generated from entities represented individually in the computer's memory. Since each entity is represented individually it can be modified and manipulated individually.

It is easy to assume that the way to enhance traditional sketch visualisation methods is by the same means of adding visual qualities, such as colour and texture, and object creation, editing, and manipulation features. In fact, this is what has happened in practice, and many computer-based two-dimensional "drawing" systems are object-oriented, or a mixture of methods allowing some object-like manipulation. In such systems, the drawing function is just one of a number of options and usually of such limited functionality and performance that only the crudest of sketch marks can be produced (not aided by the general use of the "mouse" as an input device).

It is our view that designers of computer-based painting systems have not recognised the true function and significance of sketching in the early stages of creative and design activity: that is its role in supporting visual cognition. Instead they have chosen to enhance initial visualisation through computer-based techniques more appropriate to the later "working out" stages of the design process.

However, does this misconception really matter in practice? Is it not possible that the visual reasoning supported by sketching could be just as effectively supported with an object oriented sketching tool? Isn't it just as easy to realise a mental artifact using a repertoire of predetermined shapes as it is by direct drawing? Isn't it just a small cost to have to explicitly switch modes between, say, drawing and writing when compared to the benefits that accrue from the explicit internal representation of these different sign systems?

7.5 CSCW's contribution to the understanding of sketching

In the past it has not been possible to answer these questions because, despite the great interest in sketching amongst design educationalists, art historians and critics, few systematic studies of sketching have been conducted. However, it is our contention that recent research and development in the area of computer-supported cooperative work (CSCW) has, serendipitously, provided a platform from which studies of sketching behaviour can be undertaken.

Recently a number of studies have investigated the activities taking place during group design (for example Bly 1988; Tang and Leifer 1988). Tang and Leifer proposed a framework for investigating workspace activity in terms of actions, such as listing, drawing, and gesturing, and functions, such as storing information, conveying and representing ideas, and engaging attention. They conducted empirical studies which provide evidence for both the existence of the identified actions and their relative functional use.

Bly explored the use of drawing surfaces employing a similar framework to Tang and Leifer, but extended the collaborative setting in which the activity occurred. Bly investigated three settings, face-to-face, across a "media link", and by telephone. In the face-to-face setting a pair of designers worked together at a table using pen and paper. In the media link setting the designers were separated geographically, but could talk freely via a telephone and also see a combined video image of their partner's drawing surface and head and shoulders. This setting was similar to one investigated by Goodman and Abel (1986). The third setting used only telephone as the shared medium of communication. These settings were characterised by very different patterns of action and use. Bly concluded by suggesting the following hypothesis: "the actions, uses, and interactions on a drawing artifact are as important to the effectiveness of many design collaborations as viewing the final artifact, and allowing designers to share drawing space activities increases their attention and involvement in the design task."

Bly and Minneman (1990) continued the earlier work by specifying design goals for an effective shared drawing system, as:

1. Each designer's marks and gestures must be visible simultaneously to all other designers;
2. Designers must be able to switch quickly among drawing, writing and gesturing;
3. All designers must be able to mark and gesture in the shared space simultaneously;
4. The tool should be as "natural" as possible.

Bly and Minneman built a system called "Commune" that satisfied these requirements. Comparison of the "Commune" setting to the settings investigated in the earlier study Bly suggests that the use of gesturing, writing and drawing in this setting corresponds more closely to the natural setting (i.e. face-to-face) than do the others (i.e. media link and telephone). A similar direction was taken by Tang and Minneman (1990) who proceeded to develop a system called "VideoDraw". In essence, both these systems emulate natural collaborative settings and media electronically. Bly and Minneman's results indicate that the pattern of drawing surface activity when using "Commune" is very similar to that occuring in the face-to-face setting; in other words, working with "Commune" is, in this sense, like working with pen and paper.

The ROCOCO Project: collaborative design at a distance

The ROCOCO (RemOte COoperation and COmmunication) project was also concerned with developing systems to support geographically separated designers working collaboratively during the early stages of design. The project was structured in two phases. The first phase of the project involved a study of face-to-face working (Scrivener *et al.* 1992a). In this study, six designer-dyads engaged in predefined tasks, regarded as being characteristic of the early stages of design. The designers sat opposite each other across a table. On the table, between them, was a pad of A1 plain white paper on which they could both draw using their own pens.

Throughout each of the six studies undertaken an audio-video recording was made. Two camera angles were adopted, a close up of the drawing surface and a wide angle of both participants to capture non-verbal communication. Later transcripts of the verbal discourse were produced. This raw data was systematically coded (or allocated to descriptive categories) in order to reduce it (from twelve hours of video tape, six hours of audio tape and approximately eighteen A1 drawing sheets) to a manageable form while minimising the loss of meaning. Established systems were used in the main to code verbal and non-verbal communication, whereas a scheme had to be devised for categorising drawing activity. Table 7.1 summarises the primary coding categories used in the face-to-face study.

The face-to-face study served two primary functions: first, it provided a basis for system development, in that a computer system was designed that replicated the media and communication channels available in the face-to-face setting; second, the pattern of activity occurring in the face-to-face setting provided a reference for comparison with that occurring during computer-mediated interaction.

The system designed to replicate face-to-face working is called the ROCOCO Station, and supplies pairs of geographically separated designers with an eye-to-eye video-link, a high-quality audio-link, and a shared drawing surface. Each user of the ROCOCO Station is provided with a SUN SPARCStation 1+ . A central feature of the ROCOCO Station is the ROCOCO Sketchpad, a computer-based Distributed Shared Drawing Surface (Clark and Scrivener 1992) which allows persons sitting at different computer workstations to share a drawing surface. The surface takes the form of a large "shared window" which is displayed on each workstation screen. Users have simultaneous access to the drawing surface (the ROCOCO Sketchpad). They are able to draw with a selection of "pen-types" and can point to existing drawings with a "telepointer". The drawing surface can, in principle, be shared by any number of users.

Table 7.1. Activities and primary coding categories.

Activity	Coding
Verbal	Discourse, progression through design cycles; speech acts.
Non-verbal (e.g. gesture)	Gaze (e.g. eye-to-eye contact); gesture (e.g pointing); body language (e.g. leaning forward); gestural function (e.g. accenting)
Drawing	Drawing acts.

The sketchpad is operated via a digitiser and pen. To one side of the workstation screen is a "Video Tunnel" video-link (incorporating a video camera and monitor). This arrangement, developed by Smith *et al.* (1989), uses half silvered glass and mirrors to allow eye-to-eye contact to be made over the video-link. Users also have a high-quality headset audio-link. A designer in position at a ROCOCO Station is shown in Figure 7.1.

Figure 7.1. The ROCOCO Station.

In the second phase of the ROCOCO project (Scrivener *et al.* 1992a) the communication requirements of group design were investigated in conditions where, typically, communication was impoverished. These experimental conditions were achieved by manipulating the features of the ROCOCO Station. The four configurations shown in Table 7.2 were investigated.

Table 7.2. ROCOCO Station experimental configurations.

Configuration	Sketchpad	Video Tunnel	Audio-link
1	on	on	on
2	on	on	off
3	on	off	on
4	on	off	off

Five design pairs were studied under each of these conditions (i.e. 20 one-hour experiments using the system). In all conditions the ROCOCO Sketchpad was available. In addition to the ROCOCO Project's studies, the LookingGlass project performed three similar design sessions using the sketchpad together with an "overlay" video-link and telephone audio-link (see Keen 1991; Scrivener *et al.* 1992c, 1993a). Also, a modified version of the ROCOCO Sketchpad was developed to run over a basic rate ISDN line in order to allow a product designer in Loughborough to work with a product designer in Adelaide, a distance of some 10000 miles. In addition to the sketchpad, these designers were able to talk to each other via a headset telephone link. Six one-hour design sessions were performed over this distance (see Scrivener *et al.* 1992d; Scrivener *et al.* 1993b, Scrivener *et al.* 1993c). Essentially, this study replicated Configuration 3 of the ROCOCO project.

An important feature of the ROCOCO Sketchpad is its ability to maintain a "log-file" of all drawing and telepointing activity occurring during a sketching session. Each drawing act, pen-colour change, pen-thickness change, pointing act and page change is recorded together with an identifying participant number and time stamp. The log-files generated in all of the above design sessions have been kept in computer-readable form, and constitute a large body of drawing activity data (29 hours of design activity, approaching 100Mb of ASCII files).

The ROCOCO project and related studies have been fully documented elsewhere (Clark and Scrivener 1992; Scrivener *et al.* 1992a, 1992b, 1992c, 1992d, 1993a, 1993b, 1993c). The important point to make here is that the results of the research show that the two primary configurations (i.e. 1 and 3, Table 7.2) compare favourably with the face-to-face setting both in terms of activity patterns and users' subjective assessments of the system's appropriateness for the task and usability. In other words, in these configurations the ROCOCO Station supported design at a distance (using sketching) in a natural and familiar manner.

7.6 An analysis of aspects of sketching activity during design at a distance

In the context of this paper, what is of interest about the above work is its focus on providing a medium that basically emulates traditional pen and paper - a sketchpad in other words. No attempt was made by the developers of Commune and the ROCOCO Sketchpad to exploit the computer to enhance or augment the functionality available to the users. Rather the design goal was to provide a computer-based drawing medium that would not significantly impoverish the collaborators in comparison to pen and paper. Empirical research indicates that face-to-face sketching is replicated in design sessions using these computer-mediated sketching tools.

However, this may seem rather like a case of using an sledgehammer to crack a nut. Is it not desirable to utilise the powers of the computer to go beyond sketching? However, as noted earlier, because we understand so little about sketching requirements it is difficult to see how to enhance this form of interaction with images. In what way, then, does the CSCW research described above provide opportunities for understanding sketching behaviour that will help us to determine the way ahead?

Because the sketch "marks" produced by systems such as the ROCOCO Sketchpad can be easily recorded and "replayed", for perhaps the first time since sketching was invented some 500 years ago, sketching can be conducted using technology that can also support its analysis, thereby offering increased opportunities for understanding sketching behaviour.

In the following sections, we conduct such an analysis using some of the ROCOCO data. The data examined is that produced in Configuration 3, Table 7.2 (i.e. speech and sketchpad -

the "Video-off" condition) because this condition has been most extensively studied in both laboratory and non-laboratory settings (Scrivener *et al.* 1992c, 1993a). Our purpose is to gain insights about the nature of sketching episodes. Later, we will consider the implications of these findings in respect of current and future sketch augmentation systems.

The temporal primitive: The drawing act

Before proceeding to such an analysis it is necessary to explain the drawing categories employed for coding the drawing data generated during sessions using the ROCOCO Station. In effect drawing activity is represented in the stream of data from the user's stylus and tablet. In simple terms, this stream consists of actions when the pen is "up", or not in contact with the tablet, and those when the pen is "down", or in contact with the tablet surface. In the first instance this stream is structured into "drawing acts".

When a designer is creating a mark it is not uncommon for the pen to be in intermittent contact with the drawing surface, thus leading to a sequence of disjoint strokes. In such circumstances these drawing discontinuities are all part of a single drawing act. However, there are periods when its is obvious that the draughtsperson is not drawing, when the pen and hand are held in a resting state. Such pauses, which mark the beginning and end of a drawing act, are relatively easy to detect in video recordings of face-to-face activity because the hand is clearly visible.

From analysis of the face-to-face setting a simple temporal rule was derived for segmenting the computer-logged drawing data. As defined by this rule a drawing act is a segment of the data stream that contains a set of pen-down (and interleaved pen-up) events terminated at the beginning and end by a continuous sequence of pen-up events of duration three seconds or greater.

Drawing act types

After segmentation, each drawing act is coded as belonging to one of five types: "Non-symbolic" (e.g. a doodle or a squiggle), "Other symbolic" (e.g. a line under text or an arrow) "Alpha/numeric" (e.g. labels/writing), "Pictorial orthographic" (e.g. a plan view of an object), or "Pictorial perspective" (e.g. a street view receding into the distance). These are referred to as drawing act types 1, 2, 3, 4 and 5 in the following text. In Figure 7.2, each type is illustrated using a drawing act taken from the ROCOCO data. These categories are self-explanatory, except the non-symbolic category which perhaps deserves further explanation. Sometimes marks are made on the surface which don't appear to mean anything at all even in the context of other marks. Such marks fall into the category non-symbolic. In a sense, this is a catch all category for any mark that cannot be categorised as belonging to one of the other classes. In practice the four symbolic categories proved relevant and generally accommodated the vast majority of marks; marks of category "non-symbolic" representing a very small proportion of drawing acts.

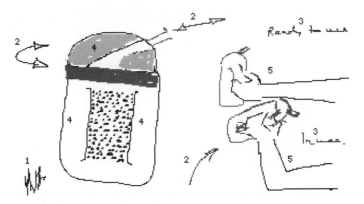

Figure 7.2. Drawing act types: non-symbolic, other symbolic, alpha/numeric, pictorial orthographic, pictorial perspective (labelled respectively 1, 2, 3, 4 and 5).

The pattern of drawing act duration and inter-drawing act intervals

Figure 7.3 shows the frequency of occurrence of intervals of between drawings acts and was produced by summing the data produced in each of the five Video-off design sessions. From this plot it is clear that over half (i.e. 61%) of intervals between drawing acts are less than 12 seconds, 33% of these being less than 3 seconds, indicating that, in general, cessation of drawing surface activity is followed swiftly by the onset of further sketching.

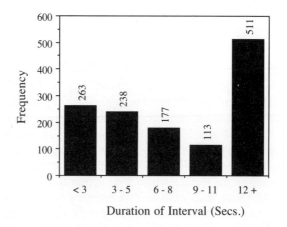

Figure 7.3. Frequency of occurrence of inter-drawing act intervals of a given duration between drawing acts.

The duration of drawing acts, categorised in terms of duration ranges, are shown in Figure 7.4. From this it is clear that the majority of drawing acts are produced in short bursts of activity (71% being less than 15 seconds in duration, and 28% less than 5 seconds).

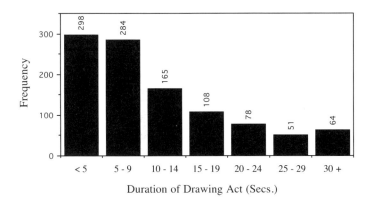

Figure 7.4. Frequency of occurrence of drawing acts of a given duration.

Drawing acts tend to be meaningful wholes

Considering the drawing acts themselves, it is interesting to note that they tend not to be arbitrary fragments of the things they represent. For example, it is not usually the case that an alpha/numeric drawing act comprises part of a word. Usually, a word or group of words is realised in a single act. In the case of writing, this is perhaps not that surprising since the word is intuitively the natural primitive of discourse. However, the natural primitive for pictorial representation is not so intuitively obvious; it could be a line or a group of lines comprising an arbitrary fragment of that which is represented. It is thus illuminating to find that, in general, pictorial drawing acts represent meaningful and structurally complex entities. For example, a figure, the top of an ironing board, or the overall structure of a shirt as shown in Figure 7.5. Furthermore, as noted earlier, the entities are drawn with great rapidity.

Split drawing acts

Figure 7.3 illustrated the intervals between drawing acts. In fact the category "< 3" is a special category because the drawing acts bounding an interval falling into this category are actually sub-divisions of a drawing act segmented by the applying the temporal rule described above. This is because a second level of processing was applied during the coding of drawing acts. Consider for example Figure 7.6 which shows a drawing act segmented on the basis of time. Clearly, it would be difficult to code this drawing act since it is composed of drawing of different types: that is pictorial orthographic (the "cross" shape) and other symbolic (the double headed arrow). To overcome this problem such drawing acts, called "split acts", are sub-divided according to their type composition.

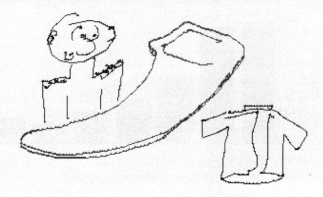

Figure 7.5. Drawing acts tend to comprise entities that are complete and meaningful in themselves rather than being arbitrary fragments of entities: in this sequence of drawing acts, first a figure is drawn, then the top of an ironing board, then a complete shirt

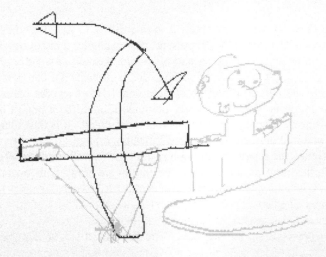

Figure 7.6. A split act composed of drawing types pictorial orthographic and other symbolic.

A segment of drawing act file derived from the raw drawing data generated during the first session of the ROCOCO Video-off condition using the temporal and type rules is shown below:

Designer	Start	End	Duration	Acts	Act Types
0	1028	1042	15	1	5
1	1061	1064	4	1	1
0	1072	1087	16	3	4 2 4

The columns record the label of the designer who generated the act, when the act started, when it finished, how long it lasted, how many "sub-acts" it comprised and the type of each sub-act. The rows represent what was captured by the application of the temporal rule. As we can see, the first two acts were not sub-divided. However, the act in row 3 comprised different types and hence were sub-divided according to type. Thus the drawing act in row 3 was split into a type 4 segment, followed by a type 2 segment, and completed by another type 4 segment. These split acts are interesting for at least three reasons. First, because they consists of marks of different mode, such as alpha/numeric and pictorial (however, occasionally pictorial split acts are of one type, say 4 and 4, in cases where different, usually extant, drawings were elaborated in one act), second, because the intervals between changes of modality must be less than three seconds, and finally, because a split act indicates a sequence of type changes the produced by only one designer.

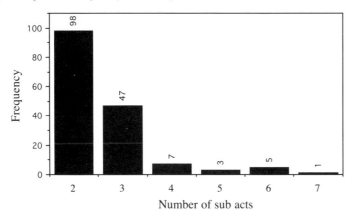

Figure 7.7. The frequency of split acts per different number of sub-acts.

Figure 7.7 shows the total number of split acts occurring in the Video-off condition divided according to number of splits or sub-acts. Clearly, the vast majority of split acts consist of two or three sub-acts, however longer sequences of modal changes are also evident. Overall, split acts represent 16% of all drawing acts. The generation and anatomy of a split act is illustrated in Figure 7.8. First a sleeve-press is added to the developing ironing board idea, then an arrow is drawn illustrating the link between this idea and an earlier design, and finally the cuff end of a shirt sleeve is added.

In Figure 7.9 the duration of drawing acts is shown for split acts. Given that the average number of sub-acts per split act is 2.9, it is interesting to note that 84% of split acts are less than 30 seconds in duration, indicating that these sub-acts, like non-split drawing acts, are also generally of short duration.

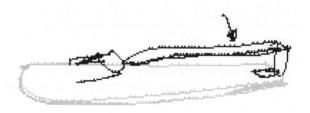

The "Split Act" is composed of three "sub Acts"

A sleeve press (Type 5)   An arrow (Type 2)   A cuff (Type 5)

Figure 7.8. The anatomy of a split act.

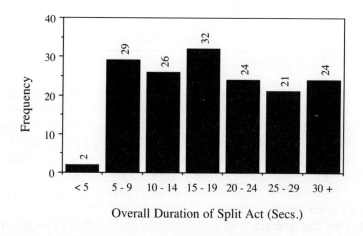

Overall Duration of Split Act (Secs.)

Figure 7.9. Frequency of occurrence of split acts of given duration.

Descriptive and depictive combinations

Figure 7.10 shows the split acts categorised in terms of the types contained in each act. Not all combinations are shown, instead the analysis focuses on acts which contain no pictorial marks, those combining pictorial and alpha-numeric (types 1 or 2 can sometimes also occur in this category), those containing pictorial and non-symbolic or other symbolic marks but no alpha/numeric marks, and finally those containing only pictorial marks.

In general, each split act contains marks of different type or mode. However, of particular interest is the category of pictorial (type 4 or 5) and alpha/numeric (type 3), since this category comprises depictive and descriptive marks as discussed by Fish and Scrivener (1991), a split act of this type is shown in Figure 7.11a. In other words, both categorical information (e.g. the words "aluminised layer") and depictive information (e.g. the shape of a flask) is realised in a single burst of activity.

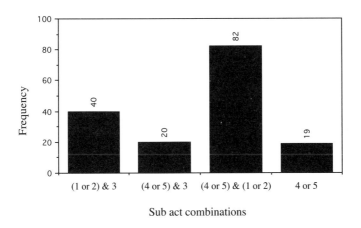

Figure 7.10. Breakdown of split acts in terms of types contained in each act.

By far the most prominent category is that of pictorial (type 4 and 5) and non-alpha/numeric (type 1 or 2). Typically, such acts consists of pictorial marks and arrows indicating movement or direction. This is illustrated in Figure 7.11b. It is worth noting that an "arrow" is both descriptive, in the sense that it stands for "movement", and depictive, in the sense that its shape generally indicates a specific direction and path of movement: such a symbol represents both the general and the specific.

It is rarely the case that split acts with pictorial marks consists of only pictorial marks (i.e. only 12% of split acts are made up only of types 4 or 5). Typically picturing is combined with describing - "seeing as" with "seeing that".

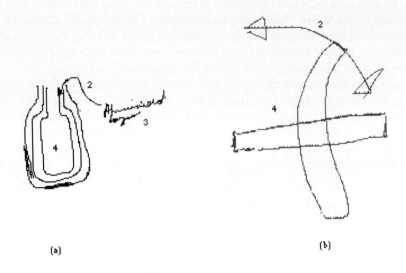

(a)   (b)

Figure 7.11. Typically split acts consist of both depictive and descriptive information: (a) illustrates a type 4, 2 and 3 combination (the text says "aluminised layer"), and (b) the use of a type 2 "arrow" showing movement together with a type 4 drawing.

The conjunction of verbal description with drawing

Given that bursts of sketching activity comprise both description and depiction, it is interesting to consider whether drawing activity is simultaneously accompanied by verbal description. Again, some insights can be gained into this question by looking at drawing surface activity, but this time focusing on the ROCOCO Sketchpad-only condition (Configuration 4 in Table 7.2). Figure 7.12 shows the data for this condition corresponding to that shown in Figure 10 for the Video-off condition. Clearly, the distributions in Figures 7.10 and 7.12 are quite different. The significant feature of this difference is the increase in split act categories that include alpha/numeric marks: in the Video-off condition these represent 37% compared to 94% in the Sketchpad-only condition. It is not surprising that writing should substitute in the Sketchpad-only condition for the absence of a audio channel of communication. However, the fact that the proportion of split acts including text increases in this condition relative to the Video-off condition indicates that in the Video-off condition packets of expressive activity consist of drawing and verbal description. This is evidenced by the fact that in the Video-off condition 17% of split acts containing pictorial marks are accompanied by alpha/numeric marks, which increases to 84% in the Sketchpad-only condition. In other words, in the Sketchpad-only condition there is a decrease in the proportion of pictorial split acts without text relative to those with text compared to the Video-off condition. This suggests that non-textual pictorial split acts in the Video-off condition are accompanied by verbal description.

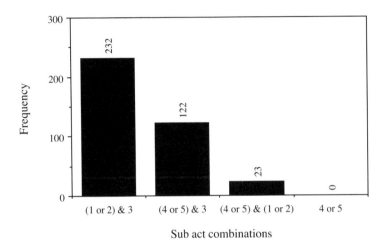

Figure 7.12. Breakdown of split acts in terms of types contained in each act for the Sketchpad-only condition.

Figure 7.13. The descriptive nature of the text in textual-pictorial split acts in the Sketchpad-only condition is clearly evident in these examples. Text in example (a) says "a scoopy thing", example (b) says "a hover person?", example (c) says "removable plastic box".

A number of textual and pictorial split acts from the Sketchpad-only condition are shown in Figure 7.13, and clearly illustrate the descriptive nature of the text.

7.7 Discussion

These observations reveal a number of important features of sketching behaviour:

1. The drawing surface is regularly accessed for mark making;
2. A good percentage of drawing episodes are separated by pauses of less than three seconds;
3. A drawing act is usually of short, and sometimes very short, duration;
4. Typically, drawing acts represent meaningful parts which may be structurally complex (for example, a shirt shape);
5. Drawing acts often consist of different representational modes (drawing act types) realised in rapid succession;
6. Drawing acts are usually accompanied by verbal description.

These findings support the theory of sketching discussed in the earlier sections. There does, for example, appear to be a rapid, continuous, intense and focused interaction between the designer and the drawing surface. The fact that drawing acts are meaningful and complex indicates a close coupling between mental structures and the process of drawing (i.e. the drawing programme operates on imaged parts as a whole). The fact that bursts of drawing activity often consist of both depictive (pictorial) and descriptive (textual) representations suggests that the visual reasoning processes involved in early design utilise different information forms (i.e. visual and non-visual). Finally, the fact that drawing acts are usually accompanied by verbalisation (in the case of the individual sketcher this would just be unspoken thought) supports the idea that sketches only partially represent ideas in mind. In general, a drawing act in sketching is not an attempt to represent a solution as such, rather it is a notational device that helps its creator to reason with complex and labile mental structures. As noted above, the "sketch" is largely in the mind of the sketcher, and is developed via internal and external movements, effected partly through the drawing surface. It is perhaps obvious then that the changes to the drawing surface must be achieved without disrupting the percept-image hybrid.

7.8 Implications for design of computer systems

If we accept the notion that the ideas formulated in the early creative stages of a design task are largely constructed, retained, compared, manipulated, and evaluated in the mind, then we can begin to see why sketching and the sketch provide such effective support. The act of sketching requires little preparation. It is automatic in the sense that the projection from idea to external representation is realised through the unconscious execution of a programme of motor actions. Marks of different type can be produced with great rapidity and in rapid succession. As such there is limited interference between the act of sketching and the cognitive processes of creation, retention, manipulation, comparison, and evaluation. Furthermore, the incompleteness and indeterminacy of the sketch minimises the interference between percept and mental images utilised by these processes, and may even stimulate invention.

If we consider drawings acts constructed from different primitive components (such as circles, rectangles etc.) it is difficult to imagine how these could be produced with anything like the rapidity characteristic of sketching, even in the hands of the skilled user - imagine for example attempting to construct the shirt illustrated in Figure 7.5 using such primitives. If the dynamics of sketching are determined by the duration and limit of working memory and attention the likely effects of reductions in rate of production are obvious: for example, ideas may be forgotten while others are being realised.

Even if complex structures could be realised at the same rate as a sketch using primitives we have argued that design objects may be imagined that have never been seen before. Is it likely, therefore, that the repertoire of shapes provided in an object-based system will be rich enough to construct the imagined objects and in the form required (e.g. orthographic or perspective)? Inevitably, the flow of interaction between internally and externally represented elements of the creation must be impeded both in terms of rate of modification, and the shape and structure of that which can be represented externally. Again, it is difficult to see how changes of mode, between say a text tool and a drawing tool, could be achieved with the fluidity of sketching, or how an "arrow" could be readily given exactly the right curvature to represent the motion of a lever or the twist-and-pull action required to remove a bottle top.

The time required to select a new mode, the explicit need to shift attention from the design task to the interaction task, the visual nature of the tool interactions typical of such systems, the difficulty of realisation using modal primitives (e.g. modelling and typing) are all features that are likely to interfere with and compete for the resources available to visual reasoning; thus rendering of little utility any object handling tools provided. On the other hand, we conjecture that the cognitive benefits provided by the sketch (through its attributes of abbreviation, incompleteness and indeterminacy) and sketching (through speed and directness of production - in different representation formats) outweigh the editorial and manipulatory limitations of the sketch: the editing and manipulation is best done in the mind.

7.9 Conclusions

We have argued that sketching is not an anachronistic activity. We have postulated that the sketch and the process of sketching supports visual reasoning during the early conceptual stages of design in ways that are barely understood, but depend crucially on the interaction between the sketch and the cognitive processes underlying conception.

From an analysis of the computer-mediated sketching behaviour of remotely located design pairs it is concluded that object-based graphics systems are likely to impose temporal, structural, and cognitive constraints on visual reasoning during creative design. This would explain why features of model-based systems that augment the later stages of design impoverish rather than enhance initial design, and are still little used for this purpose.

This would suggest that different cognitive activities are involved in the different stages of design, requiring different forms of external support. Nevertheless, it is almost inconceivable to think that digital computer technology has nothing to offer in the way of enhancements to the early stages of designing, that pen and paper is the best we can expect. This is almost certainly not the case. However, we would argue that before any such benefits can be realised we must first recognise that sketching is used preferentially, if intuitively, by designers in the early stages of design because it supports visual imagination. Such a recognition will lead us to study more systematically the nature of the sketch and sketching, the cognitive processes underlying creative design, and the how the latter is supported by the former. Only when insights have been gained in these areas will begin to see how computer-based technology can help us to go beyond sketching.

References

Beiderman I. (1987). Recognition by Components: A Theory of Human Image Understanding, *Psychological Review*, 94, No. 2, 115-147.

Bly S. (1988). A Use of drawing Surfaces in Different Collaborative Settings, *Proceedings of the Conference on Computer Supported Co-operative Work*, 250-256, Portland, Oregon, September 1988.

Bly S. & Minneman S. (1990). Commune: A Shared Drawing Surface, *Proceedings of the Conference on Office Information Systems*, 184-192, Boston, April 1990.

Clark S.M. & Scrivener S.A.R. (1992). The ROCOCO Sketchpad Distributed Shared Drawing Surface, *LUTCHI Report No. 92/C/LUTCHI/0150*, LUTCHI Research Centre, University of Technology, Loughborough, UK, 1992.

Fish J. & Scrivener S.A.R. (1990). Amplifying the Mind's Eye: Sketching and Visual Cognition, *LEONARDO*, 23, No. 1, 117-126.

Goldschmidt G. (1991). The Dialectics of Sketching, *Creativity Research Journal*, 4, No. 2, 123-143.

Gombrich E.H. (1966). Leonardo's method for working out compositions, in Norm and Form, Phaidon Press, London, 58-63.

Goodman G. & Abel M. (1986). Collaboration Research in SCL, *Proceedings of the Conference on Computer Supported Co-operative Work*, Austin, Texas, December 1986.

Huyghe R. (1962). *Art and the Spirit of Man*, London, Thames and Hudson, 1962.

Keen N. (1991). *The LookingGlass*, Masters Thesis, LUTCHI Research Centre, University of Technology, Loughborough, UK, 1991.

Scrivener S.A.R., Clarke A.A., Connolly J., Garner S., Clark S.M., Palmen H., Smyth M. & Schappo A. (1992a). *The ROCOCO Project Phase 1 Report*, LUTCHI Research Centre, University of Technology, Loughborough, UK, 1992.

Scrivener S.A.R., Clarke A.A., Connolly J., Garner S., Clark S.M., Palmen H., Smyth M. & Schappo A. (1992b). *The ROCOCO Project Phase 2 Report*, LUTCHI Research Centre, University of Technology, Loughborough, UK, 1992.

Scrivener S.A.R., Clark S.M. & Keen N. (1992c). *The LookingGlass Distributed Shared Workspace*, LUTCHI Research Centre, University of Technology, Loughborough, UK, 1992, submitted to Kleuwer International CSCW Journal.

Scrivener S.A.R., Clark S.M., Symth M., Harris D. & Rockoff T. (1992d). Designing at a Distance: Experiments in Remote-Synchronous Design, *Proceedings of OZCHI92: CHISIG Annual Conference*, 44-53, Gold Coast, Australia, November 1992.

Scrivener S.A.R., Clark S.M. and Keen N. (1993a). *The Role of Replication in the Development of*

Remote CSCW Systems, Design Issues in CSCW, to be published by Springer-Verlag.

Scrivener S.A.R, Clark S.M., Clarke A., Connolly J., Garner S., Palmen H., Smyth M. & Schappo A. (1993b). Real-time Communication Between Dispersed Work Groups via Speech and Drawing, to be published in *Wirtshaftsinformatik*.

Scrivener S.A.R., Harris D., Clark S.M., Rockoff T. & Smyth M. (1993c). Designing at a Distance via Designer-to-designer Interaction, to be published in *Design Studies*.

Sheehan P.W. (1972). A Functional Analysis of the Role of Visual Imagery in Unexpected Recall, *The Function and Nature of Imagery*, P.W. Sheehan (ed.), New York, Academic.

Tang J.C. and Leifer L.J. (1988). A framework for understanding the workspace activity of design teams, EC-CSCW *88 Proceedings* 244-249, New York, ACM Press.

Tang J. and Minneman S. (1990). VideoDraw: A video interface for collaborative drawing, *Proceedings of the ACM/SIGCHI Conference on Human Factors in computing.* 313-320, Washington.

8

Biomedical Virtual Environments

Neil Robinson

8.1 Introduction

Visualisation techniques applied in computer environments can broadly be divided into two main categories. In the first category the visualisor has only a sparse amount of information about the subject he is going to make visible. This may be an engineering drawing or a description of the way a structure deforms when pressures are applied. The visualisor then will create a geometric model of the data by taking lines (or vectors) between key points in his data structure. By joining the ends of the lines the data may then be triangulated or joined by polygons to create a surface and an image is generated. The image may then be animated to show how the vector geometry changes in various circumstances. When a user wishes to interrogate an animated sequence of this type he has the problem that very few points in the image have a direct physical existence in the data structure that was used to create the image. The visualisor must therefore generate a relatively complete virtual environment with its own rules in which the user may learn the properties of the data he is examining. In the world of medical visualisation the problem is almost a mirror image of the above scenario. The visualisor is presented with a complete description of the data environment and his task is to reduce the data so that those key aspects of it are made apparent to the user. In this process, however, he must always retain the possibility of rapid location of any visualised structure within the underlying physical data. The goal therefore of visualisation is to guide the user rapidly and accurately through his data set and provide visual models which effectively represent the diagnostic characteristics of the data.

Interacting with Virtual Environments Edited by Lindsay MacDonald and John Vince

8.2 The medical data environment

The process of medical diagnosis involves collecting and evaluating information gathered from a wide range of sources. In an increasing number of instances this information is presented to the clinician in the form of a picture based on some physical property of the structure being investigated. This could be a photographic image of the structure itself, for example a cell viewed through a microscope, however it is more common to find images derived from some physical or chemical property of the structure being studied. Examples of this include: X-ray transmission characteristics; uptake of radioactive chemicals; the para-magnetic properties of atomic nuclei; reflection of ultra-sonic sound waves. (Figure 8.1).

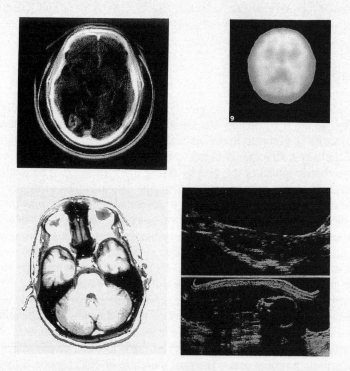

Figure 8.1. Transaxial images derived from back-projection image reconstruction. Images are shown from a number of image capture technologies:
  a) CT- X ray of the head.
  b) SPECT (Single Photon Computed Tomography) image of the head.
  c) T1 weighted MRI image of the head
  d) Real time B scan on foetus at 5 weeks and 22 weeks.

It is beyond the scope of a review of visualisation to deal with the detailed physics underlying the construction of these various images (Payne 1991). It is vital, however, that the user of any imaging modality should consider the physics and mathematics of both the methods of data generation and the algorithms used image generation to a level where the physical limitations of any methodology are understood. In any visual representation of information there is a finite limitation on the fidelity of the data; at a basic level the number of lines on a television or the grain size of a film limits the information content of the image they display. In the field of medical imaging it is usually the image capture technology that provides the ultimate resolution available within an image or picture under consideration. In many instances this may be much lower than the technology used to display the image. An illustration of this is the computer screen, where although the screen may support a resolution of beyond 1000 by 1000 pixels, the data to be viewed is often of a much more limited resolution, sometimes as low as 64 by 64 pixels. It is therefore important to bear in mind the underlying resolution of the imaging modality when changing image size in order to "improve diagnosis or inference". The traditional use of film-based technologies with resolution far beyond that contained in the data that they represent has clouded this issue in many cases.

In the past three years the ability to collect data as true three-dimensional data sets in a conventional clinical setting has increased dramatically. Although it has been possible for the past decade, in research settings to collect 3-D data from a wide range of imaging modalities the time required to collect the data has meant that such acquisitions have been impractical in a clinical environment. Advances in basic medical scanner technologies have now placed 3-D data acquisition and analysis firmly within the clinical and basic medical domain.

8.3 The computer environment

The role of computers in biomedical data analysis has experienced a chequered career over the past decade. Suppliers have compromised over the need to provide generic solutions against a desire to offer the best performance currently available. Fortunately, as we approach the mid 1990s, these compromises are no longer necessary as mainstream computer environments increasingly offer suitable performance without economic penalty. Today, standard workstations offer 256 levels (8 bit) of grey scale or colour and up to 1200x1000 pixels resolution and are well able to deal with most medical images. Although 1024 or 2048 (10 or 11 bit) may be available from the capture technology (or in the case of planar X-ray as much as 12 bit) it is generally accepted that the majority of information can be visualised using an 8 bit (256 level) data description. With these advances medical imaging is able to take advantage of the dramatic changes in price performance seen in the last decade.

The traditional approach to diagnosis has involved black and white photographic transparencies, usually of A4 (8" by 11") or A3 (11" by 16") size being held in front of a translucent illuminated box and the picture "interpreted". This method has its origins in the development of X-ray diagnosis where the films were directly exposed to the X-ray beams passing through the patient and the image generated in exactly the same way that light beams expose a conventional photographic film. It was therefore a very logical process to view directly the exposed film. The diagnosis in many cases was very straightforward, a broken bone for instance could usually be seen very clearly. As clinicians became more experienced at viewing the film plates and became very familiar with the characteristics of the images, increasingly subtle abnormalities could be seen. The skill in this process was necessarily developed by and resided within the clinician. The language that evolved to describe the subtle abnormalities was drawn from the photographic and visual world, a "shadow on the lung" describing the increase in X-ray absorption caused by tissue oedema. In some cases the texture of the image was used as a key feature, for example in bone de-mineralisation in diseases such as osteo-porosis. When new reconstruction algorithms were developed in the early 1970s these allowed transaxial slices to be calculated from data collected (Hounsfield 1973). Although the images were first viewed on video monitor the "diagnostic process" was still carried out during case conferences in which films of the video images were mounted on light-boxes in exactly the same way as standard X-ray films. At the inception of CT X-ray this was a fairly sensible procedure as only a small number of transaxial slices were usually collected and these could be displayed simultaneously at a suitable size using the film presentation. This practice has to all extents and purposes continued even with the introduction of magnetic resonance imaging (MRI) and constitutes an important part of a clinical radiologist's skill base. The only area in which VDU-based diagnosis has made any significant impact is in CINE X-ray CT and ultrasound in which lower resolution images are captured and displayed in real time to show dynamic events such as the cardiac cycle.

The computer VDU is starting to make some impact as a display or diagnostic console, however by far the most common display technology in 3-D medical imaging is pan chromatic film transparency viewed by back projection on a light box. One reason for this is the natural extrapolation from transmission X-ray. The second reason is the ability to have an almost infinite display screen and hence view a large number of different slices simultaneously. In many situations one doctor may be viewing one series of images whilst another doctor standing next to him views another. The cost and size of computer VDUs effectively precludes a direct replacement of the light box by a VDU although multiple display monitors have been introduced on some review stations. One confounding problem with the use of the computer VDU as a diagnostic console is the direct relationship between physical size of the display monitor and the pixel matrix of the image. The VDU is digitally mapped to the image and conventional displays use resolutions of around 1000 by 1000 points on a 16" or 19" monitor. If a 512 by 512 pixel matrix is used within the data then a maximum of four images may be simultaneously displayed if 1024 by 1024 pixels are available. Unfortunately standard displays have usually only offered 1024 by 768, or 1152 by 900. Larger pixel matrices offering 1280 by 1024 are now being introduced at standard pricing but the ideal matrix of around 1600 by 1200 is not yet available as a standard option (although specialist products are available but this may double the cost of the workstation).

The computer VDU must in most circumstances justify its adoption by offering rapid access to the traditional views and the ability to generate new forms of visualisation not possible on a static light box review station. One key element of the form of display offered by a computer VDU is the option to interact directly with the data and obtain instant feedback. A second unique feature is the ability to provide a dynamic display, which can allow for visual linkage of elements within the image not possible in static displays. It is through the judicious manipulation of the inherent psycho-physical characteristics of the human visual system that computer VDU displays can provide the necessary "added value" to the clinical diagnostic process to justify their more wide spread adoption (Hill 1988).

Two approaches to the use of display manipulations that are specifically designed to utilise the properties of the human visual system have been adopted. One area where this type of approach is widely used is in the production of depth cues in viewing.

In the first style of processing, it is the actual view that is manipulated such the viewer makes use of his pre-conception of the image to "see" a particular interpretation. An example of this is volume rendering using different weightings for voxels at different depths within the image (Fuzzy gradient shading - see section on rendering algorithms). The second approach is to use video sequences of different views specifically to enhance the depth cues.

As the images presented increase in complexity the limitations of the 8-bit display are becoming more apparent. If the data has 256 different levels and we now wish to add an additional parameter to indicate depth and maybe a third to indicate tissue type then clearly more displayable colours must be available.

It is probable that 24 bit full colour displays will be increasingly available at reasonable price performance, however at present they are relatively rare. The use of 24-bit colour palettes to display medical images are at present poorly developed and the acceptance of continuous colour look-up tables requires further clinical trial.

8.4 Interaction in 2-D

Although the availability of 3-D data is increasing at a very fast rate it must be recognised that at least within the clinical domain 2-D representation and analysis remain the norm. The scale and type of interactions remain very varied, ranging from simple visual inspection through data based Region of Interest (ROI) analysis to anatomical atlas based segmentation.

When assessing the impact and importance of computers in 2-D image analysis a number of fundamental questions must be addressed. These include:

- Physical size of the data matrix
- Partial volume effects
- Grey scale dynamic range of the data

Data matrix size

Medical images vary in size from 64 by 64 pixels in nuclear medicine studies to 2000 by 2000 pixels from planar or digital X-ray. In order to gain an effective view the data must either be sub-sampled or interpolated.

Partial volume effects

Although the data is inevitably viewed in a digital format pixel by pixel the structure contributing to the pixel may occupy only a fraction of the pixel. This is particularly true of lower resolution images. This effect must be taken into account when estimating the accuracy of regional measurements.

Dynamic range

The grey scale range used to show the data may be constrained or expanded relative to the original acquisition to improve identification of structures, however measurements are best made on the original data values.

For the clinician the requirements for diagnosis have changed little and at their most basic can be described by three requirements:

• Can I see the abnormality?
• Can I delineate the abnormality?
• Can I quantify the abnormality?

Computer-based displays offer clinicians a level of intimacy with their data unavailable with any other display technology. By allowing direct interaction with grey scale data regions of interest may be defined with a level of interaction unrivalled by any other method. Perversely the level of interaction available tends to increase the subjectivity of the analysis in many cases, rather than decreasing it as might be expected. One reason for this is that most biomedical sensor data does not uniquely iso-contour, by this it is implied that there is always a level of uncertainty with the assignment of grey level to tissue type. The modalities with minimum uncertainty are X-ray and radio-nucleotide (nuclear medicine) studies where some form of parametric correlation is available. Magnetic resonance imaging that can generate the most exquisite images is often totally lacking in any quantitative relationship between tissue type and data values.

The tools which are used to interrogate datasets in 2-D are all based around the definition of a "region to be measured". This is usually called the Region of Interest (ROI).

The tools for control of ROI definition range from standard "anatomical templates", which effectively map predefined pixel locations to named regions, to totally interactive region definition. This may be performed either by freehand drawing or by "region growing" where pixels connected to a seed and lying within a predetermined data range are labelled as being part of the ROI.

The ubiquitous mouse and pointer is the standard tool to move around the 2-D data field although in some cases the mouse may be replaced by a Trackerball to limit the space required for manipulation. Even with the use of a Trackerball the ergonomics requires a seated operative and does not recreate the intelligent finger and commentary that is the standard form of clinical dialogue. It is interesting that it is in the field of Tele-radiology (the transmission of images by telecommunications that image dialogue interfaces are being advanced with users having individual pointers linked to the same image.

The use of anatomical templates for ROI analysis is steadily increasing and may vary from very limited fixed templates to more sophisticated models in which landmarks within the data set are used to locate and geometrically scale the template to match the data. There is considerable research activity in the field of model-based approaches in which the shape of a structure is modelled and the model then locates the "best fit" example of the model within the data. Although these approaches offer exciting possibilities for the future they are not in clinical use at present.

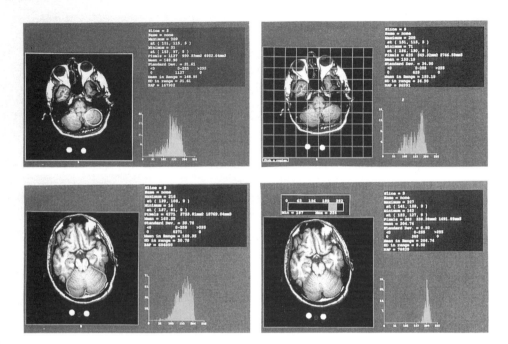

Figure 8.2. Region of interest analysis of an MRI T1 weighted image using a range of region definition tools.

- a) Geometric shape (ellipse)
- b) Grid
- c) Drawn anatomical region
- d) Data derived Region of Interest using region growing from a seed point.

Where anatomical templates are used data is often warped to occupy a standard geometric framework. One advantage of this approach is that it allows for statistical databases to be generated. The price for this statistical advantage is a loss of connection between data space, the geometric description of the data and anatomical space, "the true 3-D location of structure within the patient". The mirror of mapping data to some arbitrary or average anatomical framework is to map from a statistical anatomical framework to the particular patient geometry. Examples of both approaches are available but at present no clear consensus is available as to which will eventually be the method of choice (Figure 8.2).

8.5 Interaction in 3-D

The first and overwhelming practical limitation to 3-D interaction in a real clinical environment is the absolute requirement to limit interaction to a 2-D representation of a 3-D structure. As a result of this tools which have been developed fall naturally into four main classes:

• Manipulation of the rendering parameters to indicate depth and shape of structures,
• Pointing devices which allow registration of a 3-D surface with 2-D orthogonal planes,
• Visualisation of sequences to provide 3-D cues through motion either of the object itself or of the illuminating light source.

The first method uses the greatest sophistication of algorithmic development and as such can be difficult for the user to interpret unless the images themselves are clear in their presentation.

The second method allows connection of the newer methods of 3-D rendering with the traditional representation of medical data as a 2-D slice.

The third case makes use of the natural hysteresis of the visual system to create the illusion of a truly 3-D display from a series of 2-D images.

Rendering algorithms for 3-D visualisation

The rendering algorithms in current use fall into two main categories:

• Transmission algorithms
• Reflectance algorithms

In the case of the transmission algorithms the voxels themselves are considered as light emitters and do not require the definition of surfaces within the data. The resultant image is based on the summed strength of the emissions of the voxels along the path of each light ray cast through the data volume (Hansen *et al.* 1992 , Robb 1990). Examples of this type of rendering include:

• *Maximum intensity projection*
  This algorithm returns the value of the brightest voxel encountered along a beam of light passing through an object of interest. This may be constrained by the user to operate over a limited range of grey scale values or within a limited part of the data volume.

• *Summed intensity projection or summed voxel projection*
  This algorithm imagines each voxel as an emitter and returns the average intensity of all voxels along the line of the beam passing through the volume. Here again the algorithm may be limited to specific grey scale values and selected parts of the dataset.

- *Object constrained summed intensity projection or surface projection*
  The output is computed as the sum or average value of a defined number of voxels along the path of the ray from the surface of the object in question. In this case although the algorithm is not looking for surfaces which may reflect the light rays cast into the volume, it does require an object to have been defined within the data sets which will form the basis of the definition of which voxels the algorithm will be applied to (Figure 8.3).

In the case of reflection algorithms the model considers each voxel as a light reflector. This type of rendering has many features in common with surface rendering, but is applied to surfaces defined within a real data volume, rather than triangles or polygons connecting data points. A number of different reflection algorithms may be applied. This type of rendering requires that a surface be defined by segmentation and voxel labelling or by thresholding.

Voxel value
The actual grey value of the voxel at the surface is returned. This may be constrained by the user to operate over a limited range of grey scale values or within a limited part of the data volume.

Depth shading
The value returned is based on the depth into the data volume the light ray has travelled from light source to the intersected surface.

Depth gradient shading
The value returned is based upon the local 3-D gradient of depths of surface voxels surrounding the voxel in question.

Voxel gradient shading
The value returned is based upon the local grey value gradient surrounding the voxel in question. This type of algorithm may be constrained to use voxels only within a defined object or may include voxels outside of the object as well.

Summed opacity shading or fuzzy gradient shading
In this case each voxel is assigned an opacity related to its grey scale value on a continuum from fully transparent to fully opaque. The light ray is cast through the volume to a point of maximum opacity, the output value is then calculated from the local grey scale gradient of all voxels having non zero opacity.

Each type of rendering algorithm provides a different view of the same data and allows the clinician to interpret with the data in a different way.

Summed voxel projection algorithms can provide a good method of obtaining an overall "3-D view" of a complete data set. If a slider control and rapid view calculation are possible then the user may rapidly gain a general overview of the data characteristics. The use of sub-sampled data volumes to speed the recalculation of different views can be a great value in this

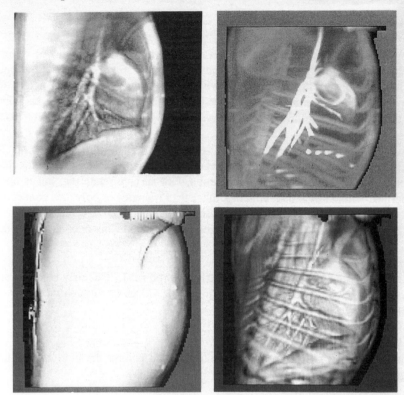

Figure 8.3. Examples of various volume rendering algorithms.
a) Summed voxel projection.   b) Maximum intensity projection.
c) Voxel gradient shading.   d) Fuzzy gradient shading.

context as the data is at present being interrogated at a very general level.

Maximum Intensity Projection images return a pixel value based upon the grey scale value of a unique voxel and as such provide a link to a specific 3-D location within the data. This can be used to great effect to visually register the computed view with the traditional planar views, which themselves may be displayed as orthogonal or oblique views. The ability to locate in 3-D space a voxel is of considerable value in the diagnostic process. A powerful interactive tool in this context is the use of a mouse and pointer which can indicate a location on the rendered image and recreate the three orthogonal views passing through this data point (Figure 8.4).

Similar 3-D location may be applied to rendered views based on reflection algorithms where the surfaces determined by threshold or other means can be located in the 3-D volume.

When multiple objects have been located and defined within an image, either by a slice by slice drawing and labelling or by selective thresholding, the ability to distinguish and locate the separate objects takes on a particular importance. Although colour has not found wide acceptance within traditional medical imaging its use in object-based volume rendering is almost essential. In multiple object volume rendering, object boundaries have already been defined so that artificial contouring of the data is due to discontinuities in colour look up tables, one of the greatest complaints levelled against colour imaging, are less critical. Mapping the object colour map onto the traditional slice image can also aid in the visual location of objects within an image.

Once an appropriate rendering approach has been adopted the next stage in analysis is often to relate the 3-D view to the original data viewed as conventional slices either in orthogonal or oblique section.

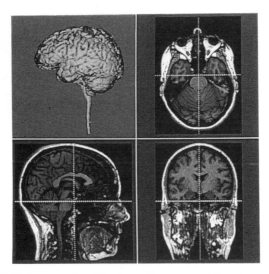

Figure 8.4. Volume rendered brain surface seen with orthogonal slices.

At this stage the ability to locate 3-D points to 2-D views in an interactive manner using a mouse or Trackerball controlled pointer allows confirmation that the boundaries set up in the definition of the rendering truly relate to boundaries within the original data. The boundary identification can be improved if each object within the data set is assigned a colour wash "grey scale" using the same colours as have been applied to the rendered view. The judicious use of colour in this arena can provide cues to the data which could not be achieved by any other method.

Visualisation of structures under or within other structures often calls for the combination of different rendering algorithms within a single view. An example of this might be to include a maximum intensity projection viewport with a surface-based gradient view.

A third class of interaction with data involves the movement of data objects relative to each other, such as may be required in reconstructive surgery. In some cases this may be performed using a predetermined sequence of movements for each object to be altered. This may be configured using a "spreadsheet" style of data entry where amounts of X, Y and Z motion are pre-set together with any rotational movement required. This can be particularly useful if an object is to be moved from one side of an image to its "mirror location" on the other side. In other circumstances an interactive "drag and drop" approach is more suitable and the object may be selected using a point and click process and then interactively moved around the data volume.

All the processes described above require that boundaries or regions are defined within the data. It is still the normal approach that this is performed interactively often on a slice by slice basis. Where thresholding can be applied 3-D region growing approaches may be applied and more recently work has been carried out on both anatomical atlas-based segmentation and model-based approaches using trainable algorithms.

8.6 Interacting with multi-modal data

As more data modalities have developed to the point where 3-D data sets are available, interest has increased in the possibility of combining information from two or more imaging modalities. This development offers unique benefit to the diagnostic process. This is especially true where the contributing modalities are able to uniquely visualise a particular tissue or property. An example of this would be bone from X-ray CT and soft tissue from MRI.

The first requirement which must be fulfilled before any cross modal analysis can occur is the accurate geometric registration of the datasets. A number of registration algorithms are now available which allow for geometric registration of data sets based on 3-D rigid body transformations. These approaches fall into two basic types. In the first type of algorithm landmark points are identified in both data sets and one set is then translated rotated and scaled to bring the points into registration (Hawkes *et al.* 1991). One very major limitation of this approach is the requirement that the landmarks can be accurately visualised and located in all the data sets to be registered. Unfortunately this is very often not the case especially when Nuclear Medicine data is to be registered with MRI data and even with CT X-ray and MRI although both provide high resolution images they are biased towards different tissues. Indeed the very reason for using multi-modal imaging - that the various modalities show different structures - would lead one to expect that landmarks would be different in the different modalities. In the second case, a different approach is taken instead of attempting to accurately locate individual landmarks, a global object is defined (Jiang *et al.* 1992). The most common examples for head data would be the skin outline or the brain outline. These are generally well visualised in most modalities. The registration is then performed using shape-based chamfer matching and again one data set is transformed to the co-ordinate frame of the other. Since object definition is a standard feature of 3-D image analysis object-based image registration builds on the standard style of data analysis and builds out of a normal 3-D analysis.

Once the data is registered, the opportunity for a completely new method of data interaction and object definition becomes possible. This form of inter-action has been given the name of Multi-spectoral classification.

8.7 Multi-spectoral classification

When multiple representations of each point in 3-D space are available, through multi-modal imaging, the relationship between two different modalities may be plotted as a scatter graph.

This graphical presentation offers the possibility of interrogating the graph by drawing ROIs on the graph and then seeing the location of the selected data points displayed on the images. For example, cluster regions may be defined on the graph and the locations seen on the images. Equally if a unique grey scale linkage exists between data in two modalities, for a particular pathology, the graphical data cluster associated with the pathology may first be identified, by defining a region on an image, and then the cluster fully marked on the scatter graph and the whole volume interrogated to find other regions of the same data characteristics and possibly pathology. The ability to move easily between images realised from different modalities and graphical presentation of the cross-modal correlation is a totally new approach to data analysis in medical imaging and still awaits clear clinical protocols to be established. At present it is being tested as a powerful research tool. One of the great advantages of multi-modal imaging based around object registration is that data classification can be used to directly create new objects for volume rendering and analysis. This direct linkage allows for very complex analysis of large data sets to be performed very rapidly and limits the inevitable increase in diagnostic time requirements as data sets increase in size and additional modalities are added (Figure 8.5).

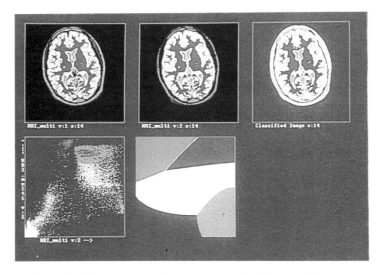

Figure 8.5. Multi-spectoral analysis of MRI T1 and T2 images.

Plates 6, 7 and 8 show three MRI images depicting transparent skin and brain ventricles.

8.8 Conclusions

The clinical use of 3-D medical imaging is still very much in its infancy and the scale of uptake will be determined by the added value which can be brought to the diagnostic process. In this context, added value has to be seen as a compromise between the time taken to reach a decision and the quality of the decision taken. Taking an infinite time to reach a perfect decision is as useless as taking a wrong decision instantly. The role of computer systems and visualisation techniques will be a central feature of the evolution of 3-D medical imaging and benefit from advances on a very wide field ranging from improvement in processor performance to new visualisation algorithms. One of the first applications of 3-D visualisation environments is likely to be in teaching systems where a number of data labelling approaches have been used to allow students to learn the link between classical anatomy and sensed image data. As these teaching systems become more widely available the resulting generation of clinicians will have been trained in 3-D and will therefore expects to practice in 3-D.

References

Hansen D.P., Larsen A., Karwoski R.A., Camp J.J. & Robb R.A. (1992). Simultaneous and Interactive Rendering of Multiple Objects. *Proc 14th IEEEMBS Conf* Rennes.

Hawkes D.J., Hill D.L.G., Bracey E.E.C.M.L. (1991). *Multimodal Data Fusion to Combine Anatomical and Physiological Information in the Head and Heart.* Kluwer Holland.

Hill C.R. (1988). *The Physics of Medical Imaging* ed S. Webb. Adam Hilger.

Hounsfield G.N. (1973). Computerized transverse axial section scanning. *Br.J.Radiol* 46 1016-51.

Payne P.A. (1991). *Concise Encyclopaedia of Biological and Biomedical Measurement Systems.* Pergamon Press.

Robb R.A. (1990). *3D Imaging in Medicine* NATA ASI series F vol60.

Jiang H., Robb R.A., Holton K. (1992). A new approach to 3D registration of Multimodal Medical Images by Surface Matching. *SPIE* vol 1808. p196.

9

Image Processing for Museums

John Cupitt and Kirk Martinez

9.1 Introduction

Many large galleries have scientific and conservation departments - these departments need records of the surface appearance of paintings. These records should be stable and accurate, so that changes in a painting can be monitored.

Until recently, the only tool available for keeping records of appearance was conventional chemical photography. Transparencies are not good at recording colour, since the colour of a transparency depends not only upon the object photographed, but also upon the lighting, the particular film stock, the length of time it spent in various developing baths, and so forth. As transparencies age, their colour moves even further away from the original. Finally, transparencies taken at different times are impossibly difficult to compare by eye.

The VASARI project aimed to digitize high resolution colorimetric images directly from paintings. Two kinds of surface appearance change were to be detected: first, change in pigment colour, and secondly, change in craquelure (hairline surface cracks). The digital images therefore had to be of the order of 10K x 10K pixels, have many colour separation bands and potentially have more than 8 bits of precision. A flexible C/UNIX-based image processing library was needed.

Birkbeck College have developed VIPS. VIPS can handle images of any size, any number of bands and any band format from byte to complex. It does not need a particularly large amount of RAM or a large swap partition. It has the usual range of functions, including arithmetic and logical operations, colour space manipulations, filtering and morphological operations. The National Gallery have developed ip (pronounced *eye-pee* in the manner of most UNIX utilities), a user interface for the VIPS library. It has a number of novel features making it particularly suitable for the scientific and technical user.

VIPS/ip currently runs on SunOS 4.1.x systems; it will be ported to Solaris 2.x in the first half of 1993 and should then run on any SVR4 X11 machine.

Interacting with Virtual Environments Edited by Lindsay MacDonald and John Vince
© 1994 John Wiley & Sons Ltd

9.2 The VIPS library

VIPS comes in several parts. At the bottom of the conceptual heap is a file format. VIPS images consist of a simple 64-byte header giving size and type information, followed by raw image data. Images can be any size, have any number of bands, and band elements can be 8-, 16- or 32-bit integer, 32- or 64-bit floating point and 64- or 128-bit complex. Integer formats can optionally be unsigned. The two floating-point formats are 32- and 64-bit IEEE respectively. Byte ordering in integer formats is most-significant first.

Above the file format definition is the VIPS input-output system. This represents images with IMAGE descriptors. These are intended to look a little like the standard I/O package's FILE descriptors. An image represented as an IMAGE can be a file on disc which has been mapped into a process' virtual memory space with the mmap(2) system call, it can be an area of memory allocated with malloc(2), or it can be an output file created with open(2). Functions that manipulate images using the VIPS I/O system do not need to know which of these types of image they have; they just see a descriptor.

Above the I/O system is the VIPS image processing library. There are roughly three hundred functions at the moment, covering the usual range of operations, but emphasising colour and filtering. The top layer of VIPS is for applications. Bare VIPS just provides a UNIX command for a selection of functions from the library. ip has been designed as a convenient replacement for this large set of UNIX commands.

There are a number of problems with the VIPS library, some of which will be fixed soon. The VIPS I/O system presents images to the processing functions as simple memory arrays. While this makes life easy for the person writing the image processing functions, it means there is no abstraction from the file format. Images in TIFF format, for example, cannot be processed by VIPS functions, unless the whole image is first passed through a conversion utility. More seriously, VIPS functions cannot be composed. If you want to pass an image through two processing functions, you must pass the image entirely through the first function, store the intermediate image somewhere, and then call the second function. This can be very time-consuming for extremely large images. Both these problems should be fixed soon when a new lazy image type is added.

9.3 The ip user interface

ip comes in a series of layers. At the top is a user interface, produced with the Motif toolkit, which is used to view images and to control the operation of the system. Below this is a simple programming language that can be used to combine image processing operations, and below that is the VIPS image processing library.

Most image processing interfaces include an imperative programming language. ip programs are written in a functional language (Turner 1986 and Bird 1988). Algorithms expressed in functional languages are concise and easy to reason about. This means that you can not only manipulate images, you can say exactly how you have manipulated them; you can prove that you have done what you intended to do. Additionally, functional programs are amenable to optimisations that imperative programs resist, since the meaning of a program

Figure 9.1. A set of thumbnails.

depends only upon its syntactic context and not upon its execution history. The very "heavy" base types make the computational overhead normally associated with functional languages negligible.

Image display

ip began life as a file viewer, and this part of its history is reflected in the many features available for browsing large images.

One or three band images of type unsigned char are copied directly to the X server for display. All other types have to be converted. Most are clipped to the range 0-255, complex types have their modulus calculated and clipped to 0-255 and histograms and LUTs (look-up tables) are graphed. VIPS supports a special format for colorimetric images in which four bytes are used to represent one CIE $L*a*b*$ colour coordinate. Images of this type are converted for display using a simple model of monitor behaviour.

Pictures are grouped into portfolios. A portfolio is a file containing a list of image names. When the user asks to view a picture, ip offers a list of all the portfolio files it can find. The user selects a portfolio, and ip then pop up a window showing a set of thumbnail images for that portfolio. A thumbnail image is a highly shrunk version of an image, just large enough to be recognisable. See Figure 9.1.

Double-clicking on a thumbnail pops up a window displaying a quicklook. Quicklooks are images shrunk to about a quarter of a screenfull, and are used for navigation. Selecting "Open high-res window" in the "Options" menu of a quicklook window opens another window displaying the associated high-res image, see Figures 9.2 and 9.3.

High-res windows display an image at full resolution. A locator box is drawn in the quicklook showing the area of the high-res file currently visible. This box can be picked up with the mouse and dropped on another part of the quicklook, causing the high-res window to move to that part of the image. Additionally, the bars along the bottom and right of the high-res window can be used to scroll about the image.

All image windows have "Magnification" menus: these allow you to select a zoom factor for the window. Various keyboard combinations are available that, along with other more arcane facilities, let you drag the image with the mouse, zoom into (or out of) the point indicated by the mouse, scroll a screenfull at a time, set particular magnification levels, and move to the extreme edges of the image.

Selecting "Open another view" in the "Options" menu will pop up an image display window that shows the same image, but at twice the magnification. Again, a locator box in the lower resolution window can be used to move about the magnified image.

All image display windows have optional status bars and rulers. The status bar gives the type, size in pixels, millimetres and bytes, number of bands, current mouse position and current pixel value. Rulers show the position of the window within the file in pixels or millimetres. There are a number of other display options: image windows can be double buffered, the contents of image windows can bounce (useful for unattended demos), windows can display in full-colour, in monochrome or as bitmaps, and finally image windows can display live video, or at least as live as standard X allows.

Figure 9.2. Thumbnails and a quicklook.

Image processing

Selecting "Open image processing" from the "Options" menu in any image display window pops up `ip`'s image processing window, see Figure 9.4. This is supposed to look rather like a desk-calculator: expressions are entered with the keypad in the bottom half of the window and results appear on the tally roll in the top half. To the right is the extended functions window.

Clicking   2 + 2 =

on the keypad will add a line to the tally roll showing the new value (hopefully 4), the symbolic name of that result (A in this example) and the text of A's definition. See Figure 9.5.

Figure 9.3. Quicklook and hi-res.

The symbolic name can be used in other expressions. Clicking

$$A + 17 =$$

will add another line to the tally roll showing the new value (21 for this calculation), the symbolic name of the result (B in this example) and the text of B's definition. See Figure 9.6.

If you now go back up the tally roll and edit the definition of A to be 2 + 3, B will be automatically recalculated, since its value depends on the value of A. This is a general principle in ip: definitions are entered which describe relationships between objects. If an object or a definition is changed, ip automatically recalculates the value of any object which is affected by the change.

This spreadsheet-style recalculation strategy avoids a traditional weakness in functional languages, that of input/output interactions with the user (Thompson 1987); additionally, the spreadsheet style of calculation encourages "suck it and see" experimentation, an important attribute for an interactive program.

You can of course manipulate images as well as numbers. If an image (D, say) is open, you can drag out a region of interest on it with the right mouse button. Regions have symbolic names, just like images and the numbers above, and can be used in expressions. If you create a region E on D, entering

```
!E =
```

makes F, the area of D inside E (given a region, ! returns the area of image inside that region). If E is now moved or resized, F will be recalculated. See Figure 9.7.

If you edit the definition of F to be

```
heq !E\1
```

then E will change to show the result of histogram equalising the second band of the area inside D. This simple enhancement operation can be quite useful. Figure 9.8 shows a small section of Raphael's Garva Madonna being enhanced. With age, the paint on the Virgin's neck has become increasingly transparent, allowing the lines of Raphael's initial sketch to become visible. These faint lines become much easier to see if the contrast is boosted. This is a slightly silly example - there are much better ways to examine underdrawing. See Billinge *et al.*

Toolkits

Choosing "enhance" from the "Toolkit" menu fills the extended functions area with tools for enhancing and correcting images. Other toolkits contain functions for resampling images, transforming between colour spaces, filtering, graphing and so on. Clicking

```
Histogram_equalise E =
```

will also enhance D, but requires a little less thought. The onus is on the user to remember the number and type of arguments for each tool. This is in contrast to packages which build dialogue boxes and prompt for each argument in turn. In defence of ip's scheme, it is quick to type (or click), and most technical users are accustomed to systems far less friendly. Selecting "Help on toolkit" from the "Help" menu pops up a window summarising the function of each of the tools in this kit and listing their arguments.

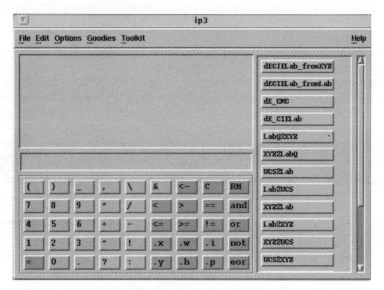

Figure 9.4. ip as it starts up.

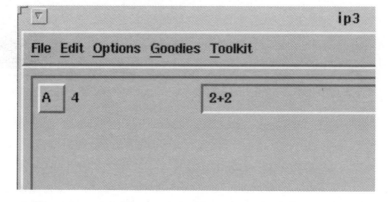

Figure 9.5. Adding two numbers.

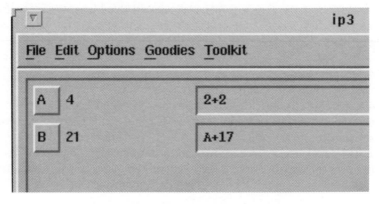

Figure 9.6. Adding two more numbers.

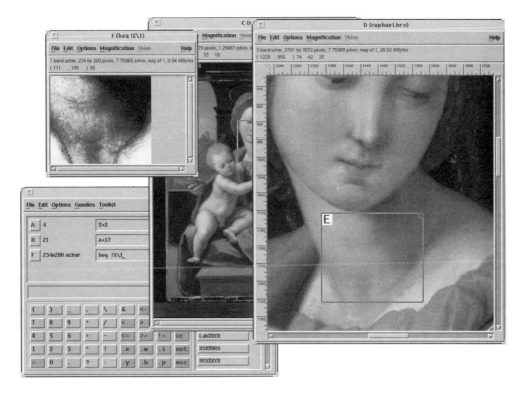

Figure 9.7. Extracting a region.

Parameterised definitions

Clicking on a tool adds the tool's name to the calculator window. Shift-clicking on a tool pops up an edit window containing the text of the tool's definition. See Figure 9.9.

ip definitions follow the syntax popularised by 1000 functional programming languages. A name is followed by a list of parameters and a list of possible right-hand sides (RHS). Each RHS has a guard attached to it; when the definition is applied to a set of arguments, guards are evaluated in turn until one of them is found to be true, in which case the value of this application is the text of the associated RHS with the appropriate arguments substituted.

Definitions can also have a list of local definitions attached to them; Pascal-style scoping rules are followed. Local definitions may themselves have further local definitions, but generally at the expense of comprehensibility.

For example, consider the text of the Histogram_equalise tool we used earlier.

```
Histogram_equalise r
{       extr a
        = !a, if is_region a;
        = a, if is_image a;
        = error "not region or image", otherwise;
```

```
        mono a
            = a\1, if a.b != 1;
            = a, otherwise
   }        = heq (mono (extr r))
```

This defines a pair of local functions, extr and mono. extr tries to return an image, no matter whether it is passed a region or an image. mono tries to return a one-band image, no matter how many bands are in the image it is passed. Histogram_equalise passes its argument through both of these local functions, and then passes the result through heq. The semi-colons and curly-brackets are, sadly, compulsory; the if and otherwise are optional.

Recursion

Any ip definition can refer to any other ip definition in scope, including itself. For example, you might define fib, a definition that given a number *n* returned the *n*th fibbonacci number, as

```
   fib n
       = fib (n-1) + fib (n-2), if n > 2;
       = 1, otherwise
```

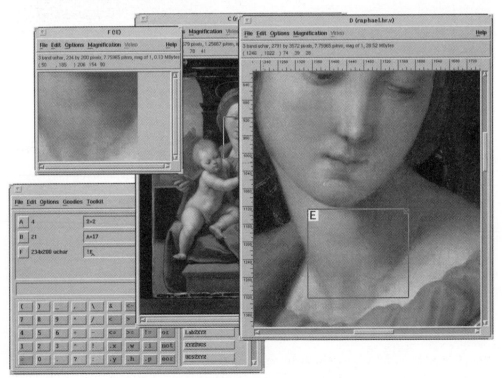

Figure 9.8. Enhancing the Garva Madonna.

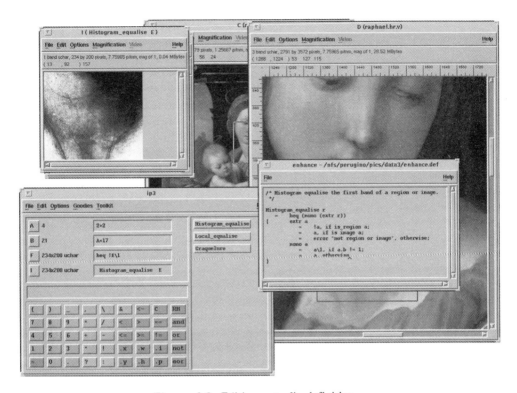

Figure 9.9. Editing a tool's definition.

More usefully, you might want to repeatedly apply a morphological operator until there was no further change.

```
skel a
    = a, if a = a';
    = skel a', otherwise
{       a' = thin a
}
```

The ' is an allowed character in variable names. A hardened functional programmer would avoid the explicit recursion by using a higher-order function.

We claimed earlier that ip definitions could be reasoned about easily. It should now be clear why - the only proof techniques needed are equational reasoning (substituting the value of the appropriate RHS) and induction (to prove properties of recursive definitions). Both techniques are simple, well understood and easy to apply. Proving properties of languages which incorporate destructive assignments is far harder, since the value of an expression depends not only upon its text, but also upon the program's evaluation history.

You also need an accurate description of the operation of your image processing primitives. This information should be provided in a manual somewhere.

Sliders

Selecting "Input slider" from the "Goodies" menu pops up a window containing a numeric slider. Dragging the slider's knob with the left mouse button changes the numeric value of the slider.

Slider objects have symbolic names, just like images. If the new slider is called A, say, and you have an image called B, then clicking

```
    B >= A
```

will pop up a new image, C perhaps, in which every pixel in B which was greater than or equal to A will be 255 (logical truth), and all other pixels will be shown as 0 (false). Moving the slider up and down will force C to be recalculated.

The menus in the slider window let you change the range of values the slider covers, select vertical or horizontal orientation, and select graphical or text input.

Matrices

ip has some support for matrix operations such as convolutions and morphologies. Selecting "Convolution", for example, from the "Goodies" menu pops up a convolution editor. Matrices can be edited, loaded and saved, convolution types can be changed, they can be rotated, and so on. Once a matrix (M, say) has been set up, entering

```
    M W
```

creates a new image which contains W filtered through convolution M. Morphological operators and colour change operators are handled in a similar manner.

Optimisation

ip performs two optimisations which can significantly increase the speed of evaluation of definitions. The first replaces any sequence of arithmetic operations on an 8-bit image (Gamma_correct, for example) with a single lookup table operation. Second, ip removes common sub-expressions within each definition. If two sub-expressions in a definition are syntactically equivalent, they are both replaced by a reference to a new local definition. For example

```
frankly mr shankly
     = morph mr + morph (morph mr) + shankly
```

is represented internally as

```
frankly mr shankly
     = A + morph A + shankly
{    A = morph mr
}
```

This sort of transformation is quite safe in a functional language, thanks to the lack of destructive assignment. The equivalent transformation in an imperative language, such as C, is far more difficult.

9.4 Video

Selecting "Open video window" pops up a live video window showing the output of the camera. A variety of options are available, allowing you, among other things, to set the refresh rate, select a video source, select a crop region and set a black and white voltage.

Liveness propagates, that is, any objects that depend upon a video window are themselves live. If you create an object which displays a histogram of a video window, the graph will also update, although the number of frames per second may well drop.

Two frame grabber boards are currently supported: the Sun VideoPix board and the DataCell S2200. Support for an SBus version of the Kontron ProgRes 3012 controller card will be added shortly.

9.5 Paintbox

Selecting "Open paintbox" from the "Edit" menu of an image window opens `ip`'s image editing tool on that image. Paintboxes are generally alien to scientific image processing, since it is very hard to say exactly what has been done to an image which has been through a paintbox. Nevertheless, they are useful in some circumstances. The paintbox in `ip` was developed with two main applications in mind: painting out peaks in Fourier images to remove specific frequency components, and annotating images. It has good support for local filtering operations (smears and smudges), and fancy text and pen tools. When you close the paintbox, any objects which depend upon the edited image are recalculated.

Editing very large images is difficult. The solution adopted by \ip\ is to request write permission for the image file `mmap(3)`ed by VIPS. Paint operations then directly affect the file on disc. This is clearly very dangerous, since a stray brushstroke could wipe out valuable data. The paintbox includes comprehensive undo and redo functions which make it possible to back out of any paint session.

The mmap(3) system call has a private copy-on-write option, in which pages which are written to are not copied to disc, but replaced by private RAM pages. This initially seems perfect for a paint program, unfortunately mmap(3) requires that you have enough space in your swap partition to be able to, if necessary, copy-on-write the whole of the file. We decided that it was better to alter the original image than require the user to have a swap at least as large as the largest image they might want to alter.

9.6 Conclusions

ip combines a fast and convenient image display system with a graphical interface to a functional programming language.

Functional programming languages are usually thought arrtactive only by theoreticians - general purpose functional programming languages, despite recent improvements in compilers, are still considerably slower than their imperative rivals. We believe we have found a niche in which functional programming languages are clearly superior.

There are a number of deficiencies in the current implementation of ip's functional language. There is no list type. This will be added very shortly. Lists of lists can be used to represent matrices, allowing the easy addition of matrix algebra. There are no higher order functions, and parameter passing is strict. The next version will feature normal order reduction, true sharing of local values, and proper higher order functions. Higher order functions are really necessary to make list processing bearable. It would also be nice to have an ML-style type system, although this is much less urgent.

Acknowledgements

The VASARI project (1989-92) was funded by the European Community's ESPRIT II scheme (project 2649). The other groups involved are: Brameur Ltd (UK), Telecom Paris, Thomson-CSF (Rennes France), TÜV (Germany), The Doerner Institute (Germany), The Louvre (France), SIDAC (Rome).

References

Billinge R., Cupitt J., Dessipris N. & Saunders D. *A Note on an Improved Procedure for the Rapid Assembly of Infrared Reflectogram Mosaics*, Studies in Conservation, accepted for publication.

Bird R., Wadler P. (1988). *An Introduction to Functional Programming*, Prentice Hall.

Burmester A., Cupitt J., Derrien H., Dessipris N., Hamber A., Martinez K., Müller M. & Saunders D. (1992). The Examination of Paintings by Digital Image Analysis, *Proc. 3rd International Conference on Non-destructive Testing, Microanalytical Methods and Environment Evaluation for Study and Conservation of Works of Art*, Viterbo 4-8, pp. 201-214.

Martinez K., Cupitt J. & Saunders D. (1993). High Resolution Colorimetric Imaging of Paintings, *Proceedings of the SPIE conference on Electronic Imaging Science and Technology*, San Jose USA, Vol. 1901.

Martinez K. (1991). High Resolution Imaging of Paintings: The VASARI Project, *Microcomputers for Information Management*, Vol. 8, No. 4, Ablex Publishing Corp., Norwood, New Jersey.

Martinez K. & Hamber A. (1989). Towards a colorimetric digital image archive for the visual arts, *Proceedings of the Society of Photo-Optical Instrumentation Engineers*, Vol 1073.

Saunders D. & Cupitt J. (1993). Image Processing at the National Gallery: The VASARI Project, *National Gallery Technical Bulletin*, Vol. 14, pp. 72-85.

Saunders D. & Hamber A. (1990). From Pigments to Pixels: Measurement and Display of the Colour Gamut of Paintings, *Proc. SPIE*, Vol. 1250, pp. 90-102.

Saunders D. (1989). The Detection and Measurement of Colour Change in Paintings by Digital Image Processing, *Proc. SPIE*, Vol. 1075.

Thompson S.J. (1987). *Interactive Functional Programs: A Method and a Formal Semantics*. University of Kent at Canterbury Computing Laboratory Report No 48.

Turner D. (1986). An Overview of Miranda, *SIGPLAN Notices*.

10

Interacting with Graphic Arts Images

Lindsay W. MacDonald

10.1 Introduction

The reproduction of coloured images in print involves a number of stages, starting with the original photographs and culminating in a printing plate ready for press printing onto paper. The workflow varies according to the type of job and the working practices of the studio, but is typified by the generic workflow shown in Figure 10.1. The constituents of image and text are converted into electronic form and composed into a page, guided by the layout instructions of the designer. Visualisation of the results is achieved through colour proofs, which may take one of three forms: a "soft" proof on a display; a "hard" proof on a digital printer; or finally a press-proof simulating the actual ink, paper and half-tone structures of the press.

The process is usually iterative, with results being presented to the client followed by one or more cycles of modification to the layout or image content or both. Only when the client "signs off" the result does the job proceed to the next stage (MacDonald 1991a). It is the objective of an efficient studio to minimise the number of rework cycles by a thorough initial understanding of the client's requirements and the use of skilled operators and high quality equipment.

Retouching of images is an optional step, which in an ideal situation might not need to be performed at all. If the original photographs are perfect **and** the scanner can produce a pleasing facsimile **and** neither the designer nor client requires any special changes to the images then no retouching may be necessary, but such is rarely the case. Image retouching is normally performed for three main reasons:

(1) To correct deficiencies in the original photograph. The original may have a colour cast due to incorrect exposure, illumination or film processing. The subject may have

Interacting with Virtual Environments Edited by Lindsay MacDonald and John Vince
© 1994 John Wiley & Sons Ltd

blemishes, such as facial skin defects or rust spots on a car. Or the photograph itself may be scratched or faded.

(2) To match the characteristics of the printing process. The final image is usually printed in the four process inks of cyan, magenta, yellow and black. Press characteristics determine the balance of the inks, as well as the need for grey-component removal, sharpness and grip (overlap of inks to accommodate changes in press registration).

(3) To make editorial corrections according to the requirements of the designer and client. The tonal range may be adjusted, for example to bring out detail in the shadow areas. Certain colours may be changed to match a specified reference, common in mail-order catalogues. Unwanted details or areas of the image may be replaced. Creative effects range from the subtle to the dramatic.

This paper describes some of the interaction techniques employed in contemporary electronic image retouching workstations, which allow the user an unprecedented degree of control over the reproduction of colour images. Their effectiveness is shown to depend upon both a sound underlying processing model and the provision of interactive tools that meet the needs of the user.

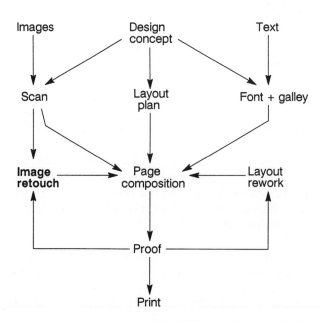

Figure 10.1. Simplified workflow in graphic arts image reproduction.

10.2   Traditional retouching methods

Before the days of scanners and digital image manipulation, retouching of images for improved reproduction was performed manually by skilled craftsman using a variety of techniques.   The cardinal rule in retouching is that the original material (artwork or photographs) should never be altered, both because of the risk of making an irrecoverable mistake and because the original is usually the reference by which the reproduction is judged. Manual retouching is therefore always carried out on photographic duplicates of originals or on the films resulting from colour separation (Field 1988).

Figure 10.2.   A traditional retouching artist at work over a back-lit light-table.   Note the high-power stereo magnifier headset that he is wearing.

Retouching of photographic transparencies is performed by adjusting the amounts of dye in the three coloured dye layers of the film: cyan, magenta and yellow.   The retoucher uses liquid dyes, such as Kodak E-6 Retouching Dye, painted on in small light strokes with a very fine sable brush, often working under a magnifying glass.   By using dilute dye the colour density can be built up very gradually.   Reduction of colour density is achieved by painting with potassium permanganate, which reduces the amount of metallic silver in the film uniformly throughout all tonal values.   In this way unwanted details such as blemishes, wrinkles or dimples in skin and creases or folds in fabric can be removed.   Unless great care is taken, however, the retouched areas may be visible in the final reproduction through the presence of brushstrokes or metameric colour differences.

Colour separations were traditionally made in a photographic enlarger by exposing the coloured original through a series of coloured filters: a red filter to produce the complementary cyan component, a green filter for magenta and a blue filter for yellow.   Each separation is then exposed through a half-tone screen, to give a dot percentage area corresponding to the colour density of the original (see Figure 10.3).   Retouching of the separation films involves the adjustment of the dot areas for the individual inks, and can be performed by either photographic or chemical means. In order to make the dots smaller, the films can either be etched by a reducer such as potassium ferricyanide ("wet etching") or re-exposed onto a second film with a spacer to allow the diffusion of light around the dots ("dry etching"). To make the dots larger the same processes are applied to an intermediate negative (Chambers 1967).

Figure 10.3. Magnified section of a half-tone magenta separation showing dot structure.

Generally only a localised region of an image needs to be retouched. The manual retouching of transparencies by brushing is naturally a localised process, whereas the etching of separations is inherently a global process that must be restricted if necessary by use of a mask. For chemical etching the areas of the image to be protected are painted with a resistant lacquer or varnish to prevent them being etched. For photographic etching, two complementary opaque masks must be made, one (positive) defining the scope of the areas to be retouched and the other (negative) defining the areas to be protected (Wentzel 1983).

Thus the traditional retoucher interacted with his images in a very tangible manner, relying on brushes, swabs of cotton wool, needles, surgical knives and high-powered magnifiers as tools of the trade. Techniques involved stroking with a brush, drawing, stippling, scraping and cutting, all to accuracies of a few thousandths of an inch. The skill and experience of these craftsmen was very considerable, although it has now largely been supplanted in Western countries by electronic image retouching.

10.3   Electronic image retouching

Image representation and masks

The graphic arts input scanner derives from the original picture an array of digital picture elements (pixels) representing the colour content at each point of the original. Each pixel consists of four bytes, containing values of the dot areas of the four process printing inks cyan, magenta, yellow and black (CMYK). A typical scanning resolution is 12 pixels per mm of output (post-enlargement) dimension, so that an A4 (page-sized) image of 210 by 297 mm will be represented by about 9 million pixels, requiring some 36 Mbytes of storage.

Retouching of an image involves modifying the pixel values, either by adjustments to the individual ink components, corresponding to the manual retouching of film separations, or by a generalised colour change affecting all inks together, corresponding to the manual retouching of the original. Through the display and graphic user interface of a computer-based workstation the user can view and manipulate the stored digital image. With a typical display resolution of 1280 by 1024 pixels the user has the option of viewing either a low-resolution (LR) version of the whole image or a small section of the high-resolution (HR) image.

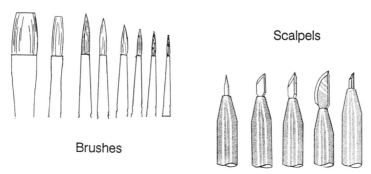

Scalpels

Brushes

Figure 10.4. Tools of the traditional retouch artist.

A mask defines the area(s) of interest in an image, and consists of an array of digital values in one-to-one correspondence with the pixels of the image. Masks are broadly of two types, hard and soft. Hard masks have one bit per pixel and their purpose is to separate the pixels of an image into two classes, one class to be processed in a certain way and the other to be processed in a different way. Soft masks, also known as *mattes* in the movie industry, have multiple (usually 8) bits per pixel. They specify for each pixel of the image a density value, which represents some attribute such as the transparency or opacity of the pixel for a subsequent mixing operation with another image (Porter and Duff 1984). Somewhere between the hard and soft forms lie soft-edged masks, which have a hard (opaque) interior but a graduated edge. These are typically used for the anti-aliased compositing of curved shapes and text fonts.

Retouch process model

A generalised model for electronic image retouching has been developed and used for some years at Crosfield, as shown in Figure 10.5. The original colour image is stored in computer memory as an array of pixels. Through a global retouch transform it may be modified to produce a second colour image, with pixels in 1-to-1 correspondence with the original. Independently the user can apply tools from the mask toolkit to create a soft mask to define the relative balance required between the original and modified images at each pixel. The two images are then mixed on a pixel by pixel basis using linear interpolation (*lerp*) under control of the mask value to produce a composite image.

This image mixing model is powerful because it offers numerous advantages to the system developer and user alike:

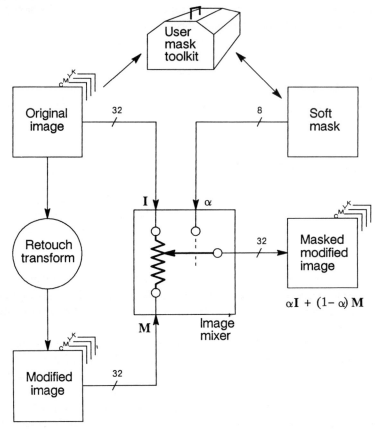

Figure 10.5. The "potentiometer mixing" model of image retouching.

- It decouples retouch and mask operations into orthogonal functions that can be defined and executed independently. This makes the task of developing and testing the software easier because retouch transform functions can be applied globally over the image without the need to consider masking.

- It provides a simple and effective mental model for the user, allowing him or her to specify retouch parameters and mask geometry as separate, sequential, operations with a lower cognitive load than would be required for one compound operation. One of the fundamental tenets of cognitive ergonomics is that good design should lead to a single, coherent mental model for the user (Manktelow and Jones 1987).

- It can be implemented in various forms through appropriate graphics hardware without affecting the operating procedures or algorithms, thus facilitating the porting of image retouching applications from one computer platform to another. We have implemented the model first in software, then in firmware on a dedicated *raster-op* graphics processor, then in an ASIC circuit in a video-rate mixer in which the output pixel stream goes directly to the display (MacDonald *et al.* 1990).

* It is equally applicable to images represented by other colour spaces besides CMYK, such as RGB, HSV and HLS, although the colour algorithms in the retouch transforms would have to be modified. The model easily simplifies to the composition of two images under a hard mask by reducing the mask plane to 1 bit per pixel and replacing the potentiometer mixer by a binary switch.

Advantages of electronic retouching

Electronic imaging systems greatly improve the quality and flexibility of the retouching process. Because no photographic duplicates need to be made there is no loss of sharpness, colour fidelity or tonal range in the image. Because no pigments or dyes are involved the colour match between retouched and unretouched areas is perfect. Because the image can be enlarged (zoomed) many times for correction of fine details, on a pixel by pixel basis if necessary, very high spatial precision can be achieved. Because the modifications are made to a digital copy of the image they are non-destructive and many cycles of change and display visualisation ("soft proof") can be performed without the need to produce any intermediate film or hard-copy proof.

The tools of the electronic image retoucher are metaphors of the actual tools used by the traditional manual retoucher: the airbrush, scalpel, etching brush and magnifier. There are several reasons for this correspondence. First, many of the operators of the new electronic equipment were trained in the traditional methods, so the metaphors are familiar. Second, the working practices and language of the trade shops are still in many cases based on the old manual methods. Third, experience has shown that these tools offer the most effective means of performing the tasks of spatial definition of mask areas and localised correction of colour in images.

Ideally the user interface should be substantially transparent (Thimbleby 1990), so that the skilled user engages it as naturally as he would the traditional tools to perform the desired image retouching task. This transparency is a composite of many factors, chief among which are the appropriateness of the input device to the control requirements of the task, the match between the phrasing of the dialogue and the transactional sequences of the task, and the degree of interactivity. When the transparency is perfect then the user's illusion of working in a virtual environment is complete: as far as the user is concerned the digital image and its manipulability become as real as the celluloid image was for the traditional retouching artist.

The choice of a digitising tablet with a hand-held stylus as an input device provides a natural simulation of hand-held graphic arts tools such as brushes, pencils and knives. The electronic stylus includes pressure sensitivity (Z-axis) and therefore provides the proper affordances for the user (Buxton 1993), who will generally have long experience and higher than average manual dexterity in the use of such implements.

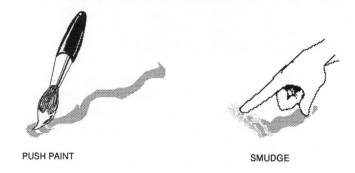

PUSH PAINT   SMUDGE

Figure 10.6. Metaphoric tools for electronic image retouching.

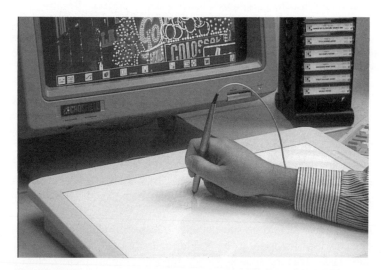

Figure 10.7. The pressure-sensitive stylus is a natural input device for the retouch artist.

The effectiveness of the electronic retouching system also relies upon its degree of interactivity. There is a dramatic reduction in productivity when system response times exceed about 200 msec during interactive sequences (Brady 1986), though at the closure points that mark the completion of transactional phrases, delays can be longer (Brown 1988). By designing special hardware in the video pipeline to perform the mixing of two images under control of a mask, the update rate of an image on the display can be made to equal the refresh rate of the monitor, eg. 16.7 milliseconds for a 60 Hz non-interlaced display. By storing all of the high-resolution image in random-access memory, so that no swapping to and from disk is required, delays are minimised (less than 100 msec) when scrolling the view window around the image during retouching operations.

10.4   Making masks

Masks define the areas of interest in images and so can serve to limit the scope of any retouching operation. There are many methods of making masks, different methods being appropriate for different images and different kinds of retouching. As shown in Figure 10.5, we provide the operator with a "toolkit" of different tools for making masks. The metaphor is that of the toolkit of a builder, who has a saw for one type of cutting task, a plane for another and a chisel for a third. The user can choose the tools in any order and combination as required, giving great flexibility of operation.

In the Crosfield *Colorspace* retouching workstation, the two framestores are known as the Image Frame and the Scratch Frame. Each has associated two 8-bit mask stores, as shown in Figure 10.8, either of which can be enabled by the operator pressing on a screen icon to control the active areas of the corresponding frame store. Masks can be displayed as a translucent tinted overlay on the image, though in subsequent use they are normally active but invisible.

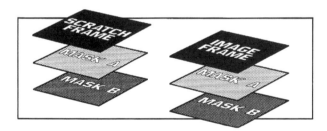

Figure 10.8. User's model of image frames and associated masks.

Mask generation from outlines

The simplest method of defining a mask is to specify an outline, or closed contour, which is then filled to create a binary mask. Open outlines,which do not close on themselves, in general cannot be filled, although the user has the option of prescribing a "tacky fill" where the filler is not permitted to leak out through gaps smaller than a certain diameter.

Outlines may be simple geometric shapes, piecewise linear or curved segments, or freehand lines drawn by the user. Intricate cut-outs may require hundreds of points to be entered, with the image zoomed to considerable magnification. Alternatively, edge-following algorithms guided by local gradients in image density can be employed to assist the user in specifying a complicated outline, for example around hair. Conventional edge enhancement algorithms, such as the Sobel filter (Gonzalez and Wintz 1987) or the Canny filter (Canny 1984), can also be used to generate edge maps, which can then be noise-filtered, thresholded and filled by the use of suitable tools as shown in Figure 10.9.

a) Original image

b) Result of applying
Sobel edge detector

c) Operator-defined
edge neighbourhood

d) Thresholding gives
noisy binary mask

e) Mask grown to Sobel
edge to remove noise

f) Mask applied to cut
out dark background

Figure 10.9. Making a mask around the complicated outline of human hair (Courtesy of Dr Richard Kirk, Crosfield Electronics Ltd.).

Mask generation from areas

Area masks have no explicit outline, except for the bounds of the image from which they are generated. Their purpose is to separate the pixels of an image into two classes, according to some criterion, so that a subsequent operation, such as retouching or image blending, may be restricted to affect the one class of image pixels but not the other.

The simplest method of making a binary mask is by density thresholding, which assigns a mask value *zero* to all pixels of the image whose density falls below a specified value, and assigns a mask value *one* to all others. The threshold may be extended to a min-max range, for example "all pixels having magenta component between 20% and 40%". The user can either specify explicit density values or "train" the computer by pointing at key areas within the image. See Plates 9 to 14 for an example of this form of mask construction.

More generally, an arbitrary domain may be defined in any perceptual colour space: any pixel whose colour falls within the region takes mask value *one* and all other pixels take mask value *zero* (MacDonald 1991b).

Soft mask generation

Soft masks have 8 bits per pixel to allow the representation of a density value at each pixel position, generally known in computer graphics as an *alpha plane* (Porter and Duff 1984). Tools are provided to allow the user to generate soft masks by a variety of methods.

The user can build up the desired density distribution in a soft mask by direct painting on the screen, with one or more types of brush. The airbrush is particularly effective at creating a soft density gradation, using the pressure-sensitivity of the stylus to control either the width or density of the "spray".

Computer-generated density profiles that cover the whole mask plane may be one- or two-dimensional, and have various profiles such as linear ramp, piecewise linear or gaussian. These are known as *vignettes* or *degradees*.

The soft mask may be created as a function of the distance of each pixel in perceptual colour space from a given colour reference. For example, the mask value may be made proportional to the lightness of the image. Alternatively it may be opaque for a specified red, semi-opaque through orange and transparent for all other colours, for use in restricting the scope of subsequent colour retouching or airbrushing operations on the image (see Section 10.5).

Text and linework are frequently digitised or converted from an outline font into a binary mask of higher spatial resolution than the images. The edges of outlines, moreover, are normally calculated to higher precision than the spacing between pixels in the image. Anti-aliasing consists of making a soft mask, known as a *coverage mask* (Fiume 1989), at the normal image resolution by counting sub-pixels at the higher resolution and assigning a corresponding density value. At edges, the appropriate fractions of the corresponding pixels from each image are combined. This has the effect of minimising unpleasant edge effects or *jaggies* on the display (Blinn 1989).

Mask conversion and combination

Tools can be provided to allow the user to convert outlines, binary masks and soft masks to one another in any manner:

Outline to binary	Fill operation
Outline to soft	Fill then expand to 8 bits
Binary to soft	Expand to 8 bits
Binary to outline	Edge extraction filter
Soft to binary	Threshold to given density level
Soft to outline	Threshold then extract edges

Masks may be complemented or formed as the logical union or intersection of masks generated by any other means. For example, an area mask may be combined with a filled outline mask (logical AND) in order to restrict its scope to a given region. A soft mask combined with a binary mask results in another soft mask, etc.

The key to a successful product is thus to provide the user with a graphic toolkit, containing a large number of tools, from which he may select as required. Often there is no single best method of making a mask - different users will select a particular method according to experience, inclination or type of image. A versatile system, therefore, does not lock the user into one rigid method of working. Figure 10.10 shows part of the iconic menu hierarchy for mask tools on the Crosfield *Colorspace*.

10.5   Image retouching techniques

Manipulation of digital images covers a vast range of techniques, ranging from almost imperceptible change of a few pixels to gross distortions and dramatic colour changes of the whole image. This section focuses on a few specific interactive retouching techniques in which some of the pixels of an image are modified or replaced without any spatial transformation of the pixel grid.

Global corrections, affecting all pixels of an image, can be used for colour correction, for example to remove a cast or to make the whole image lighter or darker. For most retouching jobs, however, the user will employ one or more masks to restrict the changes to particular classes of pixels or regions of interest within the image. All of the following techniques derive their power from the user's ability to apply them selectively through a mask.

Blemish removal

Images are frequently "improved" by removing unwanted details or clutter that detracts from the visual impact or intended message. Skin in portraits is frequently retouched to remove dimples, freckles, creases and other blemishes. Glossy objects such as car bodies may have distracting reflections from light sources or even the photographer and camera. Skylines may be marred by ugly TV antennae or telegraph poles.

Small blemishes or defects in an image can be removed by overwriting them with pixels from other parts of the image. A two-cursor technique is used to copy pixels from a small area under the source cursor to a corresponding area under the destination cursor. Interactive

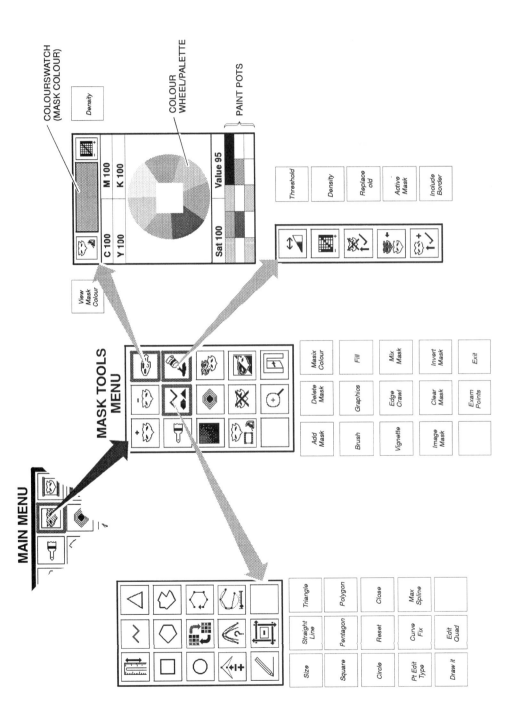

Figure 10.10. Part of an iconic mask toolkit on the *Colorspace*.

techniques consist of first setting the spatial relationship between source and destination, then with a brushing action of the stylus copying across the pixels.

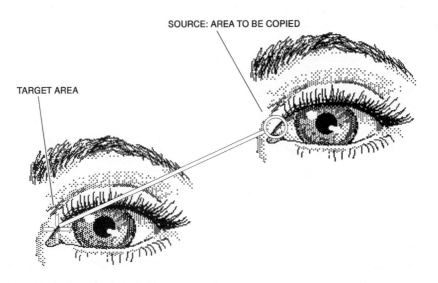

SOURCE: AREA TO BE COPIED

TARGET AREA

Figure 10.11. Source and target cursors in the pixel copy technique.

Movement of the source cursor may be related to movement of the destination cursor in a number of ways. Normally they have a fixed spatial relationship but they can also be *geared* by a fixed ratio, resulting in a magnification or reduction of the destination image, rather like the old-fashioned pantograph drawing instrument. Traversal of either cursor can be restricted to an area defined by a binary mask, or pixel copying inhibited outside the mask area, allowing the protection of specified regions of the image.

Pixel copying offers the great benefit of retaining local colouration and texture, for example by replacing a skin crease with neighbouring skin of similar visual quality. In order to prevent patterning due to repetition of structure within the image, however, an experienced user will make frequent adjustments to the relationship between the two cursors, in both orientation and distance.

Selective colour correction

Colour changes in an image frequently need to be restricted to specific colours. The requirement may be the complete replacement of a particular colour, as in cartoon line-art. In real images where there is a continuum of colour it is more commonly required to change hue whilst preserving the natural gradations of lightness and saturation of the original object, known by photographers as *modelling*.

The operation can be carried out in three stages: first by making a mask of all pixels in the image to be affected; second by processing the entire image to perform the colour change; third by combining the original and modified images under control of the mask as shown in Figure 10.5. See the colour plates for an example of selective colour correction. To prevent a noticeable edge between the original and modified areas, best results are achieved by the use of a soft mask, constructed with density proportional to the proximity of the target point in colour space (MacDonald 1991b).

Interactive technique for making the colour selective mask consists of the user pointing and sampling the image at one or more positions in the desired colour region, then moving a graphic slider to adjust the bandwidth of the profile in colour space. The mask values are displayed immediately as a translucent overlay on the image, or optionally against a plain background, giving the user instant feedback on the effectiveness of the colour control settings. The best achievable mask usually has to be further edited with other tools for filling pinholes, removing spots, excluding other regions of similar colour, etc.

Brush-through

The provision of the circuit in Figure 10.5 to combine two images under control of a soft mask offers many interaction possibilities. By filling the mask with a uniform value of 50%, for example, the two images are seen superimposed and can be scrolled relative to one another to achieve the desired alignment. By filling the mask with a gradation, for example from 0% at the top to 100% at the bottom, a cross-fade from one image to the other can be achieved.

By allowing the user to brush directly into the mask, moreover, arbitrary regions of one image can be made to show through the other. This technique, known as *brush-through*, is both powerful and versatile as an interactive retouching method. Because the soft mask provides a naturally anti-aliased merge of the two images, the joins between them can be rendered invisible. The non-destructive nature of the circuit in Figure 10.5 means that until the user is completely satisfied with the result on the screen the original image is not modified.

Three common ways of using brush-through are for montaging, revealing and retouching. To montage, the two images are placed in the two frame buffers, positioned interactively by moving one relative to the other then, by using any of the mask tools, a mask is drawn to define those areas of the overlying image to be replaced by the underlying image. The boundary region of the mask can be brushed to achieve the necessary degree of fineness and gradation.

To reveal an image in the underlying frame, the overlying frame is filled with a uniform or vignetted colour or a texture. The user then employs a brush tool, such as an airbrush, to "etch away" the mask plane to reveal the underlying image. The pressure sensitivity of the stylus (Z-axis) can be coupled in two separate ways, to control either the width of the brush or the strength of the "paint spray". Also the maximum paint density can be limited by a slider, and a second hard mask can be used to restrict the area affected. See Plate 15.

For retouching, the underlying image revealed by brush-through may be a modified version of the original image. For example to smooth out skin tones a smoothing filter may be applied to the whole image, then brushed through selectively in the pertinent regions of the image. Alternatively to emphasise detail the whole image may be sharpened by a suitable filter then brushed through in key areas, for example the eyelashes, eyebrows and lips in a portrait. An embossing effect can be achieved by offsetting the underlying image by a few pixels.

10.6   Conclusions

Although the retouching of images for reproduction in the graphic arts is not new, the traditional methods of etching film by chemicals have largely been supplanted by digital image manipulation. The methods and tools have been preserved metaphorically, however, through the interactive user interfaces of powerful image retouching workstations such as the Crosfield *Colorspace*.

The graphic user environment for image retouching must provide opportunities for exploration of the effects of image manipulation, with rapid visualisation of results, including accurate colour soft proofing, and the ability to backtrack or undo modifications if necessary. A pressure-sensitive stylus provides a natural and effective emulation of the traditional hand-held retouching tools. The partitioning of original image, modified image and mask offers both a convenient mechanism for product development and an effective mental model for the user. Given the versatility of the underlying model and the provision of a wide array of interactive tools, the range of creative possibilities open to the inventive user is almost endless (MacDonald 1992).

References

Blinn J.F. (1989). Return of the Jaggy, *IEEE Computer Graphics & Applications*, 9, No. 2, pp 82-89.

Brady J.T. (1986). A Theory of Productivity in the Creative Process, *IEEE Computer Graphics & Applications*, 6, No. 1, pp 25-34.

Brown C.M. (1988). *Human-Computer Interface Design Guidelines*, Ablex Publishing Corp., Norwood N.J., 1988, pp 115-119.

Buxton W.A.S. (1993). *The Pragmatics of Haptic Input*, Draft Manuscript to be published by Cambridge University Press.

Canny J.F. (1984). A Computational Approach to Edge Detection, *IEEE Trans. PAMI*, 8, No. 6, pp 679-98.

Chambers E. (1967). *Photolitho-offset*, Society of Lithographic Artists, Ernest Benn, London 1967, pp 43-49.

Field G.G. (1988). *Color and its Reproduction*, Graphic Arts Technical Foundation, Pittsburgh PA, 1988.

Fiume E.L. (1989). *The Mathematical Structure of Raster Graphics*, Academic Press, Boston, 1989, pp 110-112.

Gonzalez R.C. & Wintz P. (1987). *Digital Image Processing*, 2nd Edition, Addison-Wesley, Reading MA, 1987, pp 334-340.

MacDonald L.W., Mayne C. & Rassool R. (1990). *Image Generating Apparatus*, US Patent 4954912, 4th September 1990.

MacDonald L.W. (1991a). Visualising Colour Palettes for Designers, *Proc. BCS Displays Group Conf. on Human Interfaces for Design and Scientific Visualisation*, Royal College of Art, London, March 1991.

MacDonald L.W. (1991b). Use of Colour for Image Segmentation in the Graphic Arts, *Proc. IEE Colloquium on Binary Image Processing*, London, March 1991.

MacDonald L.W. (1992). Electronic Photo-Retouching - Making Photographs of Fantasy, *Proc. IOP/RPS Seminar on Image Manipulation in the Graphic Arts*, Bath, February 1992.

Manktelow K. & Jones J. (1987). Principles from the Psychology of Thinking and Mental Models, In *Applying Cognitive Psychology to User-Interface Design*, Ed. Gardiner M.M. and Christie B., John Wiley, Chichester, 1987, pp 106-111.

Porter T. & Duff T. (1984). Compositing Digital Images, *ACM Computer Graphics* (Siggraph), 18, No. 3, pp 253-259.

Thimbleby H. (1990). *User Interface Design*, ACM Press, Addison Wesley, Wokingham UK, 1990.

Wentzel F. (1983). *Graphic Arts Photography*: Color, Graphic Arts Technical Foundation, Pittsburgh PA, 1983, pp 123-130.

11

Photo CD Multimedia

Norman D. Richards and Paul J. Rankin

11.1 Introduction

Photo CD is a new consumer product which provides a highly cost-effective means to transfer standard 35 mm colour negatives in digital form to a CD-ROM compact disc. These digital images may then be displayed on standard domestic television sets, computer displays or printed as extremely high quality colour prints.

A considerable advantage to the consumer is that no special camera is required. Any normal 35 mm camera may be used to expose the negative, and existing negatives or transparencies may also be converted to the digital disc format. Each disc is capable of recording over 100 images. Because the initial capture of the image is on film, with the digitisation being performed by the photoprocessor, then the resolution and quality of the digitised pictures are far in excess of competing electronic capture systems. The disc may be updated, so that not all the pictures need to be written in a single operation. The disc is a writeable form of CD-ROM disc, which is formatted as a CD-ROM XA bridge disc.

Because the Photo CD system is offered to the market as an open system, it is possible for Photo CD images to be used as cheap high quality input to computer desk top publishing systems, or the images displayed on suitably high resolution computer graphics terminals. However, our present interest is in the display of pictures in a domestic environment.

A dedicated Photo CD player is able to display Photo CD discs and play standard Digital Audio CD from either audio or Photo CD discs. The Photo CD player displays the digital images from disc on either a 525 line or 625 line television receiver or monitor.

As an alternative to displaying the Photo CD images on a dedicated player it is also possible to playback and display the pictures on a standard CD-I player.

Interacting with Virtual Environments Edited by Lindsay MacDonald and John Vince

11.2 Why Photo CD?

The object of Photo CD is to combine the high quality and convenience of photographic film with the advantages of digital storage. The advantages of digital storage for images mirror the well known advantages of digital audio. Once the analogue image has been digitised it can be arranged that the image is substantially immune from subsequent distortion and degradation. An unlimited number of perfect copies may be made of any image, and there need be no degradation resulting from prolonged storage or repeated showing. The random access feature of the compact disc, which has been very well received for selecting audio tracks, is even more valuable for accessing individual Photo CD pictures. The final major advantage, is that digitisation makes flexible manipulation of the images a possibility. Zoom with selective cropping, exposure and colour balance correction, titling and photomontage are all possible in this new electronic darkroom.

The advantage of the Photo CD approach is that the digitisation equipment itself needs to be neither cheap nor portable and can be shared by a very large number of users. Thus a cheap, high quality digitisation service is available to all 250 million users of existing 35 mm cameras. The possibility of making direct digital imaging cameras that are compatible with the Photo CD standard remains. But for the foreseeable future the combination of film and off-line scanning is likely to provide the best combination, and is identical with the approach used by the professional graphics industry.

11.3 Requirements of the digital coding process

The design aim of the Photo CD coding system is to offer the advantages of a digital system, for both soft display on television systems and hard copy print output, without compromising the quality of the original photographic input. The first, and most obvious, aspect of quality is the spatial resolution of the digitised pictures. A resolution of 3k x 2k pixels has been adopted for 35 mm negatives, and this allows enlargements of poster size to be printed with good quality. Even higher resolutions will be available in the near future for larger format negatives.

The colorimetric aspects are also important. Here we have a problem arising from the fact that the Photo CD system is required to be suitable for generating both hard copy prints and television images on cathode ray tubes. So on the one hand we have a subtractive, non-linear colour system whose primaries are determined by the cyan, yellow and magenta dyes or printing inks, and on the other an additive, differently non-linear system, whose primaries are determined by the cathode ray tube red, green and blue phosphors.

There are also problems of dynamic range. Compared with audio, the dynamic range of the two target display media have a comparatively low dynamic range. Prints have a range from white to black that is limited by both the density of the dyes or pigments and the surface reflections. Cathode ray tubes are limited by surface reflections and internal electron scattering. In both cases the effects amount to several percent, so that achievable contrast ranges may only be in the range of 30 to 50. The source negative material has a much larger range, of at least 2.5 orders of magnitude. This is primarily to allow extended exposure latitude, and it is desirable to retain this extended range in the Photo CD system.

In addition to high picture quality, the system must have an adequate functional performance. It must be possible to pack a useful number of images on one disc, the loading time from disc must be acceptable for the display application, and the complexity of the decoding should be well adapted to the capabilities of current dedicated hardware and general purpose computers.

As a measure of this last problem, we can consider the consequences of writing the raw digital colour image directly to disc. One image would consist of approximately 30 Mbytes, thus limiting the disc to 20 pictures. Even less acceptable would be the fact that each picture would take three minutes to load from disc at normal CD-ROM transfer rates. It is thus essential that the picture data should be compressed, and preferably organised in a way that facilitates rapid access to individual images.

11.4 Coding Photo CD images

The 35 mm negatives are initially scanned by a solid state photosensitive array to give an image of 3k x 2k pixels. Because the scanning device is connected to a powerful digital workstation it is possible to enhance the quality of the initial digital image in a number of ways.

Self-calibration of the scanning device and correction of the known colour characteristics of the colour negative material (masking) are easily incorporated into the system. Relatively sophisticated algorithms for exposure compensation are also possible, and in the future it is to be expected that other means of providing digital image enhancement will be made available.

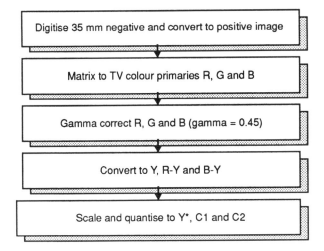

Figure 11.1. Basic Photo CD digitisation and encoding.

The coding process that is adopted (see Figure 11.1) is very similar to that used for producing digital television signals. This is no coincidence, because an important feature of Photo CD is the ability to show the pictures on a colour television display. However the coding has been adapted to the particular requirements of using the same data for making high resolution colour prints with an extended brightness and colour gamut.

The first modification to the coding process is the transformation of the three primary colour signals from the colour space of the image scanning system to that adopted for the colour television display system. The colours that can be reproduced by a colour CRT are defined by a colour triangle with vertices defined by the colours of the individual red, green and blue phosphors. This triangle lies inside the locus of pure spectral colours. It nearly, but not quite encompasses the locus of real surface colours available from pigments, but is deficient in both the magenta and cyan areas. This is shown in Figure 11.2. Although the subtractive colour processes are themselves restricted in their available gamut (and in a much more complex and non-linear way), the cyan and magenta dyes or pigments used may well be capable of reproducing colours in the area where colour phosphors are most deficient. Even television systems of the future are likely to have a colour gamut that is not limited by the current phosphor set.

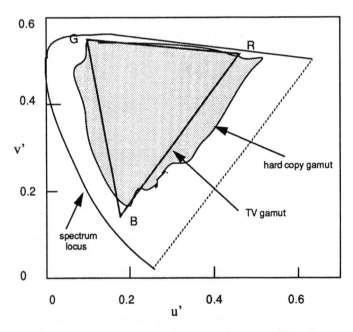

Figure 11.2. Comparison of hard copy colour gamut and TV colour gamut.

A possible solution would be to use neither colour television nor colour printing primaries for the encoding process, but to use hypothetical primaries that encompass the gamut of both display processes. However, an alternative solution is to make use of the fact that the whole of colour space may be defined by any practical set of primaries, e.g. the colour television set, provided that the red, green and blue values may take a range that exceeds the normal boundaries of zero to unity. In particular, negative values may be allowed. These negative values must be ignored by the television system, but are valid inputs to linear matrices that may be used to transform to a wider gamut colour space with alternative primaries. Adopting this approach ensures close compatibility with present video display systems, without losing the information that is required by systems with an extended colour gamut.

The first stage of coding is thus linear matrixing from the wide gamut colour space that is used by the digitising equipment to the colour space defined by the standard SMPTE phosphor set, retaining any negative values or values in excess of unity. The resulting red, green and blue linear values are then gamma corrected by the conventional 0.45 power law, to give R, G and B. This is almost identical to TV practice, except the non-linear coding preserves negative values. A luminance signal, Y, is generated from the gamma corrected R, G and B, using identically the same equations as used to generate the TV luminance signal. Chrominance signals R-Y and B-Y define the colour. The Y signal thus formed will never take negative values, but may have a value that exceeds unity. The extended colour gamut coding also results in an increased range for the chrominance signals. In order to accommodate this extended range, the gains and offsets of the Y and colour difference signals differ slightly from the standard PAL or NTSC signals. This modified type of coding is referred to as YCC coding.

Although different in detail, the coding is very similar to standard digital television coding. A simple set of look-up tables will perform the recoding that is required to convert to standard CCIR YUV components with 0.45 law gamma correction. The only further requirement for video compatibility is that the display system should be able to deal with de-matrixed RGB signals that may take negative values.

11.5 Display resolutions and data compression

It is not generally possible to convert a high resolution image to a lower resolution by a simple process of subsampling. It must be preceded by a low pass filtering process. Not only does this require computation time, but it requires that all of the data for the higher resolution image is accessed. This could result in very long access times for the display of TV images. The Photo CD system overcomes this problem by storing a hierarchy of five properly filtered and subsampled images on the disc. This is shown in Figure 11.3. The contents of an image pack ranges from the highest resolution print file, through images suitable for differing television resolutions, including HDTV, and down to reduced area overview images.

The lower resolution images i.e. from 768 x 512 downwards, consist of a Y image at the basic resolution and chrominance components subsampled by a factor of two both horizontally and vertically. This is a well established means of obtaining a factor of two data compression, with little visual loss in fidelity. Because very little of the total data resides in these lower resolution images, and because it is desirable to have the least decoding overhead for these television based images, no further compression is used at these levels.

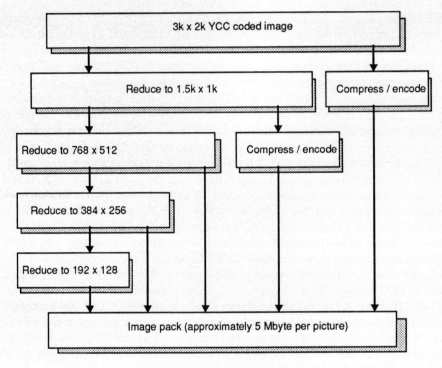

Figure 11.3. Coding of an image pack from 3k x 2k YCC image.

The two highest resolution images are encoded by a form of pyramid coding. Thus the 1k5 x 1k image is encoded by first subtracting the interpolated 768 x 512 image, to give a difference image. Because the higher resolution image only differs from the interpolated lower resolution image in the vicinity of sharp edges, the difference data has statistics that make it suitable for quantisation and variable length coding, which compresses the data from 8 bits per pixel to 2 or 3 bits.

The 1k5 x 1k image is subsequently reconstructed from the 768 x 512 resolution image plus the compressed difference data. A second stage of differencing enables the 3k x 2k image to be coded in a similar way, and at this level even higher data compressions are achieved. A complete "image pack" of the different resolution images compresses to about 5 Mbytes, thus allowing over 100 different pictures to be stored on one disc.

11.6 Combining Photo CD and CD-I

Because the coding of the images has been designed to be very similar to that adopted for digital television, it has been possible to design cost-effective hardware for dedicated Photo

CD players. These players decode the images from disc and display them on a standard domestic television receiver. Features like rotation of images, zoom magnification and favourite picture selection are all supported, as well as the playback of conventional CD audio.

Similarly, the encoding has been designed so as to present few decoding problems for the relatively powerful workstations used for image processing and quality desk-top publishing.

Each Photo CD disc includes software for CD-I players which enables them to display Photo CD images and perform all the functions of the dedicated Photo CD player.

The fundamental problem for such a program is to transform the data in the Photo CD image packs to a form that is compatible with the CD-I video display system.The standard CD-I player is capable of displaying colour images in several different modes, depending on the particular application. In common with many computer systems, graphics and text may be displayed in CLUT mode, using colour look-up tables to translate the 8-bit or 4-bit values into either one of 256 or 16 colours respectively. In addition to this display mode, natural photographic images are generally displayed using the DYUV mode. This is an 8-bit display mode that uses delta PCM coding of YUV colour components to achieve compression of the colour data both on disc and in display memory. As a result of the differential PCM coding it is possible to display the complete gamut of colours used in colour television, and in this respect its performance is exactly equivalent to a 24-bit colour display system.

In order to display Photo CD image data it is necessary first to translate the YCC values to YUV by means of a look up table. This is followed by a delta PCM encoder which compresses the 8-bit YUV data to the 4-bit delta PCM codes that are used by the CD-I display. The CD-I player is programmed to recode the data as it is loaded from disc with only a few seconds delay.

The normal resolution of the CD-I natural picture mode enables DYUV coded pictures to be displayed as either 384 x 256 non-interlaced or 384 x 512 interlaced images, which are comparable in quality with broadcast TV. However, it is possible to enhance the pictures further by means of a technique known as QHYB coding. This makes use of various unique features of the CD-I hardware to enhance the 384 x 512 images to 768 x 512, while still providing the full colour gamut that is a feature of DYUV coding. The increased resolution requires rather more time for loading and recoding, but results in displayed images which exceed the quality obtainable on most current broadcast receivers.

11.7 Photo CD as an interactive multimedia system

If we examine the basic requirements for an interactive multimedia system, we require the following features:

- natural photographic images
- text and graphics
- audio
- storage capacity
- programmable structure
- user interface

At first sight, the Photo CD system does not appear to be a strong contender. It has good features for displaying natural images, and has storage capacity for over 100 image packs but it would appear to lack the other essential requirements. It has no specific text or graphics modes and user interaction is either at the level of the individual image or restricted to showing simple linear sequences.

The first problem, the lack of an explicit mode for displaying text and graphics is readily solved. In conventional computer systems text and graphics are generated at display time from compressed data such as ASCII data or graphics primitives. Using this approach enables the data to be modified very readily by the user or the display program, but the main advantage has been in compressing data to the few Megabytes that might be available from magnetic storage media e.g. floppy or hard discs. The optical storage medium used for CD-ROM does not have this constraint, so graphics and text can be regarded as special cases of natural photographic images and can be encoded and stored as standard image packs.

Even with the large capacity of the optical disc, there is space for only a little over 100 full resolution (3k x 2k) image packs.This capacity problem may be solved by storing image packs with only the lower resolutions (768 x 512 and lower). This is fully adequate for applications that are only intended for display at standard TV scanning standards i.e. PAL and NTSC. By this means it is possible to store as many as 800 images on a single disc.

The Photo CD player includes hardware to play standard CD Digital Audio. Combined with the digital fast random access capabilities that are intrinsic to the CD, this makes possible the use of audio in an interactive manner.

We thus have the nucleus of high quality hardware resources, but appear to lack the final two essentials of a programmable structure and interactive user interface to make use of these resources.

Most interactive multimedia systems run on comparatively powerful general purpose programmable computer systems. The challenge in the case of Photo CD was to design a programmable system that would function using the very limited computational and memory resources that could be provided by the simple microcontroller within the Photo CD player. However, because the basic mechanisms of data retrieval, image display and audio playback are intrinsic to the Photo CD hardware, it has been possible to design a useful but inexpensive system that operates within these constraints.

11.8 Basic elements for interactive programs

Photo CD multimedia programming is by means of a very low level language, the PPS, that has been stripped down to only two basic data structures. The first of these is the Play Sequence - a structure that describes a sequence of either images or audio segments. The second structure is a Selection Item, which defines the way in which the user can interact with the program, so as to branch to alternative sequences or Selection Items. These data structures in turn call primitive Image Entries and Audio Entries, which describe the audiovisual assets and how they are to be played back by the system.

Play Sequences consist of simple lists of either image or audio descriptors. A simple slide show would contain only image descriptors, whereas a full audiovisual presentation would

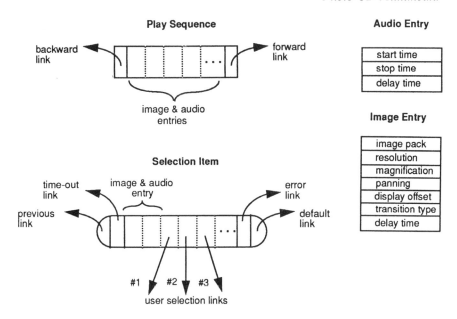

Figure 11.4. Primitive elements in PPS (simplified).

more typically consist of alternating image and audio items. On the dedicated Photo CD player the user can move forwards and backwards between successive images and their accompanying audio clip in this sequence via "next" and "previous" buttons on the remote handset. More generally, it is essential to allow the user an easy way to navigate a way through a potentially very complex data organisation.There is therefore provision in the PPS for special links that enable the user to move quickly from the end or backwards from the beginning of a Play Sequence to the next or previous Sequence or Selection Item.

There are two essential parts to a Selection Item, a user prompt and an action list. In general there must be some indication to the user that it is possible to make a choice at the current point in a program and a prompt given of the nature of the choices available. The Selection Item specifies an image that may be displayed as a menu of choices along with a segment of audio that may be played either as a supplement or an alternative to the menu image. In addition, the Selection Item contains the information that associates the actions of the user with the branches in the program that correspond to a selection. Just as with Play Sequences, backwards i.e. previous links are provided in the Selection Items to enable the users to retrace their choices. Forwards links can also be set to activate default branch choices.

Two kinds of user input are supported within the Selection Item data structure. The first is for use by simple dedicated players that use numerical input from a remote keypad for indicating selections. Play Sequences or Selection Items to which the user can branch are listed in the Selection Item in this numeric order. The second alternative is a screen-based selection using a pointing device such as a mouse, joystick or touch screen. For these types of device, screen coordinates of the selection areas are stored in the Selection Item alongside the addresses of branch links which are available to the user. Other data in the Selection Item can store both a time-out link which is activated upon elapse of the specified image and audio delays, and also an error link which is activated, e.g. to play an audio help message, if the user makes a numeric selection which is not expected.

Audio Entries describe the CD Digital Audio clips which are used in the structure. Start and stop times for these clips are specified in the PPS in terms of absolute disc time codes. A delay time can be added after the end of each clip before the next audiovisual entry is loaded.

Image Entries are described by: the image pack that is to be used, the image resolution to be employed from the pack, the magnification factor, panning and offsets for its display, the type of transition to be used between images and a delay time to elapse before loading further audiovisual entries.

Just by using these two Sequence and Selection objects as building blocks it is possible to construct a wide variety of interactive multimedia applications, as the system places few constraints on the way that the elements can be constructed and linked together. In practice, a very large number of applications are modelled around the simple hierarchical tree structure shown in Figure 11.5.

The two basic elements in the Photo CD program i.e. the Play Sequence and the Selection Item, correspond closely to the concepts of file and directory in a standard computer file system. Alternatively, a better analogy for the user who is more familiar with the text-based literary world is that of an organisation based on the concept of a hierarchy of volume, chapter, section, subsection etc.

This type of hierarchical tree structure is one of the most generally useful methods for organising information. However, the PPS has few constraints on the way that its elements are linked. It is comparatively easy to use the basic building blocks to design hypermedia applications which include arbitrary hyperlinks between different levels of the information structure. Simple quizzes or even programmed learning schemes and "adventure" games are within the capabilities of this simple program scheme.

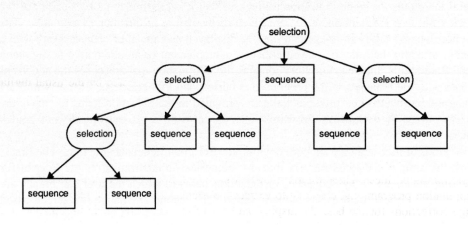

Figure 11.5a. Basic tree constructed from selection items and sequences.

Although Photo CD players or CD-I players will themselves store sequencing information which is associated with a specific disc, there is no simple mechanism for transferring this data from one machine to another. Use of the PPS enables the data to be written to the disc itself, and so the program of sequences and menus will play on any Photo CD player, or compatible system such as CD-I.

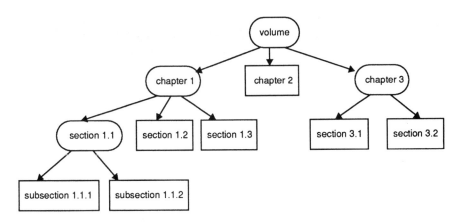

Figure 11.5b. The same tree representing the structure for an interactive book.

11.9 Authoring Photo CD multimedia

The authoring of these Photo CD discs, programmed by the addition of a PPS data structure to make "Picture Discs" is rather simple in comparison with the authoring of more advanced multimedia discs which include animation, special effects or video. It is precisely this simplification of the authoring process that keeps the production costs low- thus making specialist or local publications in this format economic- and the authoring times short- thus making it possible to track fashion, news, periodicals or other transitory interests in the market.

The bulk of the work is in production and management of the image and audio assets. Individual audio recordings required in the Picture Disc are collected by the usual digital acquisition and encoding computer tools. As the audio must be laid down on the disc at CD-DA quality, its consumption of the overall disc space can be high. It may therefore be better to author discs in different languages, rather than a single multi-lingual disc.

Source images for the slideshow sequences can be scanned from slides or negatives into digital form or read from simple Photo CD discs into the computer used for authoring via programming utilities. These digital images usually require work in a professional image-manipulation program, e.g. cropping to extract the desired views, careful gamma and other image corrections for the best TV display, and re-sizing (e.g. using cubic interpolation) to 768x512 pixels for use in the Picture Disc. Text annotation can be added at this stage to the image, paying care that an adequate font and point size is used for comfortable TV legibility, and ensuring that the text is written in anti-alias form to avoid jagged sloping lines. Such annotations should be restricted to a "safe area" of the screen, whose size depends on the tolerance on overscan found in the PAL and/or NTSC TV sets of the target market, e.g. 538x404 for 20% NTSC overscan.

A CD-I playback program is included on each Photo CD disc. This program could transcode from the image pack format stored on the disc, into DYUV or QHYB formats, on-line as required for display to the CD-I user. However, this method entails significant delays during playback of the disc due to the transcoding time between image transitions. It is therefore better to pre-code CD-I versions of the image packs in QHYB format during the production process and add those as well to the disc for instant display by the CD-I playback program. These QHYB images require some vertical filtering before storage to avoid the flicker that would otherwise result from interlaced display on a TV screen. (The dedicated Photo CD player does the same filtering in its display hardware.)

For the CD-I versions of the images of menus used in Selection Items, the annotation of keypad numbers against user's choices can be omitted. User choices on CD-I are made via the cursor and the predefined selection areas stored in the Selection Item in the PPS. These CD-I images should be sampled according to the target PAL and/or NTSC format (e.g. 768x560 pixels).

Once the audio and image assets have been prepared, the last remaining authoring task is to define the structure of sequences and menus. An object-oriented script language is advisable for the author to compose the structure, from which the low-level form of the PPS can then be automatically compiled. For example, it is convenient for the author to assign symbolic names to the Selection Items and Play Sequences, set values for the properties of each object and collect together in one place the linking of symbolic names for Audio and Image Entries to references giving the pathnames of their data files. At this time, before building a disc image, relative addresses are all that can be specified in the PPS for the links between sequences and selectors and the start and stop times of the audio clips.

This PPS script language can be generated from a graphical flow-chart editor. Not only must the forward links between Play Sequences and the branching from Selection Items be decided, but the author must also connect up the other links in the PPS for reverse play, time-out and error actions. For each Selection Item, active screen areas corresponding to each of the user choices must also be added. During this assembly process the author needs to emulate playback of the disc both on Photo CD and CD-I players both to verify the structure being built and to check the legibility of text and other aspects of the images when displayed on a TV. For more limited or repetitive Picture Disc designs, a simpler, non-graphical front-end to generate the PPS script is possible, such as some form-filling database tool. Here the labour is simply that of re-populating an existing structure with new assets.

Other stages in building the disc to the Photo CD, Bridge-XA standard format can then be performed automatically. The general flow is as outlined in Figure 11.6. The following functions must be performed during the production process:

- Compilation of the PPS script language, performing various checks for consistency and completeness of the structure defined by the author.

- Concatenation of the individual audio clips into one or more audio files to be put on the disc.

- Coding of Photo-CD image packs from the source image files and construction of the overview image pack containing thumb-nail 192x128 pixel versions of all of the images, as required on all Photo CD discs.

- Relocation of relative addresses given in the PPS script to refer instead to absolute disc addresses as required by the PPS, namely the addresses for links between PPS objects and the audio clip start and stop times.

- Generation of the low-level form of the PPS for use by the microcontroller in the dedicated Photo CD player.

- Duplication of the contents of the PPS in a computer-readable file form for other playback devices.

- Production of other information files as required by the Photo CD standard on disc format.

- Build of a disc image ready for the disc writer, constructing all of the contents of the Photo CD and CD-I directories on the disc and adding extra disc-specific header, index and copyright information.

The CD-I directory must contain an application program used for CD-I playback as well as any other CD-I specific image or audio data, such as QHYB versions of the image packs. This playback program might be a general-purpose program, driven by the computer-readable form of the PPS. The general-purpose CD-I program must explicitly create on-screen options for the "next" and "previous" buttons provided on the dedicated player's remote keypad. It can in addition provide a wider variety of types of image transition and cursor highlighting of selection areas which are not possible on the dedicated player. Alternatively, a custom-written application might be included on the disc giving many more features that exploit the additional facilities which CD-I players offer in comparison with the dedicated Photo CD player. For example, ADPCM sound across image changes could be substituted for the CD-DA audio or special facilities could be added for searching and browsing through information, marking items of interest and remembering choices made by the user.

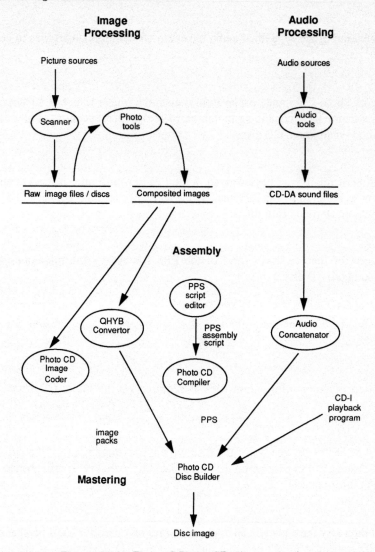

Figure 11.6. Flow of Photo CD disc production.

11.10 Design considerations

As with all multimedia productions, the slideshows provided by these Picture Discs will not be interesting for the user without a careful design. In particular, it is the audio which must provide the narrative interest which threads a sequence of images together. Certainly, in a good design the audio should draw the viewer's attention to different aspects of the content of the currently-displayed image and provide ambience. Paradoxically, the extra dimension of sound is the selling feature that these Photo CD discs can offer over conventional, glossily-printed publications.

On the dedicated player, numeric choices on menus are made with remote keypad which can be rather fast compared with targeting a joystick on a selection area. However, image changes are rather slow (about 4 seconds) in comparison to CD-I. This can make navigation through menus and submenus tedious on a Photo CD player. The menu structure for Photo CD playback may therefore be rather flatter, offering more options at each level, but fewer menu levels for the user to traverse. As a faster response (about 1 second) to the user can be made with audio rather than image changes, it is may be more effective to provide messages for help options etc. via audio clips without changing the screen.

The Selection Item representing a menu in the PPS contains a list of user branches, in order of the keypad numbers which the user must enter. Often, it is easier for the user to remember that a specific number is associated with an option throughout the disc, e.g. to return to the root menu. Numbers such as 99 may be reserved for use in all menus, by padding out the intervening unused numbers in the selection list in the PPS with "no operation" links.

The Play Sequence provides an easy way to construct an audiovisual slideshow. However, the amount of interactivity available to the user during the sequence is limited to forward and backward increments. For this reason, it is better to keep the length of such Play sequences short. A more interactive type of sequence can be constructed by chaining together Selection Items. Each Selection Item then shows one image in the sequence and will time-out to its successor, but at the same time can offer additional options for the user to key a number to explore additional side-avenues of information, or jump to other points in the structure.

11.11 Applications of Photo CD multimedia

Two main type of usage are envisaged for the programmable discs. Because the Photo CD discs use a writeable medium that is capable of being updated, it is possible to add the sequencing information to discs containing existing images. Photofinishers will provide facilities to allow customers to create PPS display programs for their own use or as custom presentations for business applications.

In addition to this ability to record sequences on individual discs, pre-recorded discs can be designed and authored at relatively low cost and duplicated by standard CD processes. As these discs may be played back on both Photo CD and CD-I players (or any other Photo CD compatible multimedia systems), this opens up the possibilities of a large market for inexpensive but high quality discs.

Authoring costs for these pre-recorded discs will be very low compared with those that are incurred in designing software for more complex multimedia systems. There is no software to be written. The design process is reduced to the logical minimum. First there is the process of creative design, followed by the acquisition of assets in the form of Photo CD images, text screens and audio clips. These assets must be linked by specifying the order of play within the sequences and then adding the selection branches. Although the PPS program data is written to the disc in a very low level form of code, this will be completely hidden from the author. Computer-based tools have been developed which allow the author to generate the

PPS data in a very simple and intuitive way. A whole disc may be structured with a few hours of relatively unskilled effort.

Effectively, the major process of authoring interactive multimedia programs for Photo CD is reduced to the essentials of applying creative design and acquiring the relevant sound and image assets. It will thus be seen that publishing for Photo CD does not differ greatly from conventional text publishing, apart from the final printing technology. The main difference is that spoken words will generally be used, rather than printed text. However, if is thought appropriate, it is simple to display images of text screens. Because the screens are designed for display on domestic TV receivers, it is desirable to limit the text screens to about 200 words, but up to about 150000 words of text are possible

As the authoring costs will be broadly similar to those incurred in text publishing, and initial capital investment will not be high while the skills required for the technology are low, it is to be hoped that Photo CD/CD-I Picture Discs will be an attractive route for existing book and magazine publishers to venture into electronic publishing.

The capability of very high quality images and sound, interactively controlled by users, combined with simple authoring, makes the medium ideal for a wide range of publishing applications. These range from illustrative picture collection discs such as art, sport and nature, news and fashion magazines, and through to more extensive works of reference.

Although it might be appropriate to use the more sophisticated multimedia systems for highly interactive educational applications, there remains a large area within the field of education that is very suited to Photo CD publishing. Extensive resources of images and sound clips may be made available to teachers and children at low cost. These may be given added value by the simplicity of including hypermedia links within sequences, so as to encourage browsing to acquire more extensive information. The potentially low costs of both discs and players, plus the inherent compatibility with CD-I, make this a very attractive educational medium.

Finally, because of the low initial costs, the technique is also suitable for all areas of product cataloguing point of sale or information systems, with economic production quantities ranging from one off, through short runs using writeable discs, and up to very large runs using pressed discs.

This is necessarily an incomplete list of applications. The salient features they have in common are the combination of high quality image and sound resources with low costs. The cost advantage is exhibited at all levels, including image acquisition, authoring, distribution medium and user hardware. In view of their fast production times, market response times for these discs can match those of the audio CD business.

11.12 An example

A typical example of the type of multimedia publication which is readily assembled with the PPS from Photo CD images with sound clips is one of a specialist interest, Formula 1 racing cars. This disc was produced from about 290 base-resolution images, annotated with about 40 minutes of 5-15 second CD-DA audio clips.

The structure of the disc consists of a a few introductory images which prefix a main menu (see Plate 16), offering six sub-topics and carrying an option for activating an audio help clip. The six sub-topics range from the history of Formula 1 racing, to a number of audiovisual slideshows on racing drivers, teams and circuits, plus a longer slideshow on technical information about the cars (see e.g. Plates 17 and 18) and a simple quiz.

The section on history is in turn divided into three slide shows covering the period from 1950-1992. Information on drivers, circuits and teams is alphabetically-organised under further sub-menus. Taking the racing circuits sub-topic, this in turn is introduced by a sub-menu screen, from which short slide shows about each circuit can be activated, automatically returning to the sub-menu on completion. The information on drivers is organised under two descending sub-menus (Plates 19 and 20) before getting to the image and audio description on a particular driver (Plate 21). A trivia quiz is added to test the user's knowledge of racing, from identifying drivers to naming famous races.

The keypad number 99 is reserved throughout sub-menus for return to the top, main menu to make it easier for the user to memorise. If the user keys an erroneous number on a menu a short audio message is played.

11.13 Future enhancements to Photo CD multimedia

One of the main deficiencies in the first generation of dedicated Photo CD players is their inability to play a continuous audio soundtrack as a background to a sequence of images. Because standard CD digital audio requires the full data bandwidth of the disc, the sound playback has to be interrupted for the player to display an image. This is not too severe a limitation to many programs, where the sequences commonly consist of images alternating with audio clips consisting of spoken commentary on the individual image, but the playing of a continuous music background is precluded. This problem is overcome in CD-I and CD-ROM XA by encoding the sound in an alternative and more highly compressed form, ADPCM. Because the audio information is more highly compressed, then the disc can be made to interleave the image and sound data. In consequence, a suitably equipped player is capable of loading images simultaneous with playing continuous sound.

A further advantage of using ADPCM sound coding is that more sound can be packed on a single disc. This is particularly desirable if it is required to author multilingual discs. A maximum of only one hour of standard CD audio is available, for division between the alternative languages. Using ADPCM, it is possible to pack as much as 16 hours of speech quality audio on a single disc, or up to 4 hours of higher quality stereo music.

The Photo CD specification allows for the use of ADPCM sound, and extended Photo CD players with ADPCM sound capability are planned in the future. Discs will be designed to be compatible with both existing players and the extended players.

11.14 Conclusions

The Photo CD disc standard is the first real multi-platform standard embracing CDROM and CD-I formats. It provides a low-cost route to digitising images, preserving a high control over picture quality while encoding to a very high resolution efficiently. The medium is attractive both for handling images in the professional spheres of publishing and photography, but also in the home for showing the consumer's own photographs on television.

CD-I offers display modes which support the complete gamut of colours shown on television, and thus is eminently suitable for showing Photo CD in a consumer environment. Via a technique known as QHYB coding, the resolution and quality of these images on CD-I can exceed normal broadcast quality and match the display quality of Photo CD when running on the dedicated players. In addition, further interactive features can be added for CD-I playback.

The Photo CD disc standard includes provision for simple interactive structures combining sequences and menus to play high quality sound and images under user control. These multimedia discs are simple and cheap to author, run on a low-cost players and therefore open up new opportunities for interactive books, periodicals and magazines.

Acknowledgements

The work described in this article forms part of a collaboration between the Eastman Kodak and the Philips Consumer Electronics development group.

The example Picture Disc described in the example was made at the Freeland Studios by Philips Professional Publishing International, Dorking, Surrey in conjunction with the AutoSport Magazine. Copyright for the disc is held by Philips Interactive Media International Ltd 1992 and Haymarket Specialist Motoring Publications Ltd 1992.

References

DeMarsh L.E., Giorgianni E.J. (1989). Color Science for Imaging Systems, *Physics Today*, pp. 44-52.

Hubbard G.R. (1991). The Photo CD System: An Overview for Consumer and Photofinishing Applications, *Digest Int. Conf. on Consumer Electronics,* pp. 316-317, Chicago.

Philips N.V. & Eastman Kodak Co. (1993). *System Description Photo CD.*

Philips N.V. & Sony Corp. CD-ROM XA, Compact Disc Read Only Memory Extend-ed Architecture Specified in the System Description

Petruzelli C., Small J., Torok A., Uebelacker J., Luyckx E., Mertens E., Terryn D., Schepers J., Timmermans J., Tijskens K. & Boggs S. (1991). PVC-1: Photo CD Video Controller ASIC, *Digest Int. Conf. on Consumer Electronics,* pp. 320-321, Chicago.

Richards N.D. (1992). Multimedia Extensions to Photo CD, *Digest Int. Conf. on Consumer Electronics,* pp. 340-341, Chicago.

Richards N.D. (1987). QHY- High Resolution Natural Picture Mode for CD-I, *Philips Re-search Laboratories (UK) Ann. Rev.,* pp. 61-63.

Richards N.D. (1990). Showing Photo CD pictures on CD-I, *Philips Research Laboratories (UK) Ann. Rev.,* pp. 11- 14.

Richards N.D. (1991). Photo CD and CD-I : A Marriage of Great Convenience, *Digest Int. Conf. on Consumer Electronics,* pp. 322-323, Chicago.

Robertson B. (1992). Disc-o-mania, *Computer Graphics World,* pp 40-48.

Shiels M. (1991). A Frame Language for Compact Disc Interactive, *Philips Research Laboratories (UK) Ann. Rev.,* pp. 56-58.

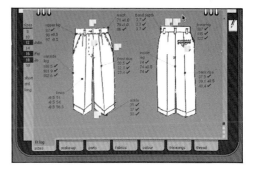

Plates 1-3 Appropriate connotation and the relationship between narrative and representation; database for fashion designers by RCA CRD Department 1993; design Charlie Hill, Stephen Camlish; research Ellie Curtis, Mike Scaife. The direct-manipulation approach of the first prototype (below left) proved impossible to represent in the final design (above and left) where simultaneous access to a large number of garments was essential

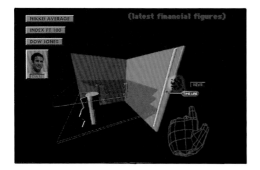

Plate 4: Density of meaning: *Virtual Stockbroking* by Dennis Poon, RCA CRD Department 1992. Five variables are expressed in this virtual space. Initial investment is shown by volume, profit by "wings", company prospects by direction, company status by colour, risk by the vertical axis and sector by the horizontal. At a glance one can judge the spread and performance of one's portfolio.

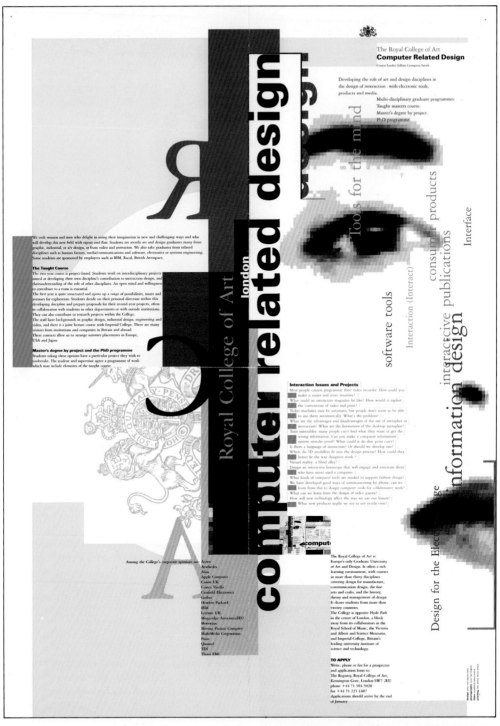

Plate 5 Layers of meaning: poster by Why Not Associates, 1991. Recent typographic design explores layering, which differentiates parts of information in a single image, implying three-dimensional relationships, not necessarily consistent, between elements. This is not yet much exploited in interface design which has emphasised precision rather than suggestion.

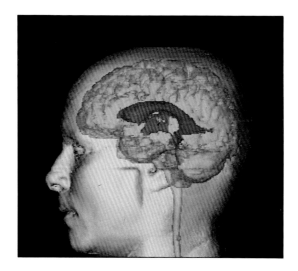

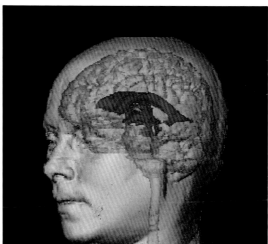

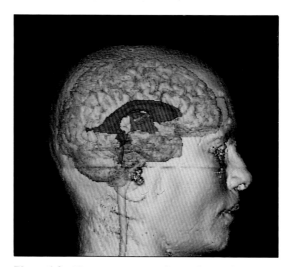

Plates 6-8 Three transparent views of a head rendered from MRI data showing skin and brain ventricles.

Plate 9 The original picture in which it is desired to change the yellow jersey to blue.

Plate 10 The result of a global colour change. Note the effect on yellows in grass and the crowd.

Plate 11 The construction of a colour selective mask to isolate the yellow jersey.

Plate 12 The slider is adjusted interactively to give the best definition of the jersey region (green overlay).

Plate 13 The final mask for the jersey, after removing unwanted areas with an etch brush.

Plate 14: The final composite image combines the original and globally colour corrected images under control of the jersey mask.

(a) Original image of Tutankhamun statue

(b) Studio shot of model in same pose

(c) Images aligned and partial brush-through

(d) Brush-through completed giving composite result

Plate 15 The brush-through retouching technique allows the seamless composition of two images.

Plate 16   The main menu.

Plate 17   The image from the slideshow.

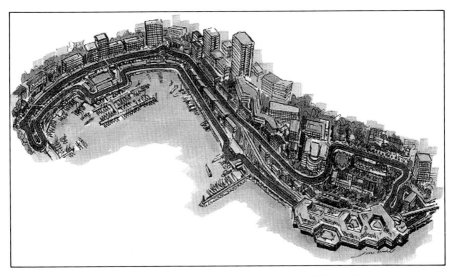

Plate 18   The image selected from section "Circuits".

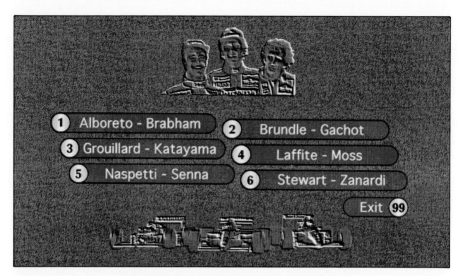

Plate 19 First sub-menu under "Drivers".

Plate 20 Second sub-menu under "Drivers".

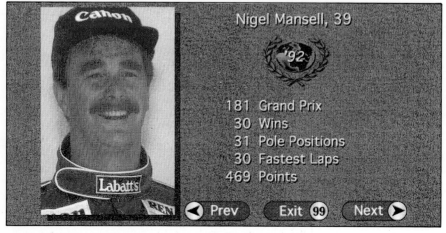

Plate 21 Final information screen on a driver.

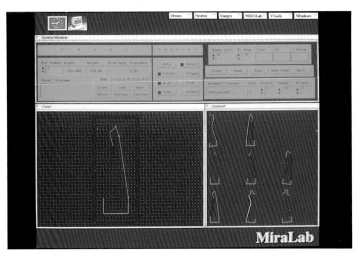

Plate 22   An example of seam pairs.

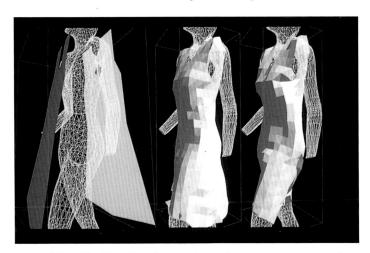

Plate 23   The three images depict the seaming process.

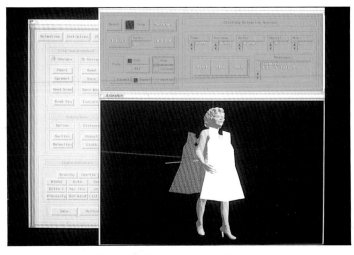

Plate 24   The Animation Window.

Plates 25-27 Three examples of different garments and materials.

Plates 28-29 Examples of synthetic actors.

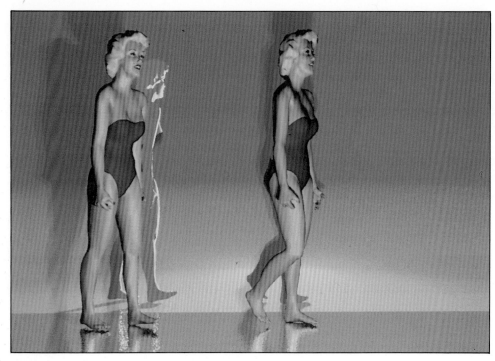

Plate 30 An example of a walking sequence.

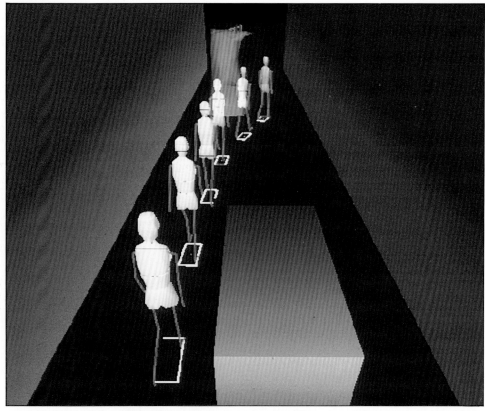

Plate 31 Autonomous actors avoiding obstacles.

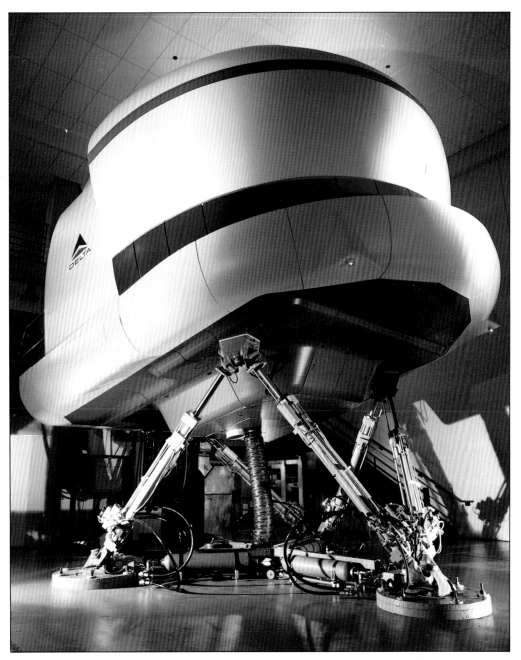

Plate 32 A full-flight simulator manufactured by Hughes Rediffusion Simulation Ltd.

Plate 33 (left): The inside of an MD-11 flight simulator. Reproduced by kind permission of Hughes Rediffusion Simulation Ltd.

Plate 34 (below): Daytime view of a synthetic airport. Reproduced by kind permission of Hughes Rediffusion Simulation Ltd.

Plate 35 Dusktime view of a synthetic airport. Reproduced by kind permission of Hughes Rediffusion Simulation Ltd.

Plate 36 A computer-generated winter scene. Reproduced by kind permission of Hughes Rediffusion Simulation Ltd.

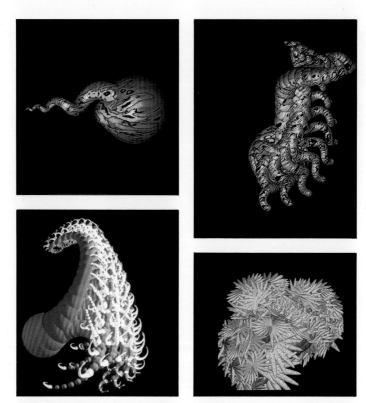

Plate 37 Complex forms: segmented horn, horn of horns, fractal and branched horns.

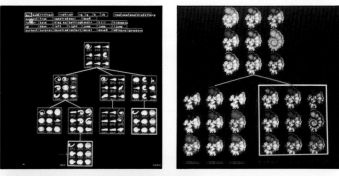

Plate 38 Display of family trees by Mutator.

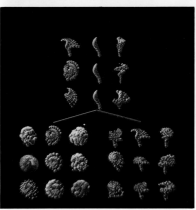

12

Information Environments

Matthew Chalmers

12.1 Introduction

Several projects at EuroPARC are aimed at merging the electronic and physical worlds. The information available in each world, and the types of interaction engendered, are too often divorced from each other. We are working to make computers more like the physical world, and to extend the physical world with the power of computers. This allows people to move from cognitive problem-solving to more natural sensorimotor strategies.

Three systems are discussed. The first, Bead, involves the visualisation of complexly structured information using three-dimensional graphics. The aim is to make interaction with a database of documents more graphically-oriented, and to move away from interaction styles requiring knowledge of query languages and the database material itself.

The DigitalDesk is a system which takes an unorthodox view of the "desktop" metaphor. It is directed towards combining the electronic and paper-based media so as to gain some of the benefits of each. It reflects the way that many people work: not solely using the computer, and not solely using paper documents, but rather combining the two so as to gain the best of both worlds.

Another focus of work is the interaction of people. The last system to be described, RAVE, concentrates on supporting collaborative work, in particular when the people involved are not physically co-located. RAVE employs video and audio communication links and a supporting infrastructure of tools for interaction.

12.2 Bead

Bead is a prototype system for the graphically-based exploration of information. In this system, articles in a bibliography are represented by particles in 3-space. By using physically-based modelling techniques, we represent the relationships between articles by their

Interacting with Virtual Environments Edited by Lindsay MacDonald and John Vince

relative spatial positions. Inter-particle forces tend to make similar articles move closer to one another and dissimilar ones move apart. The result is a 3-D scene which can be used to visualise patterns in the high-dimensional information space. The modelling techniques involved were the main focus of a description of an earlier version of Bead, published as (Chalmers and Chitson 1992).

The underlying notion of the system is one of our most familiar metaphors: spatial proximity to represent similarity in some more abstract interpretive framework. Documents are represented as particles in a low-dimensional space which behave so as to be a small distance from documents that are similar to themselves in some respect, and to be far from more dissimilar ones. The emergent structure of these particles is the model of the corpus: a landscape or map of the information within the document set. An example is given in Plate 1, which shows a landscape constructed from articles in an HCI conference, CHI91.

Low dimensionality is in accord with our everyday experience. We are used to a space of three physical dimensions wherein we perceive individual characteristics of objects and also their patterns and interrelationships. Physical spaces of high dimensionality are unfamiliar to most of us, and it is generally more difficult to present, perceive and remember patterns and structures within them. If our activities depend on judgements based on both the individual characteristics of documents and their relative properties then we will gain by employing a representation which shows both in a space of familiar dimensionality. The point was forcefully put in (Bertin 1981): "Items of data do not supply the information necessary for decision-making. What must be seen are the relationships which emerge from consideration of the entire set of data. In decision-making the useful information is drawn from the overall relationships of the entire set."

A goal of Bead is to represent a corpus of documents in a way which helps with tasks which rely on the relationships of the entire set of documents as much as the properties of individual members. A document must therefore play a dual role: it must act as an autonomous unit and it must also play a role as a component within a higher-level structure. We wish the corpus to have a layout which represents the more abstract patterns within it. The model of a corpus used in Bead emphasises patterns of thematic similarity as estimated by similarities in word usage. Individual documents take their places in these patterns by dint of the words used within them, but they also have important characteristics not used in constructing the overall layout. Bead is therefore intended to aid in tasks which rely on consideration of the overall relationships of the themes and words active in a corpus, as well as the individual elements.

As in most Information Retrieval systems, a document is represented as a tally of the words which occur within it, and some numeric measure of the relative weight of each occurring word. The most simple numeric measure is a one for a word occurring in a document, and a zero for non-occurrence. For reasons which include efficiency, not every word is actually used. Common words such as "the" and "or" are discarded, because of the large number of unique words that occur in most documents.

This representation has a geometric interpretation. It is as though each document is a point in space. The large number of words means a large number of dimensions to this space: each unique word in a corpus of documents defines one dimension, and the weight for each word is a coordinate for that dimension. Therefore, documents are close in this space if they have roughly the same words occurring with roughly the same weights. The assumption is that if this is so then the documents are similar in terms of themes and topics. Spatial distance roughly corresponds to thematic similarity.

Since the number of words in a corpus of documents can easily run into thousands, the number of dimensions is too large to display directly. We can get some information about what documents are close to each other by the more traditional means of information retrieval: we can take peeks at parts of the space near to documents known a priori. The system can then find the nearest (most relevant) documents and return them to you, usually in order of spatial distance (relevance ranking). A simple view of a query to an information retrieval system is that we make a fake, temporary document with just the keywords we give and with chosen (presumably high) weights, and then repeat the "peek" process just described. Again, we get an idea about some documents close to what we knew about before, but little global information. We find out about the locality near to the query, but we gain no idea about things further away (involving different words) and how they relate to each other.

Note that we have to start off with some a priori knowledge of what we want to find out. Unfortunately this is not always the case, for example when we want to explore and browse our way towards whatever it is we come to decide is of interest or relevance. We can only do this by many repeated peeks at sample regions, and in ourselves building up some sort of cognitive model of what there is in the corpus and how they fit together. Defining such samples means either having many well-understood documents in the corpus that one can work out from, or knowing how to put the words together in a query (i.e. how to use a query language) to sample in the region you want to know more about. It would be better for those who do such sampling less often (or who know less about the corpus or the query language) if some of the cognitive load could be taken on by the representation of the corpus.

Another approach using the same underlying representation is to partition the space into some number of regions which share roughly the same words and weights. We can then show representative members or the highly weighted words which typify each region. We therefore obtain a concise but more approximate representation which we can show in a list. We now get some idea of the overall range of the documents in the corpus, but our accuracy is limited because we can only write so much about each one on a screen or page. We could then choose one or two of these selected regions to look at more closely, perhaps by gathering in the members of the regions and then trying to spread them out again into another list of regions to select from, scatter out again and so on with ever more refined choices of documents. This is roughly the approach described in (Cutting *et al.* 1991).

This approach is better for someone browsing the corpus because at each stage they get some idea of the overall contents of the corpus presented to them, and they don't have to know a query language. They choose one or more relevant members of a list, and let the system move them closer to their goal.

There is a point of view which holds that most information retrieval tasks are better performed if the overall relationships within a corpus are presented and as this view has spread, a more general model of the use of information systems than that traditionally used in Information Retrieval has arisen. "Retrieval" suggests an action by some agent to find and bring back information to a somehow detached or uninvolved user. The agent is given a specification of what is wanted, and the user waits for the results to be returned. However, it is becoming more accepted that people may not be able to express what they want to access in a corpus in a query language or even a natural language, for that matter, because they may not know exactly what they are looking for. Instead, they may be able to do what they want to do if they can begin by finding out roughly what is available in the corpus and, in an exploratory manner, refine and adapt their inquiries.

An individual document may initially appear "relevant" but later be discarded if other documents better serve the interests of the user. There may be a great number of relevant documents, or there may be none: both are fair and on occasion appropriate results. There may be documents that are relevant in different ways, and this may lead to a continuation and adaptation of work as these different associations are assessed. Initially known documents may be dispersed among other unknown but potentially relevant ones. These examples stress the relative judgements that drive an adaptive and exploratory style of use that contrasts with and complements the less interactive "retrieval" approach. This approach has been labelled information access, and to some extent reflects the increasing awareness of the importance of exploration and dynamism in perception and model construction (Gibson 1979 and Russell *et al.* 1993).

The model of the corpus in Bead is intended to favour information access because the model better supports perception of the patterns and relationships of documents than the hidden, high-dimensional representation used in retrieval-based systems. The model of the document in Bead is one which creates a corpus model by having as the dominant factor in its behaviour the resolution of the similarities and differences with all other documents. By making visible the setting of each document within the larger-scale structure of the corpus, browsing and exploration is aided. For this to work, the layout must impart to the user relationships and structures which "make sense": they must be fair or adequate, and they must also appear so to the users in a way which lets them orient themselves within, navigate through and make use of the corpus. In other words, Bead should make the corpus "imageable" (Lynch 1960).

Individual documents are shown as coloured markers placed within the setting of the landscape, and they consequently produce collective patterns of density and locality. When a search for a keyword is made, matching documents have their colour changed. The resulting patterns of colour show the distribution of matching documents in the corpus.

As shown when comparing Figures 12.1a and b, searching shows global features such as how discriminating the search is and whether there are separate clusters of matching documents. The latter case tends to show the areas where there are different uses or aspects of the words searched for. Individual features of search match and pairwise proximity are also shown, but more information such as the title and keyword list are presented when an article is selected with the mouse (see Figure 12.1c). Finally, very simple printed 2-D maps of the layout can be made.

Movement, viewing and selection, along with simple searches for word occurrences, make up the means of access to the model. This small set seems straightforward to use; the limitations on use are pushed over more towards the model itself. Given a good corpus model, it should not be necessary to be an expert in query languages or on the database itself - that load should be taken on by the system.

The modelling process of Bead occasionally leads to peaks and valleys, and there is always a surrounding contour or "shore". These serve as reference points, or more literally, landmarks.

These are important in orientation and navigation. The peaks and valleys also show areas where the "fit" of the documents is rough. The shore circumscribes the corpus and is usually made up of documents which are not associated with any central cluster (or clusters) of documents. In the modelling process, such documents are pushed out to this periphery, which adds to the consonance of the model. Lastly, areas of density show clusters of strongly related documents, serve as landmarks and reference points, and offer bases for initial exploration of the corpus model. Although more realistic shading and texturing could make the landscape more naturalistic, it seems that such colours and textures might be better put towards informational content rather than the "framework" of the landscaping (Tufte 1990). This is a topic of current work.

The ultimate goal of this work is to make information spaces explorable both graphically, by humans, and automatically, by programs or "daemons". Ideally, the modelled information space should reflect the documents and document-related activities of the people using the system. It should help to guide and should be guided by their work with other systems and in other media. In this way, Bead might offer new possibilities for computer-based support of both individual and collaborative work in a semantically rich virtual environment, and might take a useful place amongst the more general environment of everyday work.

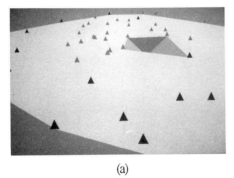

(a)

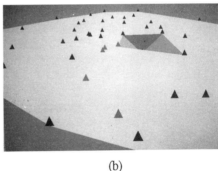

(b)

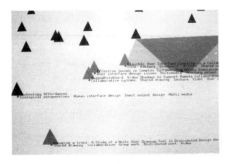

(c)

Figure 12.1 (a) Individual documents shown as coloured markers on a landscape. (b) Matching documents have their colour changed. (c) Extra information is added when an article is selected.

12.3 DigitalDesk

Another EuroPARC project looks differently at documents and how one might interact with them. Unlike Bead, it concentrates on the documents visible in our place of work. In our work, we generally interact with documents in two separate worlds: the electronic world of the workstation, and the physical world of the desk. Interaction styles in these two worlds do not resemble each other, functions available are different, and integration between the two is limited. Each world has advantages and constraints that lead us to choose one or the other for particular tasks. Unfortunately, choosing to interact with a document in one world means forgoing the advantages of the other. A great challenge to office system designers is to provide the best of both.

Electronic documents on computer workstations have wide functionality, but the ways we physically interact with them is limited compared with how we interact with paper, pencils, erasers, rulers, and other traditional tools on the desk. When interacting with objects in the physical world, we take advantage of natural skills developed over our lifetimes. We use our fingers, arms, 3-D vision, ears and kinesthetic memory to manipulate multiple objects simultaneously, and we hardly think about how we do this because the skills are embedded so deeply into our minds and bodies. Although electronic documents provide valuable functions such as spell checking, numerical calculations, and keyword searching, people must sacrifice highly developed tactile skills with paper in order to access these functions (Figure 12.2). The classic approach to solving this problem is represented by the "desktop metaphor," developed in the 1970s (Johnson *et al.* 1989). By making electronic workstations analogous to the physical desk, users can take advantage of their knowledge of the physical world, the computer becomes more familiar, and less learning is required. This approach has remained successful, and today electronic documents are still gaining more and more properties of physical documents e.g. high resolution colour, portability, pen-based interaction, etc.

When the physical world has an advantageous property over the computer, human-computer interaction (HCI) researchers tend to try and find a way of enhancing the computer with that

Figure 12.2. Contrasting electronic documents on a virtual desk (left)and paper documents on a real desk (right).

desired property. Not only are desktops and paper documents put into the computer, but many other things as well. This tendency, taken to an extreme, is virtual reality (VR), where the user abandons the real world to be completely surrounded by the computer. Enthusiasts of this approach believe that all constraints of the real world can be overcome in VR, and physical tools can be made obsolete by more flexible, virtual alternatives.

Physical tools can be hard to replace, however. At one time it seemed that paper might become obsolete, for example, and visionaries predicted the "paperless office" would dominate within a few years. But the trouble is people like paper. It is easier to read than a screen, it is cheap, universally accepted, tactile, and portable. According to some studies, paperwork in the office has increased by a factor of six since 1970, and is now growing at 20% annually (Seybold 1992). Like electronic documents, paper has properties that people just cannot seem to give up, and it is "resilient" in the face of computer-based alternatives (Luff *et al.* 1992).

As a result, we have two desks: one for "paper pushing" and the other for "pixel pushing." Although activities on the two desks are often related, the two are quite isolated from each other. Printers and scanners provide a way for documents to move back and forth between the desktops, but this conversion process is inconvenient. Wang's Freestyle system, for example, was a "paperless office" system that attempted to coexist with partially paper-based processes. A key factor necessary for adoption of this system was to minimise the printing and scanning required, because too many of these tasks would cause the process to revert entirely back to paper (Francik *et al.* 1991).

The tradeoffs between electronic and paper documents can make the choice of medium difficult, but imagine if we did not have to choose, and we had a space where documents could be both physical and electronic at the same time. Instead of putting the user in the virtual world of the computer, we could do the opposite: add the computer to the real world of the user. Instead of replacing paper with computers, we could enhance paper with computation. The Xerox PaperWorks product (Johnson *et al.* 1993) takes a step in this direction with its fax-based paper user interface to a storage and retrieval system. With this system, ordinary paper forms are enhanced to control a PC through a fax machine. These paper documents gain some properties of electronic documents, but fax machines are slow compared to computer screens. Response time is limited by the delay it takes to scan and print a page, and this limits the range of interaction techniques possible.

Another approach to enhancing paper documents with computation is to do the opposite of the desktop metaphor. Instead of making the workstation more like a desk, we can make the desk more like a workstation. This is the aim of the DigitalDesk. On this desk, papers gain electronic properties, and electronic objects gain physical properties. Rather than shifting more functions from the desk to the workstation, it shifts them from the workstation back onto the desk. No desktop metaphor is needed because it is literally a desktop.

The DigitalDesk is a real physical desk on which you can stack your papers, lay out your favourite pencils and markers, and leave your coffee cup, but it is enhanced to also provide some characteristics of an electronic workstation. A computer display is projected onto the desk, and video cameras pointed down at the desk feed an image processing system that can sense what the user is doing (see Figure 12.3).

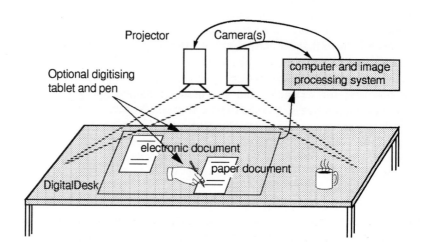

Figure 12.3. Schematic diagram of a DigitalDesk.

The first DigitalDesk prototype was cobbled together from an 1120 x 780 "ScratchPad", an overhead projector, some spare video cameras, a cooling fan, cardboard, and a lot of tape. Slicker versions based on commercial computer projection units have since been built. In general, however, the DigitalDesk has the following three important characteristics:

- it projects electronic images down onto the desk and onto paper documents,
- it responds to interaction with pens or bare fingers (hence DigitalDesk), and
- it can read paper documents placed on the desk.

The system provides a space in which paper gains electronic properties that allow it to overcome some of its physical limitations. Several prototype applications illustrate a different way that ordinary paper documents can be enhanced when placed in this space. One such is the calculator. This is a simple and familiar application that can benefit from the DigitalDesk. People using calculators often enter numbers that are already printed on a piece of paper lying on the desk, and they must copy the numbers manually into the calculator in order to perform arithmetic on them. Transcribing these numbers can constitute a large proportion of the keystrokes when using a calculator, and a large proportion of the errors.

The DigitalDesk Calculator (previously described in (Wellner 1991)) addresses this problem by providing another means of entering numbers. It allows people to place ordinary paper documents on the desk and simply point at a printed number to enter it into the calculator. In the working prototype, users can point with a pen or bare finger, and a rectangle is projected in front of the finger to indicate what number is selected. When the user taps, the system reads this number with a camera, recognises the digits, and treats them as though they had been typed into the calculator (see Figure 12.4).

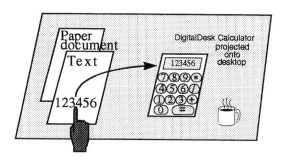

Figure 12.4. The user points at a number on a piece of paper. The number is recognised, and then entered into the calculator as though had been typed.

This example application shows how a paper document can become more like an electronic document by allowing selection of numbers for calculation. Of course, it is also possible to scan a paper receipt or annual report through an optical character recognition (OCR) program to convert the paper document to electronic form, but this is a less interactive, more batch-oriented process, and the resulting electronic document has lost all physical properties of the original. The purpose of the DigitalDesk is not merely conversion, but support for rapid and direct computer-based interaction with selected regions of paper documents.

In the working prototype, numbers are entered into a projected calculator tool, but it would also be possible to use a physical calculator that was connected to the DigitalDesk by wire or infra-red. Another possibility is to leave out the calculator, and project results back onto the paper. A "paper spreadsheet" could be designed on which pen-based interaction techniques would operate the same way on both ink and projected numbers.

Instead of making the electronic workstation more like the physical desk, the DigitalDesk does the opposite: it makes the desk more like the workstation, and it supports computer-based interaction with paper documents. Experience so far with this desk is encouraging. It enables people to do useful tasks with paper documents that are more awkward to do in other ways: tasks such as copying a long number into a calculator, translating a foreign word, replicating part of a sketch, or remote shared editing of paper documents. The interaction style supported by this desk is more tactile than "direct manipulation" with a mouse, and it seems to have a wide variety of potential applications, well beyond those described in this paper. Some issues to be addressed when implementing a digital desk include camera resolution, finger following, good adaptive thresholding and calibration, but each of these issues is solvable, as illustrated by the working prototypes.

This work can be seen as a step towards better integrating paper documents into the electronic world of personal workstations, making paper-based information more accessible to computers. The motivation for the work, however, is just the opposite. The goal is not to enhance computers by giving them better access to paper; it is to enhance paper by giving it better access to computers.

12.4 RAVE

Another project at EuroPARC has been exploring ways to allow separated colleagues to work together effectively and naturally. Bead and the DigitalDesk currently concentrate on interactions between an individual and their work, whereas RAVE looks at the interactions between people in a work environment. In this section, we discuss an example of our work in the context of three themes that have emerged: the need to support the full range of shared work; the desire to ensure privacy without giving up unobtrusive awareness; and the possibility of creating systems which blur the boundaries between people, technologies and the everyday world, providing awareness of distant colleagues.

One of the most important tools we use in this work is the Ravenscroft Audio Video Environment (RAVE). A fuller description is given in (Gaver *et al.* 1992). This is an example of a media space - a computer-controlled network of audio-video equipment used to support collaboration.

Three aspects of our research should be emphasised at the outset. Firstly, we are concerned with supporting collaboration over its entire range from the sort of casual awareness that keeps us informed about the whereabouts and activities of our neighbours to the more focused and planned work that is involved in joint problem-solving. This concern evolved in part from our experiences with a user-tailorable interface that we used to control the RAVE system. This interface allowed the functionality the system supports to emerge as a function of use.

Secondly, we are concerned about privacy, but are hesitant about achieving it at the expense of media spaces' ability to provide unobtrusive awareness. We consider the attributes of privacy as many-dimensional. Currently, we combine control and feedback in RAVE to maintain privacy without a loss of functionality.

Thirdly, we are interested in developing the RAVE system to allow a seamless transition between support for synchronous collaboration and systems which support semi-synchronous awareness over long distances and of planned and electronic events. In this way, we hope to blur the traditional boundaries between people, technologies, and the everyday world, relying both on new technologies and an understanding of peoples interactions in the everyday world (cf. (Moran and Anderson 1990)).

EuroPARC was founded in 1987 and there are currently about 30 staff members. Our building, called Ravenscroft House, has 27 rooms and 5 open areas on 4 floors. Despite the small size of the lab, the layout separates us to a surprising degree, so that the building is effectively a collection of relatively isolated sites. One of the motivations for the work described here was to turn this problem into a research opportunity: because EuroPARC is a small research lab, we were able to install complete data, audio, and video networks throughout the lab. Each room in the building has several audio and video cables running to and from a central switch as well as access to digital networks. The resulting system provides all rooms with some form of an audio-video node, consisting of a camera, monitor, microphone and speakers, which users can move and turn on or off at will. Connections among nodes are controlled via computers, so that people can display the views from various cameras on their desktop monitors; set up two-way audio-video connections, etc. (see Figure 12.5). Using this system, we live in a media space as well as the physical workspace.

Figure 12.5. The RAVE system allows us to collaborate in a media space as well as the physical workspace. Each office typically has near to a workstation a media space node:video monitor, camera, microphone and speaker.

The RAVE system provides us with a great deal of potential functionality. An important design issue concerns how best to constrain it, both to support and encourage its use in ways that enhance existing work practices and to discourage possible misuse (e.g., spying, monitoring, etc.). In considering this question, it is helpful to consider our first design theme, that of supporting the range of collaboration from casual awareness to focused engagement.

One perspective assumed implicitly by much of the current work on computer-supported collaborative work (CSCW) is of two or more people focused intensely on a single task. We prefer a broader approach, one we feel better reflects the range of activities involved in shared work.

Two dimensions characterise this framework. The first, degree of engagement, refers to the extent to which a shared focus is involved. The second, amount of planning, refers to the extent that shared activities occur spontaneously or are planned in advance. Although the space of shared work is probably characterised by many more than two dimensions, this framework allows us to consider four relevant landmarks of the space.

Underlying all is general awareness. This simply refers to the pervasive experience of knowing who is around, what sorts of things they are doing, whether they are relatively busy or can be engaged, and so on. Neither planned nor involving a great degree of interaction, this sort of awareness acts as a foundation for closer collaboration. At the other extreme is focused collaboration. This refers to occasions when people plan to work closely on a shared task. Most CSCW applications seem designed to support this kind of shared, focused activity.

There are two way-stations between these extremes. The first, division of labour, refers to the common practice of splitting a task into its component parts and allowing different people to address them separately. Division of labour does not require the intensely shared focus of attention implied by focused collaboration, but does require planning and coordination. On the other hand, general awareness often leads to serendipitous communication, in which an unplanned interaction may lead to the exchange of important information or the recognition of shared interests.

The description of collaboration illustrated by this framework suggests the need to provide support for a range of activities, from spontaneous to highly planned and from disengaged to highly focused. Moreover, we want to support the movement between these forms of shared work. In the workaday world, people move fluidly between degrees of engagement: maintaining awareness of their colleagues, engaging in serendipitous communication, collaborating intensely for a time, and dividing labour. It is important that we support not only different sorts of shared activities, but fluid movement among activities.

In providing access to the audio-video network we have emphasised its use in supporting the entire range of shared activities. Because we had few a priori notions of how audio-video connectivity would extend current work practices, we have supported access to its functionality in a flexible way, using tailorable on-screen buttons (Henderson and Card 1986 and MacLean *et al.* 1990). They are simple graphical objects which allow users to run small programs without having to enter the relevant commands explicitly. In addition, they are tailorable in a number of ways: Their on-screen location and appearance can be modified, they may be copied and emailed, they are often parameterised so that application-specific variables can be changed easily, and their encapsulated code can be edited. Their flexibility meant that we could explore our media space, developing useful control structures through use.

Initially, the RAVE buttons provided access to relatively low-level functionality, allowing single connections to be made or broken. Over time, the buttons have been modified by users to reflect the higher-level tasks they wished to accomplish. The current result is the series of generic RAVE buttons shown in Figure 12.6.

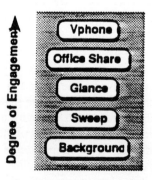

Figure 12.6. RAVE buttons reflect different levels of engagement.

These buttons reflect the range of collaboration discussed above. Indeed, the buttons and our account of collaboration evolved together. The background button, for instance, allows people to select a view from one of the public areas to display on their monitor. This is typically the default connection. Many of us, for example, maintain a view of our largest public space on screen when not actively using the audio-video system. This allows us to watch people come and go to check their mail or get coffee, to watch meetings form, or to watch for somebody with whom we want to talk. The effect is similar to having the common area outside one's door (without the noise). We can maintain a general awareness, not of our immediate surroundings, but of important areas that are more remote.

The sweep button provides another way to maintain awareness of remote locations of the building. This button makes short (~1 second) one-way connections to various nodes in the building. It is customisable, so one can sweep all nodes or a subset of relevant ones. Typically this is used to find out who is around and what they are doing. The glance button, which makes a single 3-second one-way connection to a selected node, offers more focused attention to particular colleagues. Glances are often used to find out if a particular person is in, and whether or not he or she is busy. Because both the sweep and glance buttons allow one way connections for only a short time, the effect is similar to walking by a colleague's door and glancing in: general information about presence and activities can be obtained without jeopardising privacy (an issue to which we return below).

A more focused interaction is supported by the Vphone and office share buttons. The first is a two-way audio and video connection which allows colleagues to engage in the video equivalent of a face-to-face conversation. When a vphone call is initiated, the recipient must explicitly accept the connection. Thus this sort of connection is closest to traditional telephone calls. Office share connections are identical to vphone connections, but are meant to last longer for hours, days, or even months. The effect is one of sharing an office, but because audio volume can be controlled and the video image is relatively small, the other persons presence allows but does not demand social engagement.

It is interesting to note here that the vphone and office share buttons offer exactly the same functionality, that of setting up a two-way audio and video connection. The buttons are differentiated solely in terms of the intentions with which the connections are made. Vphone calls are typically used to support relatively short and focused conversations, while office share connections typically support longer lasting shared work in which the degree of engagement varies fluidly. This is a good example of interface tools which emerged to control our system in terms of users tasks, rather than technological functionality.

In summary, the five generic RAVE buttons emerged through a process of integrated use and design supported by an interface system that affords flexible tailoring. The resulting functionality supported by these buttons reflects the range of shared work from general awareness to focused collaboration to a remarkable degree.

Accounts of cameras in every office, one-way glance connections, long-term monitoring of public spaces and so forth can often have Orwellian overtones. Clearly there is a need to protect privacy in audio-video systems such as ours but there is a trade-off between protection of privacy and provision of functionality that makes the development of such safeguards a non-trivial task.

For instance, one way to assure that work on media spaces will not add new threats to privacy would be simply to remove all audio and video equipment from EuroPARC but this would clearly do away with any and all services it offers. More subtly, privacy might be ensured by enforcing symmetrical connections, so that seeing or hearing somebody implies being seen or heard oneself (indeed, this strategy has been taken at BellCore). But one-way connections have advantages we are unwilling to give up. Glances allow us to maintain our awareness of colleagues without actually engaging in interaction with them. Thus they are a valuable prelude to communication; just as we might look in someone's door to see if they are busy before knocking, so we can look at their video image before vphoning them. Video provides an excellent means to gain general awareness unobtrusively; enforcing symmetry for the sake of privacy would undermine this functionality.

It has become clear to us that privacy is a complex issue that must be disentangled in order to understand the tradeoffs involved in its protection. In particular, four important facets of privacy which may be considered separately are:

- the desire for control over who can see or hear us at a given time
- the desire for knowledge of when somebody is in fact seeing or hearing us;
- the desire to know the intention behind the connection; but
- the desire to avoid connections being intrusions on our work.

The trade-off between privacy and functionality involves a conflict between the desirability of control and knowledge and the intrusion implied by activities needed to maintain them. Having to allow explicitly every connection made to our cameras would give us control, but the requests themselves would be intrusive. Having a face appear on our monitors every time they connect to us would similarly demand some sort of social response and might well disrupt previous connections. Having to specify and be informed of the intention of various connections would likewise transform a light-weight, unobtrusive process into a relatively effortful and attention-demanding one. The challenge of safeguarding privacy, then, is not just one of providing control and notification, but doing so in a lightweight and unobtrusive way.

At EuroPARC, our privacy protection depends to a great degree on social convention. Indeed, our culture initially provided our only protection. It is assumed that people will use the system with good intentions; that is, that they will not seek information with the intent of using it against somebody. Simply speaking, we trust one another. At the same time, social convention encourages people to control their own equipment: They are free to turn their camera to face a wall or out a window; they may keep their microphones switched off, and so forth.

We took this initial strategy for several reasons. First, being "willingly naive" about privacy meant that we did not assume the degree to which software support for privacy would be necessary, but instead could treat the question as a research issue. Second, explicitly relying on trust established clear social norms about the use of the media space instead of building software on the assumption that privacy would otherwise be invaded, we assumed it would not be and expected people to behave accordingly. Finally, this strategy allowed us to concentrate on developing the functionality of the system rather than security measures. Nonetheless, as the equipment has become ubiquitous in our own lab and we begin to ponder its eventual use in other settings, we have begun to explore other ways to tackle privacy issues. Our current system now provides services which make intentionality an implicit feature of connections and which allow us to provide both control and notifications.

A certain amount of control over connections is offered by the basic software used to control the audio-video switch. This software, called iiif (for integrated, interactive, intermedia facility), instantiates a simple patchbay metaphor in which device plugs are linked to form single point-to-point connections. Each plug and device is owned by an associated user and its access is accordingly controlled. Thus people could restrict access to their video-out plugs, for instance, to some subset of users.

In practice this strategy is awkward to use effectively. Control is offered at the level of individual connections rather than relevant tasks, while the generic RAVE services described above glances, vphone calls, etc. usually involve a number of individual connections. Although buttons can make this transparent to the initiator by combining a number of connection requests into one button, the system has no way of knowing the intention of individual connections. Thus it is difficult, using simple plug control, to design the system so that a glance can be allowed but a vphone call denied.

For these reasons, a new layer of software called Godard (Dourish 1991) has been added to the basic iiif software. Godard uses iiif's underlying protection mechanism to control device plugs so that no connections can be made without its permission. Because Godard mediates all connection requests, explicit services can be defined and control can be handled at the service level. When an initiator requests a service, Godard uses information previously obtained from potential recipients to determine whether to perform the service (and occasionally relies on interactive input to request permission for individual connections or to resolve conflicts). If permission is given and all relevant plugs are available, Godard creates a record of pre-existing connections so they can be restored, and then makes and protects the appropriate connections.

This architecture allows privacy control to exist at the level of specific services rather than individual plugs. Thus people can set permission for specific people to use specific services. Usually, a panel presents a complete list of people at EuroPARC, and allows the user to select those who will or will not be given permission to use a particular service. Control panels exist for glances, vphones, office share connections, and the like.

With the addition of Godard, our system now affords a degree of control adequate to preserve privacy: We can now explicitly allow or deny connections to our equipment. In addition, because these connections are represented as higher-level services, the system also provides a useful (if implicit) representation of the initiators intentions. Finally, it serves as a foundation for the provision of the third aspect of privacy suggested above, that of knowledge of actual events notifications about the system state.

Feelings of privacy are not only supported by control over who can connect to one's equipment using various services, but by feedback about when such connections are actually made. Because Godard knows about connections to recipients' audio-video nodes at the service level, it facilitates the provision of such feedback. Several kinds of feedback can be requested by users in current instantiations of interface software, including text messages displayed on their workstations and spoken messages played over the audio network. Less obvious than these, and in our experience quite valuable, are auditory cues used to provide information about system state (Gaver 1991b).

For example, when a glance connection is made to a camera, Godard triggers a sound (the default is that of a door opening) before the connection is actually made. When the connection is broken, another sound (typically that of a door closing) is triggered. In addition, different sounds indicate different sorts of connections (and thus the intentions behind them). A knock or telephone bell indicates a vphone request; door sounds indicate glances; footsteps might indicate sweeps; and a camera whir indicates that a framegrabber has accessed ones node. Thus auditory cues provide information about what kind of connection is being made, over and above information about the existence of a connection alone.

Playing sounds such as opening and closing doors may seem frivolous, but there are several reasons that it is a particularly effective way to provide feedback about connections:

- sound indicates the connection state without requiring symmetry that is, it provides information without being intrusive;

- sounds such as these can be heard without requiring the kind of spatial attention that a written notification would;

- non-speech audio cues often seem less distracting and more efficient than speech or music (although speech can provide different sorts of information, e.g., who is connecting;

- sounds can be acoustically shaped to reduce annoyance (Patterson 1989). Most of the sounds we use, for instance, involve a very gradual increase in loudness to avoid startling listeners;

- finally, caricatures of naturally-occurring sounds are a very intuitive way to present information. The sound of an opening and closing door reflects and reinforces the metaphor of a glance, and is thus easily learned and remembered (cf. (Gaver 1986)).

These sorts of auditory cues have provided an flexible and effective way to unobtrusively inform people that somebody is connecting to their node, and thus serve as another means of safeguarding privacy. More generally, with Godard and auditory cues, we have provided control, feedback, and intentionality three prerequisites for privacy at very little cost in terms of intrusiveness.

RAVE is useful in providing awareness of local nodes. But for technical and financial reasons, we cannot make connections to our overseas colleagues; nor can we connect to more than one node at a time. In order to extend our awareness over a greater distance and to a number of people simultaneously, we have been experimenting with distributing low-resolution video images via our digital networks.

For instance, Portholes is a system which distributes digitised images within our building every five minutes or so (Dourish and Bly 1992). The resolution of each image is low, with no grey scale, but people and objects in their environments are usually visible. Moreover, Portholes acts as an interface to the audio-video network. Portholes runs between EuroPARC and PARC, and this means that we can see not only of people in our own building, but also of colleagues in a building about 6000 miles away. This supports awareness, but it has also helped to create and develop a research community within EuroPARC and PARC. For instance, researchers who have never been co-present nonetheless speak of "knowing" one another through their experience with Portholes.

Portholes allows several remote locations to be presented simultaneously, affording passive awareness of distributed workgroups without the necessity of explicitly setting up video links and so on. This facilitates smooth transitions between general awareness and more focused engagements. In addition, the spatially-distributed but asynchronous functionality offered by systems like Portholes complements our synchronous but single-channelled video services quite well. Perhaps most importantly, Portholes allows us to extend this awareness out of our building to colleagues at geographically distant locations.

12.5 Conclusions

The RAVE, DigitalDesk and Bead projects are examples of a more general approach to interaction with computers, and also interaction between people by means of technology. Bead and DigitalDesk move towards interaction by means of imagery and work with information in a way guided by our everyday perceptual and motor skills. Video is common to the DigitalDesk and RAVE projects. Like computer graphics, it is a rich and dynamic medium that affords a great variety of powerful interaction techniques. All three projects apply images so as to work with our day-to-day skills and not against them.

There is a difference between integrating the world into computers and integrating computers into the world. The difference is in our perspective: do we think of ourselves as working primarily in the computer (and is it helpful to have access to physical world functionality) or, do we think of ourselves as working primarily in the physical world (and is it helpful to have access to computer functionality)? Much of the research in human-computer interaction seems to emphasise the former perspective, yet many useful ideas can be gained from the latter. Instead of making us work in the computer's world, let us make it work in our world.

References

Bertin J. (1981). *Graphics and Graphic Information Processing*, Walter de Gruyter, Berlin.

Chalmers M. & Chitson P. (1992). Bead: Explorations in Information Exploration, *Proc. SIGIR'92*, published as a special issue of SIGIR Forum, ACM Press, pp. 330-337.

Cutting D.R., Pedersen J.O., Karger D. & Tukey J.W. Scatter/Gather: A Cluster-Based Approach to Browsing Large Document Collections, *Proc. SIGIR'91*, published as a special issue of *SIGIR Forum*, ACM Press, pp. 318-329.

Dourish P. (1991). Godard: A flexible architecture for A/V services in a media space. *EuroPARC working paper*.

Dourish P. & Bly S. (1992). Portholes: Supporting awareness in a distributed work group, *Proceedings of CHI'92* (Monterey, California), ACM, New York, pp. 541-548.

Francik E., Rudman S., Cooper D. & Levine S. (1991). Putting Innovation To Work: Adoption Strategies for Multimedia Communication Systems, *Communications of the ACM* 34(12).

Gaver W. (1986). Auditory icons: Using sound in computer interfaces, *Human-Computer Interaction* 2, pp. 167-177.

Gaver W., Smith R., & O'Shea T. (1991a). Effective sounds in complex systems: The ARKola simulation, *Proceedings of CHI'91* (New Orleans, Louisiana), ACM, New York.

Gaver W. (1991b). Sound support for collaboration. In *Proceedings of ECSCW'91* (Amsterdam, The Netherlands).

Gaver W., Moran T., MacLean A., Lovstrand L., Dourish P., Carter K. & Buxton W. (1992). Realizing a video environment: EuroPARC's RAVE system. *Proceedings of CHI'92* (Monterey, California, May 1992), ACM, New York, pp. 27 - 35.

Gibson J.J. (1979). *The Ecological Approach to Visual Perception*, Lawrence Erlbaum.

Henderson D. & Card S. (1986). Rooms: The use of multiple virtual workspaces to reduce space contention in a window-based graphical user interface. *ACM Transactions on Graphics*, 5(3), pp. 211-243.

Johnson J., Roberts T., Verplank W., Smith D., Irby C., Beard M. & Mackey K. (1989). The Xerox Star: A Retrospective, *IEEE Computer* 22(9).

Johnson W., Rao R., Jellinek H., Klotz L. & Card S. (1993). Bridging the Paper and Electronic Worlds: Paper as a User Interface. *Proceedings of INTERCHI'93*, (Amsterdam), ACM, New York.

Luff P., Heath C. & Greatbatch D. (1992). Tasks-in-interaction: Paper and screen based documentation in collaborative activity, *Proceedings of CSCW '92* (Toronto) ACM, New York.

Lynch K. (1960). *The Image of the City*, MIT Press.

MacLean A., Carter K., Moran T., & Lovstrand L. (1990). User-tailorable systems: Pressing the issues with buttons. *Proceedings of CHI'90* (Seattle, Washington) ACM, New York, pp. 175-182.

Moran T. & Anderson R. (1990). The workaday world as a paradigm for CSCW design. *Proceedings of CSCW'90* (Los Angeles). ACM, New York.

Patterson R.D. (1989). Guidelines for the design of auditory warning sounds. *Proceedings of the Institute of Acoustics 1989 Spring Conference*. 11(5) pp. 17-24.

Russell D.M., Stefik M.J., Pirolli P. & Card S. (1993). The Cost Structure of Sensemaking. *Proceedings of InterCHI'93* (Amsterdam), ACM, New York.

Seybold A. (1992). The DOC.IT. in *Andrew Seybold's Outlook on Professional Computing*, 11(2).

Tufte E. (1990). *Envisioning Information*, Graphics Press.

Wellner P. (1991). The DigitalDesk Calculator: Tactile Manipulation on a Desk Top Display in *Proceedings of the ACM Symposium on User Interface Software and Technology* (UIST '91), Hilton Head.

13

Tailoring Clothes for Virtual Actors

Nadia Magnenat Thalmann

13.1 Introduction

Synthetic actors are clothed on the basis of a physically-based elastic surface model. Just as a dressmaker, we first cut several polygonal panels from 2-D rectangular planes and then transfer them onto 3-D surfaces around the actor. These cloth panels are seamed to each other and attached to the actor's body by a set of forces, so that a suit of clothes is created. Second, given external forces such as gravity and wind, we test for and prevent cloth-cloth and actor-cloth collisions. We calculate the changes in the shapes of the clothes with the movement sequences of actors, so that the clothing is also animated.

13.2   A survey of cloth modelling and animation

In recent years, computer technologies have begun to be used in the garment industry. Software has been developed and applied to the interactive design of 2-D garment panels and to optimising the layout of garment panels on the fabric.   In Hinds and McCartney's work (Hinds and McCartney 1990), a static trunk of a mannequin's body is represented by bicubic B-spline surfaces. Garment panels are considered to be surfaces of complex shapes in 3D. The garment panels are designed around the static mannequin body, and then are reduced to 2D cutting patterns. This approach is contrary to the traditional approach to garment design. The garment is modelled by geometric methods. To visualize the folds and drapes, harmonic functions and sinusoidal functions are superimposed on the garment panels. Mangen and Lasudry (1991) proposed an algorithm for finding the intersection polygon of any two polygons. This is applied to the automatic optimisation of the layout of polygonal garment design and manufacturing in real industrial contexts.

Interacting with Virtual Environments Edited by Lindsay MacDonald and John Vince

Computer techniques of graphics offer many other possibilities for the development of high-tech tools for garment design and manufacturing. Not only can the interactive design of 2-D garment panels be achieved by general computer graphics, but the sewing of garment panels and the examination of garment movement on the human body can also be visualized through cloth animation based on dynamic surface models. Terzopoulos *et al.* (1987) and Aono (1990) both proposed elastically deformable surface models to simulate and animate the movement of cloth in various physical environments. Another interesting approach by Kunii and Gotoda (1990) incorporates both the kinetic and geometric properties for generating garment wrinkles. Other models (Weil 1986; Lafleur *et al.* 1991; Yang *et al.* 1992; Breen *et al.* 1991) have been proposed to animate deformable and soft objects such as rubber, paper, cloth, and so on. But it is somewhat difficult to realistically animate complex objects consisting of many surface panels like trousers or jackets without proper dynamic constraints. Problems include seaming the surface panels together, attaching them to other rigid objects, and calculating collision responses when cloth self-collides or collides with a rigid object.

Successful fashion hinges on ideas and imagination, and it is the designers that first come up with the concept for their new garment. Shape, material, colour, movement and flow - all these qualities give a piece of clothing its uniqueness, and the designer uses drawings to communicate his intentions. Sketches of various views of the garment provide the clues needed for the next person involved in the garment design process: the tailor.

Tailors create two-dimensional patterns from the designer's drawings. These patterns, once cut out and sewn together according to the tailor's specifications, allow the garment to make the final step toward realisation of the designer's dream.

In our approach, we work as a tailor does, designing garments from individual two-dimensional panels seamed together. The resulting garments are worn by and attached to the synthetic actors. When the actors are moving or walking in a physical environment, cloth animation is performed with the internal elastic force and the external forces of gravity, wind, and collision response.

Our work is based on the fundamental equation of motion as described by Terzopoulos *et al.* (1987) with the damping term replaced by a more accurate one proposed by Platt and Barr (1989). When a collision is detected, we pass through the second step where we act on the vertices to actually avoid the collision. For this collision response, we have proposed the use of the law of conservation of momentum for perfectly inelastic bodies. This means that kinetic energy is dissipated, avoiding the bouncing effect. We use a dynamic inverse procedure to simulate a perfectly inelastic collision. Such collisions between two particles are characterised by the fact that their speed after they collide equals the speed of their centres of mass before they collide.

The constraints that join different panels together and attach them to other objects are very important in our case. Two kinds of dynamic constraints (Barzel and Barr 1988; Carignan *et al.* 1992) are used during two different stages. When the deformable panels are separated, forces are applied to the elements in the panels to join them according to the seaming information. The same method is used to attach the elements of deformable objects to other rigid objects. When panels are seamed or attached, a second kind of constraint is applied which keeps a panel's sides together or fixed on objects.

The main new aspects of our system for the design and creation of clothes are:

- a new data structure
- an improved physics-based deformable model
- the introduction of seaming and attaching forces
- a more general collision algorithm
- a user interface for creating clothes

13.3   The data structure

The garment data structure is maintained as a pointer to the first panel, and a total number of panels. In the linked list of panels, each element contains a record for colour, a number of vertices counter, a pointer to the head of a linked list of panel vertices, a bounding box showing size limits, and the panel's value for grid density (in cloth coordinates). Finally, a pointer to the next panel in the garment.

Seams are maintained in a doubly linked list. Ordering in the list determines which seams are sewn together. For instance, in a dress with three seams, there would be six elements in the seam linked list. The first would be sewn to the second, the third to the fourth, and so on in pairs. Each half of the seam makes up one element of the list. Each element of the list tells which panel the seam belongs to, its "seam number" (used basically to tell if a seam is the first or second in the pair, which is important when deleting seams), how many vertices are in the seam, a pointer to the head of the vertex list, and pointers to the previous and next elements of the list.

As seam pairs are drawn in the panel and garment windows of the interface, they are drawn in colours identifying which seam line joins which other seam line. For instance the first pair might be drawn in red, the second in blue, etc. Plate 22 shows an example. The data structure used is just a circular linked list containing seam colours. When a seam is drawn on the screen, a pointer points to the next seam colour. If there are m seams and n colours (m>n), the wrap-around at the end of the list makes seam m+1 get drawn in colour 1.

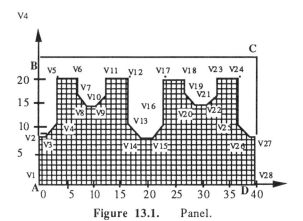

Figure 13.1.   Panel.

From the geometric data on a panel, we can derive its shape, size, position, normals, and so on. The physical data on a panel includes its mass, damping factor, speed, forces, stretch factor, curvature factor, elastic energies, etc. The seaming information for one garment dictates which edges of which panels should be seamed together. It includes the number of nodes on the edges and the coordinates of the nodes in the 2-D mesh plane, and indicates which node is seamed to which. The attaching information indicates which edges of the panel are attached to specific points on the actor's body. Figure 13.1 shows an example.

13.4   An improved physics-based deformable model

After some comparisons (Magnenat Thalmann and Yang 1991), Terzopoulos' elastic surface model (Terzopoulos *et al.* 1987) was chosen for our system with the damping term replaced by a more accurate. The fundamental equation of motion corresponds to an equilibrium between internal forces (Newton term, resistance to stretching, dissipative force, resistance to bending) and external forces (collision forces, gravity, seaming and attaching forces, wind force):

$$r(a)\frac{d^2 r}{dt^2} + \frac{d}{dr}\int\int_W \|E\|^2 da_1\, da_2 + \frac{d}{dv}\int\int_W \|\dot{E}\|^2 da_1\, da_2$$

$$+ \frac{d}{dr}\int\int_W \|B - B_0\|^2 da_1\, da_2 = S\, F_{ex} \tag{1}$$

$$\dot{E}_{ij}(r(a)) = \frac{d}{dt} E_{ij} = \frac{1}{2}\dot{G}_{ij} = \frac{\partial r}{\partial a_i}\cdot\frac{\partial v}{\partial a_j} + \frac{\partial r}{\partial a_j}\cdot\frac{\partial v}{\partial a_i} \tag{2}$$

We choose to replace the third term (dissipative force) because the one used in (Terzopoulos *et al.* 1987) is scalar. So, no matter where energy comes from, it will be dissipated. For example, gravitational energy is dissipated, resulting in a surface which achieves a limiting speed and is not continually accelerated. In our case (Carignan *et al.* 1992), we use Raleigh's dissipative function (Eringen and Suhubi 1974) generalized for a continuum surface (Platt and Barr 1989). As E is the strain (a measure of the amount of deformation), dE/dt is the "speed" at which the deformation occurs. This means that the surface integral may be considered a rate of energy dissipation due to internal friction. This implies that the variational derivative with respect to velocity of the surface integral will minimise the "speed" of the deformation. With this approach, no dissipation occurs when the surface undergoes rigid body displacement like when falling in an air-free gravity field. This improves the realism of motion.

   To apply the elastic deformable surface model, the polygonal panel should be discretised using the finite difference approximation method. We have proposed a new algorithm to calculate the elastic force on an arbitrary element. This algorithm is effective for discretising not only an arbitrary polygonal panel (concave or convex), but also other kinds of polygonal panels with holes inside them.

13.5   The introduction of seaming and attaching forces

In the animation of deformable objects consisting of many surface panels, the constraints that join different panels together and attach them to other objects are very important.   In our case, two kinds of dynamic constraints are used in two different stages.   When deformable panels are separated, forces are applied to the elements in the panels to join them according to the seaming information.   The same method is used to attach the elements of deformable objects to other rigid objects.

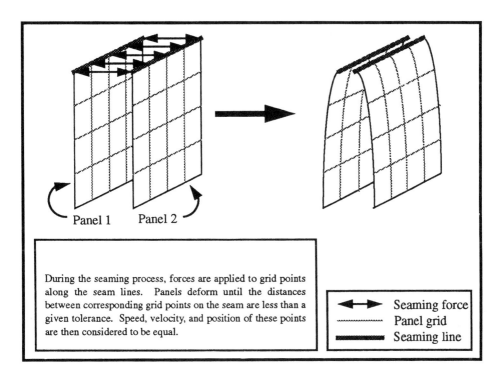

During the seaming process, forces are applied to grid points along the seam lines.   Panels deform until the distances between corresponding grid points on the seam are less than a given tolerance.   Speed, velocity, and position of these points are then considered to be equal.

◄──► Seaming force
··········· Panel grid
▬▬▬▬ Seaming line

Figure 13.2.   Principle of seaming process.

After the creation of deformable objects, another kind of dynamic constraint is used to guarantee seaming and attaching.   For the attaching, the elements of the deformable objects are always kept on the rigid object, so they have the same position and velocity as the elements of the rigid object to which they are attached.   For the seaming and joining of the panels themselves, two seamed elements move with the same velocity and position, but the velocity and position depend on those of the individual elements.   According to the law of momentum conservation, total momentum of the elements before and after seaming should remain the same.   Figure 13.2 shows the principle of the seaming process.   The three images in Plate 23 depict the seaming process from the initial 2-D garment to the final, stable dress.

13.6   A more general collision algorithm

Basically, collisions are detected before a cloth's vertices come through the body's polygons and we have to find the position of the point of impact on the polygon, the velocity, and the normal of that point. Moreover, all forces (including internal forces) acting on vertices should be computed.

We have also described a method of collision avoidance (Lafleur *et al.* 1991) that creates a very thin force field around the surface of the obstacle to be avoided. This force field acts like a shield rejecting the points. Although the method works for a simple case of a skirt, use of this type of force is somewhat artificial and cannot provide realistic simulation with complex clothes. In fact, the effect degrades when the force becomes very strong, looking like a "kick" given to the cloth. To improve realism, we have proposed (Carignan *et al.* 1992) using the law of conservation of momentum for perfectly inelastic bodies. This means we consider all energy to be lost within a collision. The collision detection process is almost automatic. The animator has only to provide a list of obstacles to the system and indicate whether they are moving or not. For a walking synthetic actor, moving legs are of course considered a moving obstacle. Figure 13.3 shows the principle of collision detection.

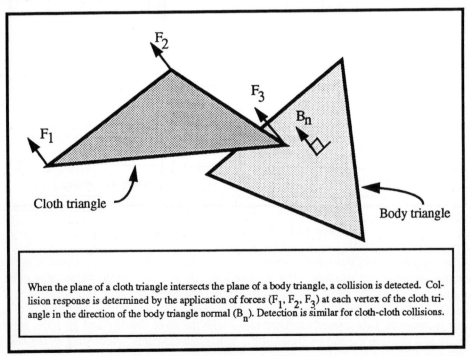

When the plane of a cloth triangle intersects the plane of a body triangle, a collision is detected. Collision response is determined by the application of forces (F_1, F_2, F_3) at each vertex of the cloth triangle in the direction of the body triangle normal (B_n). Detection is similar for cloth-cloth collisions.

Figure 13.3.   Principle of collision detection.

We have also developed an automatic method that allows us to increase or decrease locally the density of faces used to render an 3-D object modelled as an irregular mesh of triangles, without losing too much shape information. The method (Moccozet and Magnenat Thalmann 1992), is based on the Delaunay triangulation. If we take the example of an actor dressed with synthetic clothes, one time consuming process in the animation of clothes is collision detection of the clothes with the body. The complexity of these algorithms is dependent on the number of faces of the colliding objects. Moreover, most of the body parts involved in collision detection are covered by the clothes during the animation. There is no need for a very precise body.

13.7 The user interface

The designing of clothes and garments for synthetic actors presents some interesting interface design issues. Users of the software require ways of duplicating already-developed or imagined styles in a natural way. Provisions should exist for controlling not only the way a garment appears but also the way it behaves (seams, physical properties, etc.).

Our approach to synthetic fashion is divided into two distinct stages. First, garments are planned and laid out in two dimensions. Then, they are sewn around the body and animated in three dimensions.

Toolkit for application development

The high level man-machine interactions are handled efficiently with the object oriented Fifth Dimension (5-D) Toolkit (Turner *et al.* 1990). We use the 2-D class subset of this toolkit (Figure 13.4) to design and manage the multiple window interface to our system. This work is facilitated by the use of the dedicated interface builder First_step. The interface layout can be built out of multiple windows, hierarchical panels, and many input-output items such as buttons, radios, 1-D and 2-D sliders, toggles, text and browser widgets, menus, etc....

Object instances in the 5-D Toolkit communicate with each other by sending messages. The event message is a formal type of message in order to respond to user-generated input and implement the dynamic behaviour of objects. All event messages have two parameters which specify the source and destination objects. This mechanism has several advantages: first, one can query the source to get additional information about the event. Second, this strict form of event messages allows events to be manipulated as objects, and the distribution of events to be specified at run-time.

The 5-D Toolkit also integrates recent three-dimensional input devices as the SpaceBall and Polhemus that are very important for human animation. Another useful functionality provided by the 5-D Toolkit is Inter Process Communication (IPC). It is very useful for coordinating specialised software, running on different machines. For example, a motion control process can send joint level information to a physically-based surface deformation process (Figure 13.5), both programs running concurrently.

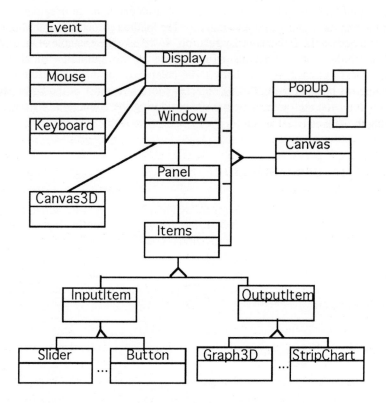

Figure 13.4. Object-relation diagram of the toolkit.

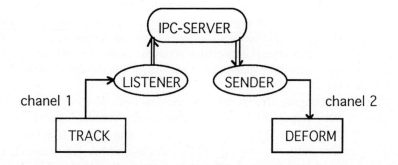

Figure 13.5. The IPC communication flow.

The 2-D interface to design garments and panels.

The first step in creating a synthetic garment is specifying the panels that comprise the garment. In this sense, the term "panel" refers to the individual pieces of cloth that are sewn together. A simple T-shirt, for instance, may have only two panels, whereas a more complex jacket could have five or more.

Because the panel is the basic unit for garment construction, the two-dimensional interface employs the notion of a "current panel". Changes to a panel in the garment are made by selecting the desired panel as "current" and then changing the current panel.

There are basically three primitives used in the construction of synthetic garments: the panel, the seam, and the attach line. The divisions lead us to the four modes of operation in the Panel Window: Polygon, Seam, Attach, and Select. The first three are used for creating new panels, seams, and attach lines. The last mode is used for selecting any of the available primitives, so that vertices can be added, edited, or deleted.

In creating a panel, the user works in the Panel Window and defines a polygon with the mouse. An optional grid guides placement of polygon vertices, and the closed polygon's edges symbolise where a tailor cuts a panel out of a roll of fabric. Many operations can be performed on defined panels. Users can edit, add, or delete vertices. They can resize panels. Panels can be saved, and pre-defined panels can be loaded. When panels transfer to become part of a garment, they either add to the garment's existing panels or replace one that has already been defined.

Once a panel is transferred to the Garment Window (i.e., it becomes *part* of the garment) the user can enter "Seam Mode" and begin defining seams on that panel. Seams are basically line segments composed of any number of vertices. They are defined in pairs, consecutively, and for easy identification both halves are shown in the same colour in the Garment Window.

Similar to the seaming line but slightly different in function is the "attach line." Currently used mainly at the waist of a synthetic actor, attach lines fix panels to the body. This capability is quite useful in the design of skirts, for example. The waistband of the skirt can be made to directly attach to the waistline of an actor, like a belt. Ensuring that skirts stay in place during an actor's walk, attach lines can also be used on dresses, pants, cuffs and collars. There is also mechanism for specifying that the attach line should take effect at a small distance above or below the "physical" waist of the actor.

The 3-D interface to design clothes

Importing 2-D designs into the three-dimensional application is simple enough. But certain changes occur to the panels as they are converted. Panels are no longer considered only as vertices and edges defining an interior. They are discretised and become collections of nodes in a three-dimensional mesh.

After we import the 2-D garment file, we are ready to begin using the three-dimensional interface for positioning the garment's panels around the body. We then continue, activating the seaming and attaching processes.

The first step is to turn "on" the parts of the body that are required for the particular garment at hand. (In practice, we have found it extremely useful to divide a synthetic actor's body into a number of sections, and use only those sections we need.) Because we perform collision detection on all active sections of the body during seaming, turning some of them "off" decreases computation time drastically.

Next, we activate the Animation Window (see Plate 24). This window is used for two things: initial positioning on a non-moving body and animation on a moving body. First, we position our clothes around the body of the synthetic actor. At this point, the garments are two-dimensional, so we only place them approximately, and at distances far enough away from the body so they don't intersect the actor. In order to move these panels and garments around the actor, we use the mouse to select which panels or garments we desire, and then use a 3-D input device such as the Spaceball to position the selected objects.

We can now begin seaming and attaching. Attach lines jump to their specified locations on the body, and seaming pairs try to join together around the body. As seaming forces cause panels to collide with the actor, the clothes respond according to a physically-based elastic model.

Once the dress is stable on an unmoving actor, we can animate the actor according to a generated movement sequence. Collisions with the moving body apply, to each node in the clothing mesh, a small velocity and force that displace the node and, more generally, deform the garment. We can control the way a specific garment responds to these collisions by modifying certain characteristics with the three-dimensional interface's main menu. From these values, we can re-create, for instance, a dress made of silk or a jacket of heavy leather. Garment positions, saved at proper intervals, provide a smoothly animated clothing sequence. Plates 25-27 show examples.

13.8 Conclusions

The things described above provide us with the means to create complex, realistic, and beautiful clothes. Once at this stage, we can begin to generalise our techniques and methods to model other kinds of soft-surface objects. When we have control over the elastic model parameters and panel boundary behaviour, we need not limit ourselves any more to only clothing; we can begin to model other kinds of soft objects.

In the panel-based two-dimensional portion, we are working on incorporating more garment-oriented features. A skeleton or simple representation of an actor would be useful as well, to convey size information to the designer. Also, the ability to add buttons or other decorations to panels would make simple dresses spectacular.

Significant research is going towards creating a much more comfortable environment for users in the three-dimensional part of our clothing software. It proves difficult for users to get an accurate feel for the objects they are manipulating when positioning panels and garments around an actor.

Just as an engineer would start from 2-D drawings or sketches of an object, we would create 2-D polygonal surfaces which we would then deform as desired in three dimensions using an expanded version of our virtual reality interface. Data gloves and goggles could be used to modify and apply forces on an object's surfaces to obtain the desired shape. Finally, once an object is modelled, we need to be able to animate it and subject it to gravity, wind, and other natural physical forces.

Ideally, we should be able to model and animate objects like shoes, hair, and other things that might not exactly be considered "soft" in the traditional sense.

Acknowledgments

This research was supported by "Le Fonds National Suisse pour la Recherche Scientifique," and the Natural Sciences and Engineering Research Council of Canada.

References

Aono M. (1990). A Wrinkle Propagation Model for Cloth. In *Proc. Computer Graphics International '90*, Springer, Tokyo, pp.96-115.

Barzel R., Barr A.H (1988). A Modeling System Based on Dynamic Constraints.In *Proc. SIGGRAPH '88, Computer Graphics*, Vol. 22, No4, pp.179-188.

Breen D.E., House D.H., Getto P.H. (1991). A Particle-Based Computational Model of Cloth Draping Behaviour, in: Patrikalakis NM, *Scientific Visualization of Physical Phenomena*, Springer-Verlag, Tokyo, pp.113-134

Carignan M., Yang Y., Magnenat Thalmann N., Thalmann D. (1992). Dressing Animated Synthetic actors with Complex Clothes, *Proc. SIGGRAPH '92*, Computer Graphics, Vol. 26, No 2, Chicago, pp. 99-104.

Eringen A.C., Suhubi E.S. (1974). *Elastodynamics*, Vol.1, Academic Press, NY.

Hinds B.K., McCartney J. (1990). Interactive garment design, In *The Visual Computer*, Vol. 6, pp.53-61.

Kunii T.L., Gotoda H. (1990). Modeling and Animation of Garment Wrinkle Formation Processes. In *Proc. Computer Animation'90*, Springer, Tokyo, pp.131-147.

Lafleur B., Magnenat Thalmann N., Thalmann D. (1991). Cloth Animation with Self-Collision Detection. In *Proc. IFIP Conference on Modeling in Computer Graphics*, Springer, Tokyo, pp.179-187.

Magnenat Thalmann N., Yang Y. (1991). Techniques for Cloth Animation, in: *New Trends in Animation and Visualization*, edited by N. Thalmann and D. Thalmann, by John Wiley & Sons Ltd., pp.243-256.

Mangen A., Lasudry N. (1991). Search for the Intersection Polygon of any Two Polygons: Application to the Garment Industry. In *Computer Graphics Forum*, Vol.10, pp.19-208.

Moccozet L., Magnenat Thalmann N. (1992). "Controlling the Complexity of Objects based on Polygonal Meshes", *Proc. Computer Graphics International '92*, Tokyo.

Platt J.C., Barr A.H. (1989). Constraints Methods for Flexible Models. In *Proc. SIGGRAPH'89 , Computer Graphics*, Vol.23, No.3, pp.21-30.

Terzopoulos D., Platt J., Barr A., Fleischer K. (1987). Elastically Deformation Models, Proc. SIGGRAPH'87, Computer Graphics, Vol. 21, No.4, pp.205-214

Turner R., Gobetti E., Balaguer F., Mangili A., Thalmann D., Magnenat Thalmann N. (1990). An Object-Oriented Methodology using Dynamic Variables for Animation and Scientific Visualisation, *Proc. Computer Graphics International '90*, Singapore, Springer-Verlag, Tokyo, pp. 317-328.

Weil J. (1986). The Synthesis of Cloth Objects. In *Proc. SIGGRAPH'86, Computer Graphics,* Vol.20, No.4, pp.49-54.

Yang Y., Magnenat Thalmann N., Thalmann D. (1992). 3D Garment Design and Animation - A New Design Tool For The Garment Industry, *Computers in Industry*, Vol.19, pp.185-191.

14

Automatic Control and Behaviour of Virtual Actors

Daniel Thalmann

14.1 Introduction

An important part of the current animation consists in simulating the real world. To achieve a simulation, the animator has two principal techniques available. The first is to use a model that creates the desired effect. A good example is the growth of a green plant. The second is used when no model is available. In this case, the animator produces "by hand" the real world motion to be simulated. Until recently most computer-generated films have been produced using the second approach: traditional computer animation techniques like keyframe animation, spline interpolation, etc. Automatic motion control techniques (Wilhelms 1987) have been proposed, but they are strongly related to mechanics-based animation and do not take into account the behaviour of characters. However, high-level animation involving human beings and animals may be produced using behavioural and perception models. Reynolds (1987) introduced the term and the concept of behavioural animation in order to describe the automatisation of such higher level animation.

This new approach of computer animation has less and less to do with the techniques of traditional animation but more and more with the techniques of actor direction. The animator is responsible for the design of the behaviour of characters from path planning to complex emotional interactions between characters. His job is somewhat like that of a theatrical director: the character's performance is the indirect result of the director's instructions to the actor. The computer director directs at the video screen synthetic actors, decors, lights and cameras using a natural language. If it is in real time, it will be like directing a real film but in a synthetic world. We will enter into the era of real computer-generated films, produced in a virtual world and directed by real human directors. The use of synthetic actors will be interesting. Due to the personality of the actors, their reactions may sometimes cause surprises. For example, it should be almost impossible (as in a theatrical scene) to exactly

---

Interacting with Virtual Environments Edited by Lindsay MacDonald and John Vince

play the same scene twice. You cannot walk exactly the same way from the same bar to home twice.

A synthetic actor (Magnenat Thalmann and Thalmann 1987) is defined as a human-like autonomous actor completely generated by computer. Applications of synthetic actors are unlimited: in the near future, any human being, dead or alive, may be recreated and placed in any new situation, with no dependence on any live action model. Digital scene simulation will be possible for landscapes with human beings, cinema or theatre actors, and spatial vessels with humans; any human behaviour may be simulated in various situations, scientific as well as artistic. From a user point-of-view, TV announcers may be simulated, or people may walk inside their dream house before the house is built.

However, the problems to be solved to achieve this are also numerous and unlimited: computer-generated motions must be as natural as possible. Unfortunately, we know that walking, object grasping, and true personality are very complex to model. Researchers will need years to be able to represent real looking and behaving synthetic actors. And if we will not have all synthetic actors behaving in the same way, we have to introduce interactive psychological description capabilities.

Then new problems arise: how to model the personality, the intelligence? We need to know concrete and mathematical models of domains which are still very soft and not quite formally described. This may be the challenge in modelling human using computers for the coming century.

In this chapter, we discuss the various methods available for the direction of these actors. We classify these methods into three categories: local control, global control and autonomy. We illustrate this classification by several examples of systems developed in our laboratory: the TRACK system, biomechanics walking and vision-based behavioural animation. We also explain how to compose motions using the Coach-Trainee methodology.

14.2   Control versus autonomy

There are a lot of methods for controlling motion of synthetic actors. For example, Zeltzer (1985) classifies animation systems as being either guiding, animator-level or task-level systems. Magnenat Thalmann and Thalmann (1991) propose a new classification of computer animation scenes involving synthetic actors both according to the method of controlling motion and according to the kinds of interactions the actors have. A motion control method specifies how an actor is animated and may be characterised according to the type of information it privileged in animating the synthetic actor. For example, in a keyframe system for an articulated body, the privileged information to be manipulated is the angle. In a forward dynamics-based system, the privileged information is a set of forces and torques; of course, in solving the dynamic equations, joint angles are also obtained in this system, but we consider these as derived information. In fact, any motion control method will eventually have to deal with geometric information (typically joint angles), but only geometric motion control methods explicitly privilege this information at the level of animation control. Plates 28 and 29 shows examples of synthetic actors.

The nature of privileged information for the motion control of actors falls into three categories: geometric, physical and behavioural, giving rise to three corresponding categories of motion control method.

- The first approach corresponds to methods heavily relied upon by the animator: rotoscopy, shape transformation, parametric keyframe animation. **Synthetic actors are locally controlled.** Methods are normally driven by geometric data. Typically the animator provides a lot of geometric data corresponding to a local definition of the motion. For example, we may consider rotoscopy, a method which uses sensors to provide coordinates of specific points of joint angles of a real human for each frame. Also keyframe systems are typical of systems that manipulate angles; from key angles at selected times, they calculate angles for intermediate frames by interpolation. Inverse kinematic methods may be also considered as being in this category. They determine values of joint angles from values of end effectors. The extension of the principle of kinematic constraints to the imposition of trajectories on specific points of the body is also of geometric nature. With the advent of Virtual Reality devices and superworkstations, brute force methods like rotoscopy-like methods tend to come back.

- The second way guarantees a realistic motion by using kinematics and dynamics. The problem with this type of animation is controlling the motion produced by simulating the physical laws which govern motion in the real world. The animator should provide physical data corresponding to the complete definition of a motion. Kinematic-based systems are generally intuitive and lack dynamic integrity. The animation does not seem to respond to basic physical facts like gravity or inertia. Only the modelling of objects as they move under the influence of forces and torques can be realistic. Forces and torques cause linear and angular accelerations. The motion is obtained by the dynamic equations of motion relating the forces, torques, constraints and the mass distribution of objects. Typical physical motion control methods for single actors which consider no other aspect of the environment animate articulated figures through forces and torques applied to limbs. The physical laws involved are mainly those of mechanics such as the Newton-Euler equations, the Lagrange equation, the Gibbs-Appel equation or the D'Alembert principle of Virtual Work. As trajectories and velocities are obtained by solving equations, we may consider **actor motions as globally controlled.** Functional methods based on biomechanics are also part of this class.

- The third type of animation is called behavioural animation and takes into account the relationship between each object and the other objects. Moreover the control of animation may be performed at a task- level, but we may also consider **the actor as an autonomous creature.** In fact, we will consider as a behavioural motion control method any method consisting of driving the behaviour of this actor by providing high-level directives indicating a specific behaviour without any other stimulus. A typical example is the definition of a command to impose a degree of fatigue on an actor like suggested by Lee *et al.* in their method of Strength Guided Motion (Lee *et al.* 1990).

In summary, we may design a scene involving an actor walking among obstacles using the three approaches. For example:

1. Using a keyframe system: by interpolating the values of parameters at given key times;

2. Using a dynamic-based system: by calculating the positions from the motion equations obtained with forces and torques;

3. Using a behavioural animation system: by automatic planning of the motion of an object based on information about the environment (decor and other objects).

However, it is clear that no method is convenient and complete to produce such a realistic scene. Using keyframes, not only is the task tedious, but also it is very difficult to be sure of avoiding collisions, to guarantee a respect of feet support on the floor. Moreover, even an excellent animator is unable to design a correct walking balance using keyframes.

As there is no general method applicable to complex motions, only a combination of various techniques may result in a realistic motion with a relative efficiency.

Integration of different motion generators is vital for the design of complex motion where the characterisation of movement can quickly change in terms of functionality, goals and expressivity. This induces a drastic change in the motion control algorithm at multiple levels: behavioural decision making, global criteria optimisation and actuation of joint level controllers. By now, there is no global approach which can reconfigure itself with such flexibility.

14.3   Local motion definition and edition

We have designed an interactive tool for the visualisation, editing and manipulation of multiple track sequences. A sequence is associated with an articulated figure and can integrate different motion generators such as walking, inverse kinematics, and keyframing within a unified framework. The TRACK system provides a large set of tools for track space manipulations and cartesian space corrections. This approach allows an incremental refinement design combining information and constraints from both the track space (usually joints) and the cartesian space. We have dedicated this system to the design and evaluation of human motions for the purpose of animation. For this reason, we also insure the real-time display of the 3-D figure motion with a simultaneous scan of the 2-D tracks.

The TRACK software structure

Figure 14.1 represents the hierarchy of modules used to construct the TRACK system. The Motion Generator includes keyframing functions, inverse kinematics, and the walking function model. At the track manipulation level, there are functions to manipulate track data structure, e.g. reading, saving, selecting, editing, filtering, zooming, and multiple sequence manipulation. The user interface is the top level. It is built with the 5-D Toolkit (Turner *et al.* 1990). For keyframing, TRACK provides functions to define and edit the key values for each joint, then the user can display the motion in real time or ask for the posture at any time by skimming the sequence.

Inverse kinematics: Reaching a target with an end effector

Motion may be produced by inverse kinematics. At first, the animator picks the root and end joint, e.g. shoulder and wrist. Then, the SpaceBall or the Trackball can be used to define the target position and/or orientation interactively. The SpaceBall is a 6 DOF interactive input device. This is essentially a "force" sensitive device that relates the forces and torques applied to the ball mounted on the top of the device. These forces and torques are sent to the computer in real time where they are interpreted and may be composed into homogeneous transformation matrices that can be applied to objects. In Figure 14.2 example, one FREE node_3D with 6 DOF is used to represent the target, that is the frame xyz on the left of Figure 14.2. The position of the target can be interactively changed with the SpaceBall. First an open chain is specified with a root node_3D and an end effector node_3D. After these definitions, the end effector moves so as to reach the target by inverse kinematics. All the angles of joints between the root and the end effector are automatically evaluated.

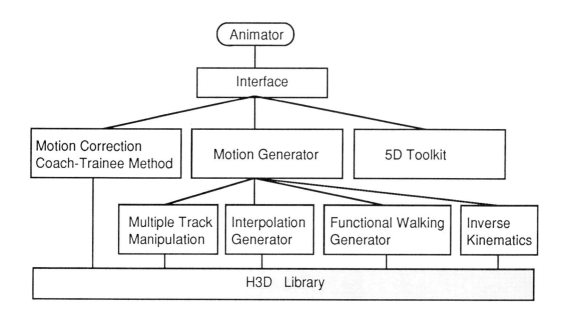

Figure 14.1. The TRACK software structure.

Walking with different relative velocities

In TRACK, human walking is produced by a model built from experimental data based on a wide range of normalised velocities (Boulic *et al.* 1990). The user can change the current velocity in real time.

We have designed a new tool (Bezault *et al.* 1992) including path and speed profile design with real-time visualisation of the step locations. This ability gives the animator both spatial and temporal control over the human figure's trajectory: for example, walking on the white squares of a chessboard or following stones in a Japanese garden path; the motions becomes easy to define. This tool is particularly efficient in that the higher level of the walking model work independently from the effective play of the low-level joint trajectories by the figure. This independence is gained by means of a transfer function calibrating the figure's normalised velocity with respect to the theoretical normalised velocity. Two real-time display functionalities greatly ease the design of trajectories in complex environments. First, the current range of permitted velocities indicates the potentialities of the local dynamic of the walking behaviour. Second, the set of step locations shown on the desired path allows precise placement. Plate 30 shows an example of walking sequence.

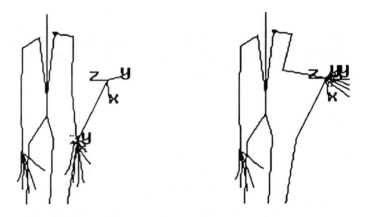

Figure 14.2. Reaching the target.

14.4 Motion composition

We have introduced two types of operations: a concatenation operator and a blending operation.

Concatenation operator

This operator concatenates a sequence A followed by a sequence B and puts the result into a sequence C. There are two parameters:

1) The concatenation mode manages the absolute positioning of the resulting sequence.

   •   A remains fixed and B is shifted after.
   •   B remains fixed and A is shifted before.
   •   A and B remain fixed.
   •   A is shifted so as to begin at time 0, and B is shifted after.

2) The gap value specifies the delay between A and B.

The sequences A, B and C can be the same so, combined with the mode and the gap, we provide a very powerful operator. For example it is straightforward to construct a periodical motion with 2^n periods from n successive concatenation operations.

Motion blending

Blending is necessary whenever two sequences overlap in time and we need to keep their respective time-base and migrate continuously from one to the other. We can do this by defining a normalised cubic step function which varies from 0 to 1 on the overlapping zone. This function is used to weigh the contribution of the sampled sequences on this zone for the evaluation of the blended key values. The resulting sequence is compressed afterwards to return to a standard Hermite spline form.

The Coach-Trainee correction method

The Coach-Trainee correction method is based on a combination of direct and inverse kinematic control (Boulic and Thalmann 1992) over an open chain (no closed loop). We just recall here the basic definitions of inverse kinematic control and the principle of our motion correction approach.

Inverse kinematic control is based on a linearisation of the geometric model of a chain at the current state of the system. As a consequence, its validity is limited to the neighbourhood of the current state and, as such, any desired motion has to comply with the hypothesis of small movements.

The basic idea of the Coach-Trainee correction method (Figure 14.3) is to consider the joint motion delivered by a motion generator as a reference model whose tracking is enforced through the secondary task while the main task insures the realization of desired Cartesian constraints over some specified end effector(s).

The user is more interested in local reshaping of the motion both in time and space. For this reason we prefer to use half-space constraints (planar, cylindrical, spherical). Then, we duplicate the 3-D hierarchy over the controlled chain with an associated parallel control. The initial 3-D hierarchy is simply controlled by the reference motion and serves as a guide for the correction control over the duplicated chain. For this reason, we refer to the reference motion as the *Coach* motion and the corrected motion as the *Trainee* motion. This *Coach-Trainee* metaphor is suggested by sport training as the adaptation of the coach reference movement into a trainee movement, being the closest possible with respect tò a different context of body structure and/or Cartesian constraints.

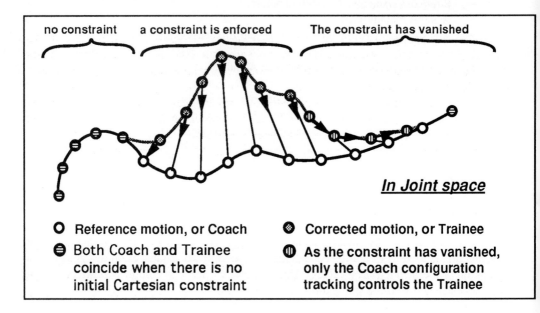

Figure 14.3. The *Coach-Trainee* metaphor.

Even with the Coach-Trainee parallel control, the solution presents a first order discontinuity at the interface of the half-space constraint. For this reason we confer a thickness on the boundary of the half-space constraints and we operate smooth switching on the resulting *transition zone* by means of a *transition function*. Then, the formulation of the combined "direct and inverse" kinematic control method is given by the following equation (one dimensional constraint case):

$$\Delta q = J^+ (f \Delta x + (1 - f) J \Delta z) + (I - J^+ J) \Delta z \quad \text{with } 0 \le f \le 1 \quad (1)$$

where Δq is the unknown vector in the joint variation space, of dimension n. J is the Jacobian matrix of the linear transformation, representing the differential behaviour of the controlled system over the dimensions specified by the *main task*. J+ is the unique pseudo-inverse of J providing the minimum norm solution which realizes the main task. I is the identity matrix of the joint variation space (n x n) (I-J+J) is a projection operator on the null space of the linear transformation J. Any element belonging to this joint variation sub-space is mapped by J into the null vector in the Cartesian variation space. Δz describes a *secondary task* in the joint variation space. It is usually calculated so as to minimise a cost function. f is the *transition function* (see Boulic and Thalmann 1992 for details)

14.5   Autonomous actors

Autonomy and behaviour

Virtual humans are not only visual. They have a behaviour, perception, memory and some reasoning. Behavioural human animation is a new topic consisting of developing a more general concept of autonomous actors reacting to environments and making decisions based on perception systems, memory and reasoning. Behaviour is often defined as the way animals and humans act, and is usually described in natural language terms which have social, psychological or physiological significance, but which are not necessarily easily reducible to the movement of one or two muscles, joints or end effectors.

A typical human behavioural animation system, is based on the three key components:

- the locomotor system
- the perceptual system
- the organism system

A locomotor system is concerned with how to animate physical motions of virtual humans in their environment. A perceptual system is concerned with perceiving the environment. The modes of attention are: orienting, listening, touching, smelling, tasting, and looking. The organism system is concerned with rules, skills, motives, drives and memory. It may be regarded as the "brain" of the actor.

Synthetic vision

As an example of behavioural animation, we have recently introduced a way of animating actors at a high level based on the concept of synthetic vision (Renault *et al.* 1990). The objective is simple: to create animation involving a synthetic actor automatically moving in a room, avoiding objects and other synthetic actors. To simulate this behaviour, each synthetic actor has synthetic vision for perception of the world, the sole input to his/her behavioural model.

Although the use of vision to give behaviour to synthetic actors seems similar to the use of vision for intelligent mobile robots, it is quite different. This is because the vision of the synthetic actor is itself a synthetic vision. Using a synthetic vision allow us to skip all the problems of pattern recognition and distance detection, problems which still are the most difficult parts in robotics vision. However some interesting work has been done on the topic of intelligent mobile robots, especially for action-perception coordination problems. For example, Crowley (1987), working with surveillance robots states that "most low level perception and navigation tasks are algorithmic in nature; at the highest levels, decisions regarding which actions to perform are based on knowledge relevant to each situation". This remark gives us the hypothesis on which our vision-based model of behavioural animation is built.

Our approach is based on the use of Displacement Local Automata (DLA), which is similar to the concept of script introduced by Schank (1980) for natural language processing. For vision, a DLA is a black box which has the knowledge allowing the synthetic actor to move in a specific part of his environment. Examples are the DLA *displacement-in-a-corridor*, the DLA *obstacle-avoidance*, the DLA *crossing-with-another-synthetic-actor* , the DLA *passage-of-a-door* etc. This concept of DLA has the advantage of being able to increase or decrease the description grain. For example, the displacement in a corridor may be one of the uses of a more general DLA *displacement-between-two-obstructions-not-far-away-one-from-the-other*. An obstruction may be a river, a wall, a road etc. This means that the DLA may be used in a corridor, on a sidewalk or a bridge. Similarly, *to circumvent the swimming-pool* corresponds to going around an obstruction. The DLA system allows for the creation of a kind of assemblage game where, using simple and modular elements, it is possible to react to a lot of everyday simple situations. It should be noted that our DLA's are strictly algorithmic; they correspond to reflexes which are automatically performed by the adult and they only use vision as the information source.

Once we have access to DLA's, how do we use them? How and when do we activate them and stop them? One solution consists of using a blackboard approach. The current situation is described on a blackboard and each DLA comes and sees if it has to react to the situation or not. There are two drawbacks to this approach. First, we have to add to each DLA the ability to know that it must react (this is opposed to reflex). Second, for the same situation, several DLA's may react and there is a conflict to handle. Another approach consists of using a controller which, in an unknown environment, analyses this environment and activates the right DLA. This controller also has to handle the DLA end, the DLA errors and other messages coming from the DLA's. The controller is the thinking part of our system. It makes decision and perform the high-level actions. In any known environment, the controller should be able to activate the DLA associated with the current location. This means that an environment description has to be stored somewhere. This is the role of the navigator. From information provided by the controller, the navigator builds step by step a "map" of the environment. The navigator then gives to the controller the location of the synthetic actor in the map, and of course, it should plan the path from a known location to another known location (at a high level: e.g. go to the kitchen). Another function of the navigator is to allow the controller to change the initialisation of some DLA's and anticipate the DLA changes. This description of the navigator functionalities emphasise the role of the map which should be more a logical map than a geographical map, more a discrete map than a continuous map. In fact, human being only remember discrete properties like *the tree is on the right of the car*. This suggests that to give to the behaviour of the synthetic actor a maximum of believability and a maximum of developing possibilities, it is essential to give the actor a world representation similar to the representation that human beings have.

Vision simulation is the heart of our system. However, we do not attempt to recreate human vision. Our purpose is to obtain a 2-3/4 D vision, which means 2D + 1/2D + 1/4D. The 1/2D is due to the fact that for each point of the 2-D vision, we know the distance between the eye and the point from which it is the projection. The 1/4D corresponds to the fact that for each point of the vision, we know to which object it belongs (e.g. object 34, which is a table). This 2-3/4D has the advantage of avoiding all problems of pattern recognition involved in robotic vision. Our system is implemented on IRIS 4-D Workstations using an object-oriented extension of the C language. For input, we have a hierarchy containing the description of 3-D objects, the environment, and the camera characterized by its eye and interest point. For output, the vision is built as a 2-D array of pixels on which the actor's view of the world is projected. Plate 31 shows autonomous actors avoiding obstacles based on their synthetic vision.

14.6   Conclusions

The long-term objective of our research is the visualisation of the simulation of the behaviour of human beings in a given environment, interactively decided by the animator. Behavioural techniques make possible the automating of high-level control of actors such as path planning. By changing the parameters ruling this automating, it is possible to give a different personality to each actor. This behavioural approach should be a major step relatively to the conventional motion control techniques. Our main purpose is the development of a general concept of autonomous actors reacting to their environment and taking decisions based on perception systems, memory and reasoning. The animation system with autonomous actors will be based on the three key components: the locomotor system, the perceptual system, the organism system. With such an approach, we should be able to create simulations of situations such as actors moving in a complex environment they may know and recognise, or actors playing ball games based on their visual and touching perception.

Acknowledgements

The research was partly supported by "le Fonds National Suisse pour la Recherche Scientifique. " The author is grateful to Arghyro Paouri and Agnes Daldegan for the design of pictures.

References

Bezault L., Boulic R., Magnenat Thalmann N. & Thalmann D. (1992). An Interactive Tool for the Design of Human Free-Walking Trajectories. *Computer Animation'92*, Geneva, Springer, Tokyo, pp. 87-104.

Boulic R. & Thalmann D. (1992). Combined Direct and Inverse Kinematic Control for Articulated Figures Motion Editing, *Computer Graphics Forum*, Vol. 2, No. 4, pp. 189-202.

Boulic R., Magnenat Thalmann N., Thalmann D. (1990). A Global Human Walking Model with real-time Kinematic Personification, *The Visual Computer,* Vol. 6, No 6, pp. 344-358.

Crowley J.L. (1987). Coordination of Action and Perception in a Surveillance Robot, *IEEE Expert*, winter, pp. 32-43

Lee P., Wei S., Zhao J., Badler N.I. (1990). Strength Guided Motion, *Proc. SIGGRAPH '90, Computer Graphics*, Vol. 24, No 4, pp. 253-262

Magnenat Thalmann N., Thalmann D. (1987). The direction of synthetic actors in the film Rendezvous à Montréal. *IEEE Computer Graphics and Applications* 7(12), pp. 9-19.

Magnenat Thalmann N., Thalmann D. (1991). Complex Models for Visualizing Synthetic Actors. In *IEEE Computer Graphics and Applications*, Vol. 11, No5, pp. 32-44.

Renault O., Magnenat Thalmann N., Thalmann D. (1990). A Vision-based Approach to Behavioural Animation, *The Journal of Visualization and Computer Animation,* Vol. 1, No1, pp. 18-21.

Reynolds C. (1987). Flocks, Herds, and Schools: A Distributed Behavioural Model, *Proc. SIGGRAPH '87, Computer Graphics*, Vol. 21, No4, pp. 25-34

Schank R.C. (1980) Language and Memory, *Cognitive Science*, Vol. 4, No3, pp. 243-284

Turner R., Gobetti E., Balaguer F., Mangili A., Thalmann D., Magnenat Thalmann N. (1990). An Object-Oriented Methodology using Dynamic Variables for Animation and Scientific Visualisation, *Proc. Computer Graphics International '90*, Singapore, Springer-Verlag, Tokyo, pp. 317-328.

Wilhelms J. (1987). Towards Automatic Motion Control, *IEEE Computer Graphics and Applications*, Vol. 7, No 4, pp. 11-22

Zeltzer D. (1985). Towards an Integrated View of 3D Computer Animation, *The Visual Computer,* Vol. 1, No4, pp. 249-259

15

Virtual Actors and Virtual Environments

David Zeltzer and Michael B. Johnson

15.1 Introduction

A *virtual environment* (VE) is a computer-simulated world consisting of mathematical and software representations of real (or imagined) agents, objects and processes; and a human-computer interface for displaying and interacting with these models. The interface has two parts: 1) a *logical* interface that specifies what parameters of the virtual environment and its models can be changed, and when; and 2) a *physical* interface consisting of one or more visual, auditory or haptic displays for presenting the virtual world to the human participant, and a set of sensing devices to monitor the human's actions (Zeltzer 1992a).

While current VE systems often use *head-mounted displays*, as well as various gesture and motion sensing devices, not all VE applications require an *immersive* interface. For example, we have implemented a VE for planning plastic surgery procedures on the human face which uses a conventional workstation CRT and a mouse-and-window interface (Pieper *et al.* 1992). This design decision is supported by the physicians who have evaluated the system (Pieper 1991). In contrast, VE or teleoperator systems which must support manipulation or command-and-control tasks, would benefit from stereo, head-tracked, wide field-of-view displays (Hirose *et al.* 1990, Kim *et al.* 1988, Zeltzer and Druker1992b).

Many applications would benefit from emerging VE technologies, including education and training; human factors analyses (Bolt *et al.* 1992); equipment and facilities design and prototyping (Brooks 1986a); and operations planning, rehearsal, command and control (Zeltzer *et al.* 1992b). And in many of these application areas, e.g., a VE system for training personnel to perform multi-person maintenance tasks, the VE system must be able to display accurate models of human figures that can perform routine behaviours and adapt to events in the virtual world. After all, the real world operates according to the laws of physics, and it is populated by a multitude of animal and human figures. The goal of the research described here

Interacting with Virtual Environments Edited by Lindsay MacDonald and John Vince
© 1994 John Wiley & Sons Ltd

is to implement a VE system that includes prototypical autonomous and interactive synthetic humans. In this chapter we will describe the research program we are pursuing to achieve this goal.

15.2 Virtual actors: guided and autonomous

We will call a computer model of a human figure that can move and function in a VE a *virtual actor*. If the movement of a virtual actor is slaved to the motions of a human VE participant using cameras, instrumented clothing, or some other means of *body tracking*, we will call that a *guided* virtual actor, or simply, a guided actor. *Autonomous* actors operate under program control and are capable of independent and adaptive behaviour, such that they are capable of interacting with human participants in the VE, as well as with simulated objects and events in the VE.

Beyond the added realism that the presence of virtual actors can provide in those situations in which the participants would normally expect to see other human figures, autonomous actors can perform several important functions in VE applications:

- *Autonomous actors can augment or replace human participants.* This will allow individuals to work or train in group settings without requiring additional personnel.

- *Autonomous actors can serve as surrogate instructors.* VE systems for training, education, and operations rehearsal will incorporate various instructional features, including knowledge-based systems for intelligent computer aided instruction (ICAI) (Ford 1985). As ICAI systems mature, virtual actors can provide personae to interact with participants in a VE system.

- *Autonomous actors can escort and assist users in navigating through complex synthetic environments.* Navigation in an unfamiliar environment is not easy. The task is hard enough in the physical world, but in computer-synthesised environments, many sensory cues and visual landmarks are often absent. Virtual actors can help a human participant to accomplish some task in a VE, especially if it involves orientation, exploration and navigation in a virtual space.

15.3 Interacting with virtual actors

Conventional animation techniques, such as keyframing, are wholly inadequate for the end-users of VE systems. Such users need to interact with synthetic humans in real time at the *task level,* through language and gesture, in ways familiar from everyday life. Our focus therefore is on modelling elementary human motor skills, integrating these skills into a repertoire of behaviours for an autonomous actor, and developing a task level, language-based interface.

Rather than capturing nuances of timing or expressiveness, we are primarily interested in understanding how to represent nominal and unaffected human interactions with physical objects and other humans. Descriptions of dance or athletic skills, for example, are somewhat special cases we will not focus on, since these acts primarily involve detailed specification of the motion of body parts, rather than interaction with objects.

In particular, we are interested in accounting for the kinds of mechanical operations on physical objects encountered in everyday activites, such as reaching and grasping, walking through cluttered environments, and so on. Healthy adult humans seem to perform these kinds of routine, stereotypical behaviours without much conscious attention. Most of the behaviours in the animal kingdom seem to fall into this category and, indeed, a large portion of human behaviour can be described as *automatised.* Walking, for example, seems to involve low-level motor programs that can execute without any conscious intervention. That is, we are capable of walking over uneven ground while reading a newspaper, as long as the path we're to follow is not too cluttered.

We have initially concentrated on simulating an individual virtual actor or multiple, *uncoupled* actors that interact with no contact and do not need to coordinate their movements (Zeltzer 1992c). Ultimately, virtual actors should be capable of coordinating their behaviour with the actions of other actors or human VE participants, but for the time being we will not deal with the issues of temporal constraints or planning for *tightly-coupled* or *loosely coupled* multi-agent activities.

In the remainder of this chapter we will describe our approaches to the twin problems of designing VEs and virtual actors, and interacting with them at the task level. Complex systems are built of many interacting components and assemblies of components. A VE system, for example, may consist of a collection of distributed computing resources and I/O devices, coordinated and controlled by any number of system-level software modules (Appino *et al.* 1992, Zeltzer *et al.* 1989, Zyda *et al.* 1992). In addition, we expect that any VE system will support a set of computational models and simulation processes that make up the virtual world, each of which may be arbitrarily complex.

Every virtual actor in a VE must have a set of behaviours it can perform, whether the actor represents a robot capable of only a few simple actions, or whether the actor is a synthetic human possessing a wide range of adaptive motor skills. The mechanism for selecting and sequencing motor skills to generate the routine behaviours of a virtual actor must link *perception* with *action*, in a process we call *motor planning.* In earlier work we have described the architecture for a *skill network* we have implemented to model the routine behaviours of virtual actors, and we have also characterised the kinds of behaviours the skill network can capture, and the sorts of behaviour it cannot model (Zeltzer and Johnson 1991). For each actor we need to construct a skill network, which will enable it to respond to simulated events and human input adaptively, and in real time. Later we will briefly review the skill network architecture, and we will describe *WavesWorld,* a development environment for designing, building and debugging distributed VEs and virtual actors. WavesWorld includes tools for assembling a collection of motor skills into a skill network, as well as runtime tools for controlling and visualising the output of the skill network.

In general, there will be multiple "points of contact" with a VE system, and it is especially important to interact with the models, simulation processes, and system components at the right levels of detail. For example, the human figure has over 200 degrees of freedom

(DOFs), yet providing the user with 200 knobs for interactively controlling joint rotation doesn't seem to be the answer. Simply put, the control task becomes unmanageable if we try to interact with the model at the wrong level of detail.

Typically there is more than one kind of user: system developers and end users, for example, who may often be one and the same person. Developers require access to editing and debugging tools that will operate on VE system components or the programs and data that make up elements of the virtual world. *WavesWorld* provides such a toolset. End users - that is, human participants in an executing VE - require transparent access to the various VE system "control knobs", as well as appropriate means for manipulating virtual objects and communicating with virtual actors. *Motor goal parsing*, in part, will enable such communication. In Section 15.5 we will describe the process of *motor goal parsing* which underlies the language-based, task level interface we are developing for interacting with virtual actors.

15.4 WavesWorld: designing and debugging virtual actors and environments

WavesWorld is a collection of software for designing, building, and debugging distributed simulations. The intent of this work is to allow a user to quickly build a graphically-simulated character - a virtual actor - that can act autonomously in a networked virtual environment. WavesWorld uses a reactive planning algorithm which was outlined in earlier work (Zeltzer *et al.* 1989), later independently elaborated by Maes (Maes 1989, Maes 1990), and which has been significantly extended for dealing with asynchronous and parallel execution (Johnson 1991). A comprehensive sensing structure has also been added to the planner, complementing the high-level controls the reactive planner provides by allowing time varying sampling rates to be integrated into the perception mechanisms. In addition, this system integrates *computational economics* at the lowest level, so that all processes in WavesWorld are "bid" at runtime. Finally, a networked, multi-modal, interactive development environment that supports debugging as well as design is essential to building complex VE systems. Therefore, WavesWorld has been seamlessly integrated into the NeXTSTEP development environment, which acts as a direct-manipulation, or guiding front-end to a large set of heterogenous computing resources.

Active objects and the skill network

When approaching the task of designing a development environment for a VE and the virtual actors that inhabit it, the problems of distributed computing and parallelism come to the forefront. We want our system to be able to run in parallel as much as possible, and we want to take advantage of distributed computational resources over the network, but how do we present the information such that the developer is not overwhelmed?

In our system, we have developed system level tools for managing and distributing computation, as well as tools for organising, steering, and visualising the ongoing computations. We have developed our own process abstraction, which we call an *active object*, which is the level at which we can distribute computation and allow parallel execution.

Computational actors in WavesWorld are implemented as collections of *active objects*, which are distributed, object-oriented, message-passing entities. Each of these processes maintains its own "read-eval-print" loop so that active objects can send complete programs to each other, and thus embed code inside of other active objects. Active objects are flexible enough to trade off computational power for communications bandwidth "on the fly." In other words, active objects have facilities for determining, at runtime, if it is cheaper to:

- send another process a message, polling it for information, or,

- download some piece of code (i.e. a set of messages) which will run locally in the remote process and communicate the information to the sending process when appropriate.

An active object is a single, sequential process running on some computational resource. It comes on-line somewhere on the network and makes itself available for communication with other processes that "speaks its lanaguage". After initialising itself and making itself available for communication, an active object drops into an endless loop, checking for new connections and evaluating the messages from previously established connections.

Perceiving the virtual environment

Since an actor's skill network maintains no explicit world model, all of the data about its relationship to the virtual world comes to the actor via its *sensor* agents and *receptors* (Zeltzer and Johnson 1991). Active objects have facilities for defining sensor agents and receptors.

Sensor agents each compute some property of the VE that has meaning for its actor. Sensors are exectuable code that measure some Boolean proposition using information derived from receptors. See Figure 15.1.

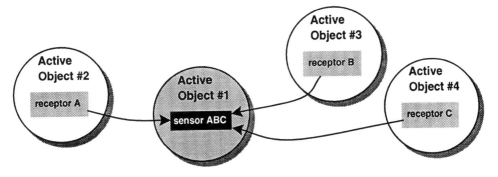

Figure 15.1. Schematic diagram showing the relationship among sensor agents and receptors.

A receptor is a code fragment used by a sensor agent: it gathers the information in the VE that is necessary for the sensor to compute its own value. Receptors are executable code (i.e., a set of valid messages that an active object responds to) that are embedded in some other active object. The receptors have a sampling frequency and lifespan associated with them. Whenever a receptor is evaluated, if its current value is different than the last time it was evaluated, a message is sent off to the active object which embedded it. Receptors can be shared by many active objects at once, and their frequencies can be modulated over time.

For example, the sensor agent **myFavoriteSongIsPlaying** might have two receptors: one embedded in the actor's **BodyManager** which measures the actor's listOfFavouriteSongs, and one embedded in the **EnvironmentManager** which measures the currentSong (see below for a discussion of the **BodyManager** and **EnvironmentManager**). Each receptor has some frequency associated with it that specifies how often the host active object (i.e. the **BodyManager** or the **EnvironmentManager**) must re-evaluate the receptor. In the case of the listOfFavouriteSongs receptor, it might have a very low frequency since the list will probably not change very often, while the currentSong receptor might have a higher frequency - say, half the average song length.

In addition to supporting sensor agents and receptors, active objects have facilities for acting as a host for *goal* agents and *skill* agents. Goal agents represent a fleeting or permanent desire that some sensor be measured *true*. The presence of a goal agent implies the existence of a corresponding sensor agent, somewhere in the actor, capable of sensing when the goal has been accomplished.

Acting in the virtual environment

Skill agents are the mechanisms that implement and control the behaviour of a virtual actor in the virtual environment. They are represented by their name, a list of pre-conditions, and a list of post-conditions. The pre-conditions are called the *condition list*. The condition list contains the names of the sensor agents that must be true in order for the planning algorithm to be able to select that skill agent for execution. The post-conditions are called the *add list* and the *delete list*. The add list contains the names of all the sensor agents that will become true immediately after the skill executes. The delete list contains the names of all the sensor agents that will become false immediately after the skill executes. Note that the post-conditions are only predictions - the sensor agents in question actually measure the state of the VE, which may or may not correspond to how the skill agent believes it will affect the VE.

In addition to pre- and post-conditions, skill agents can store a list of skill agents which have been known to be selected immediately after this skill agent was selected, i.e., in a given context skill *B* followed skill *A*. This is called the *followers list*, and it is used to influence the planning of skill agent selection. This enables the encoding of adaptive patterns of behaviour without the need for "hard-wiring".

Finally, for each skill agent, three other lists are derived at runtime from the other skill agents in the skill network, and from the pre- and post-conditions of that skill agent: *successors, predecessors,* and *conflicters*.

The successors list has pointers to all of the skill agents possessing a sensor agent on their condition list which is on this skill's add list. The predecessors list has pointers to all the skill agents possessing a sensor agent on their add list, which is on this skill's condition list. That is, if skill U enables one of skill V's pre-conditions, V is a successor of U, and U is a predecessor of V. The conflicters list has pointers to all the skill agents possessing a sensor agent on their delete list which is on this skill's condition list.

Note that whenever a skill agent is added to the skill network, the successor, predecessor, and conflicter links of each skill agent must be updated to reflect the addition. This contrasts with other systems where the equivalent skill network is assumed to be compiled (Brooks 1986b).

At runtime, activation energy spreads through the skill network at each time step from seven different sources, all flowing to the individual skill agents. When a skill agent's activation level exceeds a certain threshold, it may execute if, and only if, all of its pre-conditions are currently true. A sensor agent sends activation to each skill agent possessing the proposition on its condition list which the sensor agent computes. A goal agent has a proposition that should be satisfied, and it sends activation to each skill agent that has this proposition on its add list. Goal agents are either once-only or permanent. A goal agent is said to be protected if it is permanent and currently satisfied. For each protected goal, the associated goal agent sends negative activation (i.e., inhibition) to each skill agent that has that goal agent on its delete list.

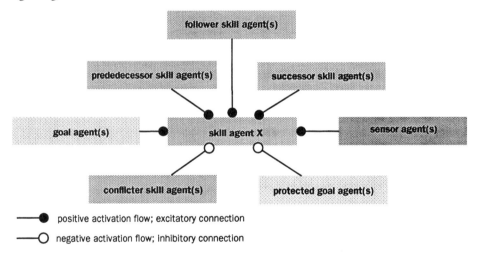

————● positive activation flow; excitatory connection

————○ negative activation flow; inhibitory connection

Figure 15.2. Schematic diagram showing the propagation of activation energy through the skill network.

A skill agent that has all of its pre-conditions true is said to be *executable*. An executable skill agent spreads activation forward to each of its successors for which their shared proposition is currently not measured to be true. A non-executable skill agent spreads activation backwards to each of its predecessors for which their shared proposition is currently not measured to be true. Each skill agent spreads inhibition to each of its conflicters for which the shared proposition is true. Each skill agent spreads activation forward to each of the members of its followers list. See Figure 15.2.

In this way, instantiated motor goals invoke a process - guided by the measurement and evaluation of current conditions in the virtual world - by which appropriate motor skills are selected for execution.

The virtual actor: from active objects to autonomous animation

The ability to act as a host for any number of goal, sensor, and skill agents is built into the core **ActiveObject** superclass. This allows a virtual actor's various goal, sensor and skill agents to be running asynchronously on a heterogenous set of computational resources. Any active object which acts as a host for any agents is referred to as an **AgentManager.**

While the computation involved in sensing and acting in the virtual environment is distributed over a potentially wide-area network, the actual planning algorithm for a given virtual actor runs in a single active object. The various agents register with an instance of this subclass of **ActiveObject** called **Planner.** The **Planner** instance executes the planning algorithm, sending messages to the various skill agents to tell them to begin executing, and updating its local information concerning the various agents as messages stream in. If any agents "die" (e.g., the agent's host machine crashes) during the course of a **Planner**'s life, it deletes them from the skill network, and updates the various interconnections of activation flow.

In addition to a **Planner** and some set of **AgentManagers**, a virtual actor needs some shared locus of state, both internal (e.g., energy level, likes and dislikes, etc.) and external (geometric, kinematic and dynamic properties associated with the actor). This is implemented as an active object called the **BodyManager.**

In summary, a virtual actor is a collection of active objects and agents:

- a **Planner**

- a **BodyManager**

- some number of **AgentManagers**, each of which is managing some set of agents:
  - goal agents
  - skill agents
  - sensor agents, each of which has some number of receptors injected in other active objects.

The EnvironmentManager

To a given virtual actor, the virtual environment is everything other than itself. In addition to other virtual actors, there are several active objects with which the component parts of a virtual actor will connect and exchange messages. The most obvious is the

EnvironmentManager, which is the active object that acts as the shared locus of activity, managing the data not associated explicitly with any one actor (e.g., the environment, props, laws of physics, etc.). An **EnvironmentManager** has the ability to render the VE directly, but it can also delegate the rendering to other active objects.

Although each active object has its own private notion of time, many active objects use the **EnvironmentManager** clock to modulate their activity. This simple expedient allows various parts of a given virtual actor to synchronize with each other, as well as other virtual actors, without explicitly communicating. In a very real sense, the **EnvironmentManager** acts as a blackboard (Erman and Lesser 1975) for the various virtual actors to interact with each other.

In addition to the subclasses of **ActiveObject** that have been discussed, there are classes for playing and recording sounds (**Voice, Nagra**) and images (**Photog, Arri**), for manipulating props in the VE (**DJ, VJ, PropMaster**), and for receiving input from various multi-dimensional and multi-modal input devices (e.g., SpaceBall, DataGlove, Bird, Ear). Since we have extensive tools for auto-generating the bulk of the code associated with a given **ActiveObject** subclass, a developer need only implement the new methods of a given subclass to build a new active object.

A simple example: sanderWorld

Now that we have some notion of what agents are, what active objects are, and how they interrelate, let's look at the process of building a relatively simple world. Called sanderWorld, this example is based on one given in Maes (Maes 1990). The scenario consists of a single virtual actor: a two-handed robot which has the dual tasks of spray painting itself and sanding a board. There are a few props in the world: a vice, a sprayer, a board.

Our actor, the robot, consists of a **BodyManager**, a **Planner**, and (say) two **AgentManagers**. Note that the number of **AgentManagers** is arbitrary, as is the decision of how and where to partition the various goal, sensor, and skill agents. Other than for performance reasons (e.g., not wanting to have two computationally intensive agents running inside the same **AgentManager**) there is no compelling reason to put a given agent in a given **AgentManager**. We'll need the following agents:

- goal agents: boardSanded, selfPainted

- skill agents: pickUpBoard, putDownBoard, pickUpSander, pickUpSprayer, putDownSprayer, sandBoardInHand, sandBoardInVice, sprayPaintSelf, placeBoardInVice.

- sensor agents: operational, board-Somewhere, sanderSomewhere, boardInVice, boardInHand, sanderInHand, sprayerInHand, handIsEmpty, boardSanded, selfPainted

- The sensor agents will use the following receptors, which have been embedded in either the robot's **BodyManager** or the **EnvironmentManager**:

robotMobility(**BodyManager**), robotLocation(**BodyManager**),
viceLocation(**EnvironmentManager**), boardLocation(**EnvironmentManager**),
sanderLocation(**EnvironmentManager**),
sprayerLocation(**EnvironmentManager**),
leftHandLocation(**BodyManager**), rightHandLocation(**BodyManager**),
iAmHoldingSomethingLeft(**BodyManager**),
iAmHoldingSomethingRight(**BodyManager**),
boardHasBeenSanded(**EnvironmentManager**), iAmPainted(**BodyManager**).

As mentioned earlier, WavesWorld has been integrated into the NeXTSTEP development environment. Concretely, this means that a set of objects have been written which are grouped together in palettes and loaded in to the NeXT InterfaceBuilder application. These objects allow a complete virtual environment and its constituent actors to be composed by direct manipulation guiding tools, and run without ever having to leave InterfaceBuilder or compile any code. A program in WavesWorld is really a set of archived objects and their interconnections. Some of these objects represent agents and receptors, some represent active objects, and some represent interface objects. To start building our sanderWorld, we open a new archive and drag objects corresponding to our active objects from the palette in the upper right into our archive's window in the lower left.

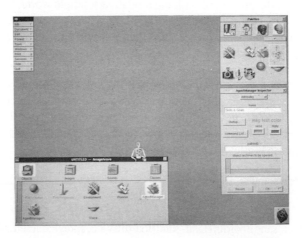

Figure 15.3. Dragging a BodyManager from the Active Objects Palette.

We then connect the various active objects to each other, e.g., each **AgentManager** needs to be connected to the **BodyManager**, the **EnvironmentManager**, and its **Planner**, and the **BodyManager** needs to be connected to the **EnvironmentManager**, and so on.

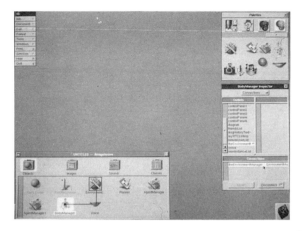

Figure 15.4. Connecting a **BodyManager** to the **EnvironmentManager.**

We then drag some interface objects and connect them to active objects. Some of these interface objects are themselves active objects (e.g., **Voice**) while others are simply subclasses of NeXT objects (e.g. the **Diagram**).

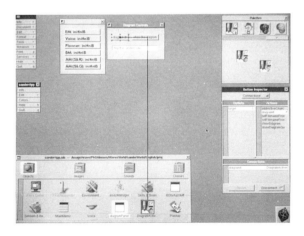

Figure 15.5. Connecting a button to the **Diagram** object.

Some active objects have a relatively complex set of interface objects associated with them. To reduce clutter, these collections of interface objects can be kept in a separate object archive, where they can be loaded at runtime when the active object unarchives itself.

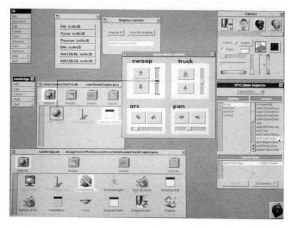

Figure 15.6. Some camera objects for the EnvironmentManager.

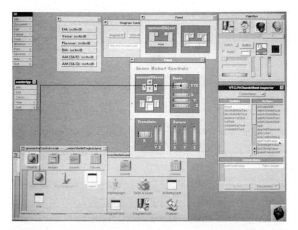

Figure 15.7. Some geometry controls for the BodyManager.

Goal agents, skill agents, sensor agents, and receptors are also manipulated graphically, and stored as an archive of objects. A given set of agents can be dragged to an **AgentManager**, which then unarchives the agents when it unarchives itself. This has the advantage that a single archive can be shared among multiple **AgentManagers**, corresponding to several different virtual actors, although in this example we only have one actor.

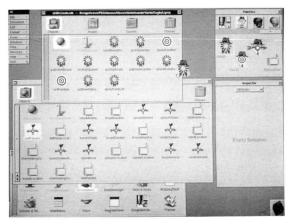

Figure 15.8. Adding a skill agent to an archive of skill and goal agents.

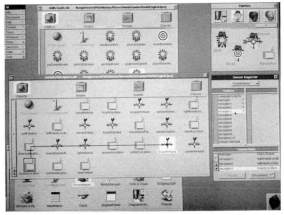

Figure 15.9. Connecting a sensor agent to one of its receptors.

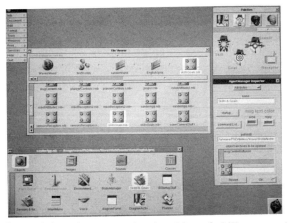

Figure 15.10. Dragging and dropping a completed archive of skills on an AgentManager's inspector.

The various agents are written in our message parsing language, which is an extended version of **tcl** (Ousterhout 1990). The agents can be directly manipulated inside of InterfaceBuilder via their inspector panel. For example, the inspector panel may include a slider which sets some value, and in the process generates or edits some **tcl** code which will be sent as a message and executed at runtime. In general, a given agent is only a few lines of code, as the underlying **AgentManager** should provide the facilities the agent needs to compute itself. Once the objects have been inspected and connected, the user can test the robot in its virtual environment. We use a NeXT machine as the interface host, and an SGI SkyWriter as a back-end graphics engine. We also use various computers scattered around the network to run some number of active objects which are not intimately tied to certain hardware resources (e.g. sound/image input/output). In order to test our sanderWorld, we select "test Interface" in InterfaceBuilder. This causes all of our active objects to be instantiated, at which point they load in all their object archives, which contain agents, receptors, and interface objects.

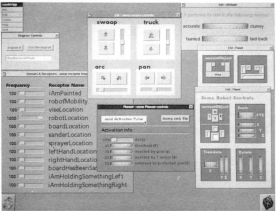

Figure 15.11. The user interface for SanderWorld.

By telling the planner to spread activation (by pressing the "send Activation pulse" button), our virtual actor eventually decides to pick up the sander, place the board in the vice, sand it, and then paint itself. As the robot makes up its mind, the various agents send messages to the **Voice** active object, telling it to say things (i.e. "I want the board sanded", "I picked up the sprayer", "I am painted", etc.). This multi-modal (the virtual environment is also being rendered in real-time on the SGI) output helps the developer debug the world being built.

We are also developing automatic graphing and layout objects which can help the developer visualize the various interconnections between agents and active objects. One difficulty in building and debugging VE systems is visualising running programs and understanding the information flow and connectivity between the component parts. The system of objects we're developing allows the developer to move at various levels of detail and abstraction. They can concern themselves with the hosts the active objects are running on, what agents are contained in which active objects, which agents are connected to which others, where activation is flowing, and so on. This is an ongoing area of development.

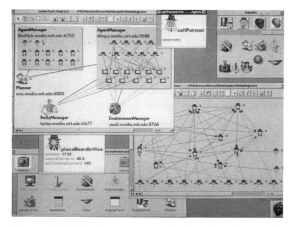

Figure 15.12.   Some network visualisation tools.

15.5 Task level programming and agents: motor goal parsing

Now that we have briefly described the process of constructing the virtual environment and virtual actors, we turn to the issues involved in interacting with synthetic humans. *Task level* interaction requires that virtual actors have the capability to respond to spoken or text-based input. Since we are not conducting research in natural language understanding *per se,* text-based or spoken input will necessarily need to be appropriately restricted to descriptions of mechanical operations on physical objects - akin to theatrical stage directions - that roughly correspond to the "activities of daily living" (ADLs), such as brushing one's teeth or making breakfast (Reed *et al.* 1992). In addition to responding to the typed or spoken utterances of human participants, a virtual actor should be capable of interpreting simple task protocols that describe, for example, maintenance and repair operations. Given a set of one or more motor goals - e.g., "Pick up the wrench and loosen the retaining bolts," or "Put the book on the desk in my office" - a virtual actor should be capable of generating the appropriate motor acts, including necessary and implicit motor subgoals.

Human tasks and actions, however, are remarkably difficult to categorize, quantify and specify (Badler and Webber 1991, Fleishman and Quaintance 1984, Reed *et al.* 1992). This is due, in part, to what has been dubbed the "accordion effect" - varying levels of intention and scope can be ascribed to any given act (Feinberg 1970). For example, at one and the same time it can be said that one is moving one's foot, putting on one's shoe, preparing to walk outdoors, or getting ready to go the theatre. In addition, complex activities like "making breakfast" are composed of component acts such as "make coffee" which are in turn composed of yet other behaviours - get the coffeepot, boil the water, get the coffee cups, and so on.

Jappinen implemented a reactive planning system for a simulated mobile robot in the late 1970s. His system made use of motion primitives in a methodology related to ours for matching actions and target objects (Jappinen 1979, Jappinen 1981, Jappinen 1984).

Schank and his colleagues developed Conceptual Dependency (CD) theory which served as the basis for a great deal of natural language understanding research. Our task primitives are based in part on CD theory. A good introduction to CD theory can be found in (Schank 1975).

Schwartz *et al.*, have developed an Action Coding System (ACS) system for precisely describing everyday human activities for clinical purposes (Reed *et al.* 1992, Schwartz *et al.* 1991). This is important in the treatment of patients who, either due to stroke or other trauma, have suffered injuries to the brain so that their motor performance is impaired. For example, a patient may perform common tasks out of order, such as putting on shoes before socks, or they may perform inappropriate acts, such as putting milk on their eggs instead of in the coffee. Consistent and unambiguous descriptions of these movements are helpful in diagnosis and treatment. We describe our use of ACS primitives below.

Finally, Agre has written extensively on representing everyday activities, and much of his work is similar in spirit to ours (Agre 1988). Unlike the work here, however, Agre focuses almost exclusively on planning mechanisms rather than the interaction of language and action.

In the remainder of this section, we discuss the need for multiple representations for motor acts. As reflected in Gibson's notion of *affordances* (Gibson 1977), an actor's motor behaviour is intimately bound to the world - virtual or physical, and we describe how affordances are modelled and used in our system. Finally, we describe the set of task primitives used by the motor goal parser (MGP).

Multiple representations of motor skills

The hierarchical structure of motor control systems (Gallistel 1980, Greene 1972) - ranging from "high-level" drives and motivations to the coordinated action of muscle groups, muscles and muscle fibres through which they are ultimately expressed - implies that different computations are involved at varying stages in the processing of voluntary motor behaviour. This has been nicely characterised by Saltzman in a hypothesised seven-level hierarchy of movement representation (Saltzman 1979). Briefly, to paraphrase Saltzman, the levels are:

1. **Conceptual**. The motor act is specified in terms of symbolically coded action units, e.g., "reach" for the cup, "grasp" it and "move" it across the table, and "place" it next to the butter dish.

2. **Environmental-space motion**. The relevant objects are located in the world coordinate system, and spatio-temporal trajectories are computed as needed.

3. **Effector**. The effector-system or systems, e.g., arm and hand, are selected for the task.

4. **Body-space motion**. Spatial relations among objects, effectors and trajectories are computed in a body-centered coordinate system.

5. **Joint motion.** Effector system joint angles for the given act are specified as functions of time, i.e., joint angles, velocities and accelerations are calculated.

6. **Joint torque.** The torques required at the effector system joints for the given motion are computed.

7. **Muscle.** The muscle forces required to generate the called-for joint torques are determined, and the muscle innervation need to produce these forces is calculated.

As defined in earlier work (Zeltzer 1983, Zeltzer and Johnson 1991), in our system, the interface agent that attends to user input is called the *task manager*. The first three levels of Saltzman's hierarchy - conceptual, environmental-space, and effector - are the domain of the task manager. Input to the task manager is in the form of constrained NL descriptions of a specific movement sequence called a *task description*, e.g., "Go to the door and open it." In *motor goal parsing* (MGP), the task manager must decompose each task description into a set of well-defined motor units - *task primitives* - that can be named and simulated. In this example, these primitives might include, "move_to(door)," "grasp(doorknob)," and "rotate(doorknob)." Thus we need to specify the set of task primitives that corresponds to the everyday activities we wish to simulate.

For two reasons, however, the mapping from these task primitives to specific motor skills cannot be one-to-one *a priori*, and the task primitives must be effector-independent at the conceptual level. First, a given motor goal, say, "Pick up the pencil," can be accomplished in various ways: one can pick up the pencil with either the left or right hand, one can grasp it with one's teeth, or in a pinch, shoes can be removed and the pencil can be grasped with one's toes. Many authors, starting with the Russian psychologist Bernstein, have commented on this problem of *motor equivalence* (Bernstein 1967). Second, the objects named in the task description may determine which skill or skills are necessary to accomplish the task. If, instead of "Go to the door," the command were "Go to the Smithsonian," we would expect the task manager to output a very different list of skills. Once the task primitives have been identified from the input task description, the task manager must consider the states of the virtual actor, the targeted objects, and ongoing events in the virtual world, and then determine the appropriate effector systems and motor skills to invoke. Therefore, the task primitives must constitute an *intermediate, effector-independent* representation which drives the selection of the underlying motor skills to be performed.

Motor skills incorporated into the skill network, operate at levels 4 and 5, body space motion and joint motion, and possibly level 6, joint torque, if a dynamic simulation is being performed. Currently, we do not control joint motion by simulating muscle contraction, as in level 7. Motor skills themselves are implemented by motor programs and local motor programs, as described in (Zeltzer 1982, Zeltzer 1983, Zeltzer and Johnson 1991). That is skill agents in the skill network must maintain pointers to appropriate procedures - motor programs - for executing the motions they represent.

Atomic skills and composite skills.

For a given virtual actor, we need to know what motor skills to implement, and we need to know what task primitives are required. Should "signing a check" be a task primitive? More likely, we would like to decompose check-signing into component acts - grasping the pen, grasping and moving the paper, moving the pen to trace out one's signature, and so on. Each of these component acts achieves a "concrete, functional result or transformation describable as the movement of an object from one place to another or as a change in the state of an object, (e.g., from open to closed, on to off ...)" (Schwartz *et al.* 1991).

Many ADLs can be described as composite actions consisting of some number of component acts that are identifiable as unitary operations on physical objects. Since these components cannot be further subdivided at a functional level, we will consider these effector-independent, functionally-defined, *atomic* skills to be the task primitives that must be extracted from task descriptions.

The notion of deriving underlying action primitives from informal behaviour descriptions can be found in early NL work by Schank (1975), as well as in recent research by clinicians and psychologists interested in developing a well-specified and psychologically valid system for consistently and unambiguously describing human movement (Reed *et al.* 1992, Schwartz *et al.* 1991). In the late 1970s, Jappinen designed and built a reactive planner for a simulated mobile robot which also used a set of action primitives (Jappinen 1979, 1981).

Schank's Conceptual Dependency (CD) theory incorporated a small set of primitive "ACTs", some of which describe physical actions, and some which describe abstract "mental actions" (Schank 1975). Those primitive ACTs that describe physical actions are in good agreement with the basic action units used by Reed and Schwartz, who describe an action coding system (ACS) based on four task primitives, the "A-1 action units" *give*, *take*, *move* and *state change* (Schwartz *et al.* 1991). They have demonstrated that naive subjects do in fact produce consistent descriptions of ADLs, e.g., making coffee, or brushing one's teeth, using ACS primitives.

Both the physical ACTs of CD theory, and the ACS "A-1s" of Reed and Schwartz satisfy our requirements for a small set of well-defined and effector-independent task primitives. It is especially interesting that ACS has been rather successfully evaluated with human subjects, since that strongly suggests that the task primitives actually correspond to the way people tend to verbally describe motor behaviour. The task primitives we use are based on ACTs and A-1 action units, and they are listed and discussed below.

While atomic skills serve as our task primitives, composite skills presumably represent behaviours that are learned. In our current work, the immediate objective is to model an adult human with a repertoire of developed motor skills. We are not attempting to model motor learning, although that will ultimately prove extremely useful, if not necessary, for constructing virtual actors. However, we feel that the motor planning architecture reported earlier (Zeltzer and Johnson 1991) can be extended in a principled way to account for certain kinds of motor learning.

Apparently humans construct composite skills, i.e., learn *routines* (Agre 1988), by remembering a sequence of actions that successfully satisfied some motor goal, or by being told or shown the appropriate sequence by some teacher. Badler and Webber at the University of Pennsylvania are currently pursuing natural language as a means of instructing virtual actors (Badler and Webber 1991). In addition, it is possible for a human user to demonstrate a skill to a virtual actor, since body tracking devices now make it possible to consider teaching a virtual actor by example. The difficult problem in this case is enabling the virtual actor to appropriately generalise from the given example (Cypher 1993, Ridsdale 1990).

For the time being, we will handle composite skills in two ways:

- Composite skills can be explicitly defined using a script-like mechanism to list the component skills and their sequence of execution.

- The virtual actor will ask for help when given a task description for which there are no corresponding motor skills or routines in its behaviour repertoire.

Affordances

The execution of motor skills is intimately bound to objects, events and other actors in the environment. Before an actor can "Pick up the cup," it must determine whether the cup is "pick-up-able." Is it too big or too small to grasp? Is it too heavy or too hot? Does it have a handle? That is, does the cup *afford* grasping, as Gibson puts it (Gibson 1977, Mace 1977)? The theory of affordances as proposed by Gibson holds that humans and animals *directly perceive* those properties of objects and their environment that are necessary pre-conditions for executing particular acts. For example, a surface affords walking if it is flat and level. Ecological psychologists, as those who follow Gibson's research program are known, have shown that apparently humans are quite good at estimating how much a surface can be inclined before they can no longer walk upon it (Kinsella-Shaw *et al.* 1992). This maximum slant angle was shown to be fairly constant across all subjects. Ecological psychologists would say that in order to make these judgements we perceive relationships among invariant properties of the visual (or auditory or haptic) field. Here we make no commitment with respect to the direct perception of affordances, but we will argue that the notion of affordances suggests the right approach for representing the commonsense knowledge that makes it possible for us to perform our everyday activities of moving through the world, manipulating objects and avoiding, for the most part, harmful encounters.

We could try to build a database of objects in the world, and for each object in the database, we might try to store the salient facts about its use and functionality. However, most objects can be used in a variety of ways for various purposes, and their functionality might change with changing circumstances. For example, one can certainly sit in a chair, but one can also stand on it to change a light bulb, use it like a table to hold objects, or throw it through a window to escape from a burning building. Is a chair "movable" when someone is sitting in it? Is a chair no longer "sit-able" when someone else is sitting in it? Since the simplified, simulated world Jappinen constructed consisted of a series of rooms with a few objects in each room, he was able to represent the objects in a taxonomy of equivalence classes, in which the classes roughly corresponded to affordances, e.g., "pick-up-able", "go-into-able", "movable" (Jappinen 1984).

Such a scheme, however, would quickly become unwieldy as the virtual world increased in scope and complexity. Norman estimates that there are 20000 "everyday things" to be attended to in our daily environment (Norman 1988), and Biederman puts the number closer to 30000 (1987). It is daunting to consider the task of representing 20-30000 objects - each with its own set of object properties, functional constraints and rules. Object-oriented class hierarchies offer certain efficiencies, but a fixed class hierarchy is inadequate since it is the intentions of the actors modulated by events and changing physical configurations that determine the functionality of objects. Due to multiple functionalities, a given object might belong to a number of possibly contradictory classes. New classes would need to be created as new functions were encountered for objects. Class membership in a dynamic world would be continually changing, e.g., a chair becomes "movable" or "not-movable" depending on whether or not it is occupied.

This is essentially a restatement of the "no-function-in-structure" principle of de Kleer and Brown which was developed in the course of their research on "qualitative physics" (Kleer and Brown 1984). Briefly, the principle states that when representing a device, one should take care not to encode descriptions of device behaviour with descriptions of the structure of the device. For example, a description of the mechanism of an electrical switch that includes the statement "when the switch is closed, electricity flows" is incorrect for switches connected in series. This principle leads us to conclude that we should carefully separate descriptions of the function and behaviour of objects from descriptions of their geometric and mechanical properties.

Where should this kind of behavioural and functional knowledge about objects be stored? Gibson suggests a solution: an affordance is "equally a fact of the environment and a fact of behaviour...that points both ways, to the environment and the observer" (Gibson 1977). When a virtual actor is given a command to "Pick up the cup," the task manager has access to representations of both the object, *cup*, and the motor act, *grasp*, which specifies what is to be done with the cup. At the time the act is determined, the intent and context for the act are known, so affordances should be stored with the task primitives. When *grasp* is invoked, the affordances attached to it specify the size, shape and weight of objects that can be grasped. No information specifying functionality need be attached to the cup itself; all we require are the physical and geometric properties of the object. In this way we place no *a priori* restrictive constraints on object functionality - we can pick up the *cup*, put coffee in it, stand on it if we have to, or throw it through the window. This will also allow us to deal with *motor equivalence* in an efficient and principled way. We can *pick up* objects in any number of ways to match the object and the behavioural context: with the fingers, with one hand, with two hands, with the teeth, or with other pairs of opposable body parts.

Task primitives

Jappinen's robot skills, the ACTs of Schank's CD theory and the A-1 units of ACS are all based in part on case grammars (Fillmore 1968, Samlowski 1976), which, in turn, are based on the notion that every verb phrase has a certain number of grammatical "slots" that get "filled in" by appropriate noun phrases and modifiers. For a transitive verb, for example, there are slots that specify the *agent* that is performing the action, the *object* of the action, the *instrument* that was used to perform the act, and possibly other descriptors that specify when and where the action took place. We note that one of the complicating features of natural language discourse is that quite often many of these slots are unfilled, and must be inferred by the listener. Schank's group expended considerable effort, in fact, on this process. However, since we are not focusing on NL understanding *per se*, we will restrict the discourse and assume that a more sophisticated NL processor may be added later. In any event, it is the case structures of our task primitives, along with the affordances, that enable the task manager to select the appropriate motor skills.

In the listing that follows, CD ACTs are capitalized, and ACT case assignments are the same as Schank's; all task primitives require instrumental case. The four cases we will use are:

- object: the thing that is acted upon,
- recipient: the receiver of an object as a result of an action,
- direction: the location toward which an action is directed, and
- instrumental: the object or action that is used to accomplish the given act.

The task primitives are:

- *reach-and-grasp* and its correlate, *reach-and-ungrasp*. The corresponding ACT is GRASP, and the A-1s are *take* and *give*. We explicitly combine reaching and grasping since experiments with human subjects have demonstrated that while reaching for objects, humans begin shaping the hand into grasping configurations that roughly match the shape of the target object (Klatzky *et al.* 1987, Pellegrino *et al.* 1989). Therefore, reaching and grasping together form an atomic skill, i.e., a task primitive. Both *reach-and-grasp* and *reach-and-ungrasp* take the objective and directional cases.

- PTRANS. The corresponding A-1 unit is *move*. PTRANS denotes the physical transport of an object from one location to another. Its cases are objective, instrumental and directive. The instrument will most often be reach-and-grasp or walk.

- PROPEL. The application of a force to an object. Its cases are objective and directive. The instrument will most often be the motion of a body part.

- ATRANS. Transfer of ownership, possession or control. As defined by Schank, ATRANS indicated a much more general transfer of an "abstract relationship", but here we restrict its meaning. It takes objective and recipient cases. The instrument is usually PTRANS.

- *alter*. This denotes causing an object to change state, e.g., from "closed" to "open". This is an A-1 action unit, but was not defined as an ACT in CD theory. It takes objective and instrumental cases.

- MOVE. Moving a body part. Its cases are objective and directive.

- INGEST and EXPEL mean to take something into the body or force something out. They take objective and directive cases.

- ATTEND. To focus a sense organ towards a stimulus. It takes objective and directive cases.

- SPEAK. To produce a sound. It takes objective and directive cases.

In addition to the cases, ACS prescribes a "manner" for each primitive, which is essentially a modifier. CD theory provides a similar mechanism, "action aiders", and we provide a like feature also.

We remind the reader that at this stage of our research, we are primarily interested in understanding how to represent nominal, commonplace and unaffected actions, and we are much less interested for the time being in capturing nuances of timing or expressiveness. In addition, neither the ACS A-1 action units nor the task primitives we have just described are intended here to support general NL understanding other than to transform a task description of mechanical operations on physical objects into a list of task primitives.

Motor Goal Parsing (MGP)

In this section we will consider the input sentence "Go to the kitchen and get me a beer," and step through the process of motor goal parsing. Briefly, we map input verb phrases to task primitives, and we need to fill in all the open case slots. For the objective and recipient cases, we need to identify appropriate objects and actors. For the directive slots we need to determine appropriate geometric information. The instrumental slots may be filled by other task primitives during the course of processing, but we are not done until all instrument slots are filled by specific motor skills. In this example, assume there is a single virtual actor, Dexter.

The input is first directed through the standard UNIX™ parsing tools, LEX (Lesk and Schmidt 1975) and YACC (Johnson 1975). MGP will output two conjoined acts - the context free grammar specified in YACC source maps "go" to PTRANS with "kitchen" filled in as the directive case, and "get" has been mapped to ATRANS, with "beer" in the object slot. The CD diagram for "go to the kitchen" looks roughly as follows:

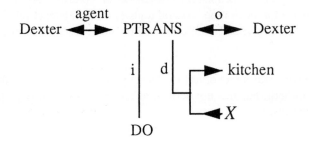

Dexter is both the agent and the object, i.e., he is to transport himself (PTRANS) from his (unspecified) current location to the "kitchen" (directive case). Following Schank, the instrument is filled in by a placeholder - "DO" - for an as yet unspecified motor skill.

The affordances attached to PTRANS are essentially a list of rules, if-then-else clauses that suggest motor skills or routines, based - among other things - on the computed distance from the starting and ending locations specified in the directive case slots. Since this instance of PTRANS denotes self motion, the task manager first must determine whether the kitchen affords walking. Here, the task manager simply consults the virtual world database of objects to determine the locations of both Dexter and the "kitchen". Once this information is filled in, the task manager can determine that the kitchen is indeed close enough, and the instrument slot can be filled by a pointer to the "walk" motor skill.

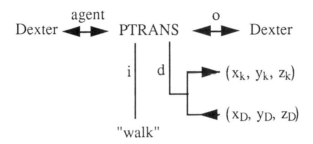

The motor goal (walk, x_k, y_k, z_k) can now be posted on the *blackboard* (Erman and Lesser 1975, Bolt *et al.* 1992) as a *protected goal*; and it will be passed to the skill network (as a *sensor*) when parsing is completed.

"Get me a beer" has been mapped to the ATRANS primitive, with the default instrument, PTRANS, filled in. It remains to fill in the instrument slot for PTRANS.

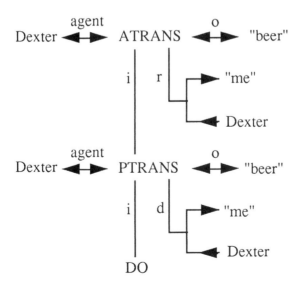

Since the object and agent are not the same, the task manager must determine whether or not the object affords *reach-and-grasp*-ing, which is the default motor skill for PTRANSing an object.

In general, the grasp may be accomplished by moving the fingers of either hand, by either the left or right hand, or by both hands acting in concert, depending on the affordances - the geometric and physical properties - of the target object. In principle, we could enumerate all the opposable parts of the body that may be used for grasping, since, in general, humans (and other prehensile primates) are rather ingenious at manipulating objects. However, in most routine situations, hands and fingers suffice, and as we have argued elsewhere, motor planning cannot accomplish general problem-solving (Zeltzer and Johnson 1991). Therefore, if none of the motor skills for routine grasping will work, either because both hands of the virtual actor have been pre-empted by other *protected* motor goals (i.e., we have already asked Dexter to use his hands for other tasks), or because the target object does not afford grasping, the appropriate course for the virtual actor will be to stop and ask the human for advice.

In this case, the target object does indeed afford one-hand grasping, and the instrument slot for this PTRANS can be filled in. We now have two motor goals that can be passed to the skill network. This is expressed by asserting that a sensor should detect that Dexter is walking to the kitchen, and another sensor should detect that Dexter is handing "me" a beer (Zeltzer and Johnson 1991).

In operation, these sensor data structures will propagate *activation energy* through the skill network, such that all those skills that have these goals as post-conditions (i.e., the goals will become true after the skill executes) will accumulate activation energy until they finally exceed their activation threshold and can execute (Zeltzer and Johnson 1991). Using its planning mechanisms, the skill network is able to generate the motor subgoals necessary to this task. After the first two goals are asserted, walk_to(kitchen) and reach-and-ungrasp("beer", to "me"), the following subgoals will be generated (comments are in brackets):

- reach-and-grasp("beer") [Dexter must have the "beer" in order to give it to "me"]
- walk_to(refrigerator) ["beer" is in the refrigerator, and Dexter must be near it to grasp it]
- alter(refrigerator,open) [open(refrigerator) is a pre-condition for grasping "beer"]
- walk_to("me") [Dexter must be near me to give me the "beer"]

15.6 Conclusions

We have presented our approaches to the twin problems of designing virtual environments and virtual actors, and interacting with them at the task level. *WavesWorld* is a development environment for designing, building and debugging distributed VEs and virtual actors, and it includes tools for assembling motor skills into a distributed and adaptive behaviour repertoire for a virtual actor.

We have described the representations we feel are necessary to transform descriptions of everyday activities into a series of motor goals that can be executed by the skill network. In order to account for *motor equivalence* and the *affordances* of objects in the environment, an effector-free set of *task primitives* must be defined and used as an intermediate representation in the parsing process. We have presented a set of task primitives from which composite motor actions can be assembled, and which can serve as the intermediate representation. And we have given a brief example showing how the task manager, the motor goal parsing process, and the skill network interact.

The task manager and MGP are currently being programmed in Objective-C on a NeXTstation. WavesWorld and the skill network have been implemented as a parallel, distributed system that currently runs on SUN, DEC, NeXT, Silicon Graphics, Thinking Machines and Kubota computers.

The challenges ahead of us include designing and implementing the affordance functions for each of the task primitives, and developing a motor skill modelling system that will provide a graphical programming interface for designing the individual motor skills for a virtual actor.

Acknowledgments

This work was supported in part by NHK (Japan Broadcasting Co.), the Office of Naval Research, DARPA/Rome Laboratories, and equipment gifts from Apple Computer, Hewlett-Packard, and Silicon Graphics.

References

Agre P.E. (1988). *The Dynamic Structure of Everyday Life.* AI-TR 1085, M.I.T. Cambridge MA.

Appino P.A. *et al..* (1992). An Architecture for Virtual Worlds. *Presence: Teleoperators and Virtual Environments,* 1(1), pp. 1-17.

Badler N.I. & Webber B.L. (1991). Animation from Instructions, in *Making Them Move: Mechanics, Control and Animation of Articulated Figures,* N. Badler, B. Barsky and D. Zeltzer, Morgan Kaufmann: San Mateo CA, pp. 51-93.

Bernstein N. (1967). *The Coordination and Regulation of Movements,* Pergamon Press: Oxford.

Biederman I. (1987). Recognition-by-Components: A Theory of Human Image Understanding. *Psychological Review,* 94, pp. 115-147.

Bolt, Baranek & Newman (1992). Virtual Environment and Teleoperators Research Consortium. Virtual Environment Technology for Training, *BBN Report No. 7661*

Brooks F.P. Jr. (1986a). Walkthrough: A Dynamic Graphics System for Simulating Virtual Buildings, in *Proc. 1986 ACM Workshop on Interactive 3D Graphics,* pp. 9-21.

Brooks R.A. (1986b). A Robust Layered Control System for a Mobile Robot. *IEEE Journal of Robotics and Automation,* RA-2(1), pp. 14-23.

Cypher A. (1993) ed. *Watch What I Do: Programming by Demonstration,* MIT Press: Cambridge MA.

Erman L.D. & Lesser V.R. (1975). A Multi-level Organization for Problem-solving Using Many Diverse Cooperating Sources of Knowledge, in *Proc. 4th International Joint Conf. on Artificial Intelligence,* pp. 483-490.

Feinberg J. (1970). *Doing and Deserving,* Princetown University Press: Princetown NJ.

Fillmore C.J. (1968). *The Case for Case,* in *Universals in Linguistic Theory,* E.B. & R.T. Harms, Holt, Rinehart and Winston: New York.

Fleishman E.A. & Quaintance M.K. (1984). *Taxonomies of Human Performance,* Academic Press: Orlando FL.

Ford L. (1985). Intelligent Computer Aided Instruction, in *Artificial Intelligence: Human Effects*, M.Y. & A. Narayanan, Wiley: Halsted Press: New York, pp. 106-120.

Gallistel C.R. (1980). *The Organization of Action: A New Synthesis*, Lawrence Erlbaum Associates: Hillsdale NJ.

Gibson J.J. (1977). *The Theory of Affordances, in Perceiving, Acting, and Knowing: Toward an Ecological Psychology*, R. Shaw and J. Bransford, Lawrence Erlbaum Associates: Hillsdale NJ, pp. 67-82.

Greene P.H. (1972). Problems or Organization of Motor Systems. *Progress in Theoretical Biology*, 2303-338.

Hirose M., Myoi T., Liu A., & Stark L. (1990). Object Manipulation in Virtual Environments, in 6th *Symposium on Human Interface*, Tokyo, pp. 571-557.

Jappinen H.J. (1984). A Model for Representing and Invoking Robot Bodily Skills, in *Advanced Software in Robotics*, A.D. & M. Geradin, North-Holland: Amsterdam, pp. 333-342.

Jappinen H.J. (1979). *A Perspective-based Developmental Skill Acquistion System*, Ph.D. Thesis, The Ohio State University.

Jappinen H.J. (1981). Sense-controlled Flexible Robot Behaviour, *International Journal of Computer and Information Sciences*, 10(2), pp. 105-125.

Johnson M. (1991). *Build-a-Dude: Action Selection Networks for Computational Autonomous Agents*, M.S. Thesis, Massachusetts Institute of Technology.

Johnson S.C. (1975). Yacc: Yet Another Compiler Compiler, *Computing Science Technical Report No. 32*, Bell Laboratories: Murray Hill NJ.

Kim W.S., Liu A., Matsunaga K. & Start L. (1988). A Helmet Mounted Display for Telerobotics, in *Proc. IEEE COMPCON*, San Fransisco CA.

Kinsella-Shaw J.M., Shaw B. & Turvey M.T. (1992). Perceiving "Walk-on-able" Slopes. *Ecological Psychology*, 4(4), pp. 223-239.

Klatzky R.L., McCloskey B., Doherty S., Pellegrino J. & Smith T. (1987). Knowledge about Hand Shaping and Knowledge about Objects. *Journal of Motor Behaviour*, 19(2), pp. 187-213.

Kleer J.D. & Brown J.S. (1984). A Quantitative Physics Based on Confluences. *Artificial Intelligence*, 24(1-3), pp. 7-83.

Lesk M.E. & Schmidt E. (1975). Lex: A Lexical Analyzer Generator, *Computing Science Technical Report No. 39*, Bell Laboratories: Murray Hill NJ.

Mace W.M. (1977). James J. Gibson's Strategy for Perceiving: Ask Not What's Inside Your Head, but What Your Head's Inside Of, in *Perceiving, Acting and Knowledge: Toward Ecological Psychology*, R. Shaw and J Bransford, Lawrence Erlbaum Associates: Hillsdale NJ, pp. 43-65.

Maes P. (1989). How To Do the Right Thing, *A.I. Memo 1180*, Massachusetts Institute of Technology: Cambridge MA.

Maes P. (1990). Situated Agents Can Have Goals. *Journal of Robotics and Autonomous Systems*, 6(1&2), pp. 49-70.

Norman D.A. (1988). *The Psychology of Everyday Things*, Basic Books: New York.

Ousterhout J.K. (1990). Tcl: An Embeddable Command Language, in *Proc. 1990 Winter USENIX Conference*.

Pellegrino J.W., Klatzky R.L. & McCloskey B.P. (1989). Timecourse of Preshaping for Functional Responses to Objects. *Journal of Motor Behaviour*, 21(3), pp. 307-331.

Pieper S. (1991). *CAPS: Computer-aided Plastic Surgery*, Ph.D. Thesis, Massachusetts Institute of Technology.

Pieper S., Rosen J. & Zeltzer D. (1992). Interactive Graphics for Plastic Surgery: A Task-Level Analysis and Implementation, in *Proc. 1992, ACM Press*: Cambridge MA, pp. 127-134.

Reed E.S., Montgomery M., Schwartz M., Palmer C. & Pittenger J.B. (1992). Visually Based Descriptions of Everyday Action. *Ecological Psychology*, 4(3), pp. 129-152.

Ridsdale G. (1990). Connectionist Modelling of Skill Dynamics. *Journal of Visualization and Computer Animation*, 1(2), pp. 66-72.

Saltzman E. (1979). Levels of Sensorimotor Representation. *Journal of Mathematical Psychology*, 20(2), pp. 91-163.

Samlowski W. (1976). *Case Grammar, in Computational Semantics,* E.C. & Y. Wilks, North-Holland Publishing Co.

Schank R.C. (1975). *Conceptual Information Processing,* American Elsevier Publishing Company: New York.

Schwartz M.F., Reed E.S., Montgomery M., Palmer C. & Mayer N.H. (1991). The Quantative Description of Action Disorganization after Brain Damage: A Case Study. *Cognitive Neuropsychology,* 8(5), pp. 381-414.

Zeltzer D. (1982). Motor Control Techniques for Figure Animation. *IEEE Computer Graphics and Applications,* 2(9), pp. 53-59.

Zeltzer D. (1983). Knowledge-based Animation, in *Proc. ACM SIGGRAPH/SIGART Workshop on Motion,* pp. 187-192.

Zeltzer D., Pieper S. & Sturman D. (1989). An Integrated Graphical Simulation Platform, in *Proc. Graphics Interface '89,* pp. 266-274.

Zeltzer D. & Johnson M. (1991). Motor Planning: Specifying and Controlling the Behaviour of Autonomous Animated Agents. *Journal of Visualization and Computer Animation,* 2(2), pp. 74-80.

Zeltzer D. (1992a). Autonomy, Interaction and Presence. *Presence: Teleoperators and Virtual Environments,* 1(1), pp. 127-132.

Zeltzer D. & Drucker S. (1992b). A Virtual Environment System for Mission Planning, in *Proc. 1992 IMAGE VI Conference,* Phoenix AZ, pp. 125-134.

Zeltzer D. (1992c). Human Figure Modeling for Virtual Environment Applications, in *Proc. IEEE International Workshop on Robot and Human Communication,* Tokyo, pp. 117-122.

Zyda M.J., Pratt D.R., Monahan J.G. & Wilson K.P. (1992). NPSNET: Constructing a 3D Virtual World, in *Proc. 1992 Symposium on Interactive 3D Graphics,* ACM Press: Cambridge MA, pp. 147-150.

16

Flying in Virtual Worlds

John Vince

16.1 Introduction

Flight simulators are central to today's military and civilian aviation industries, and without them it is difficult to imagine how pilots could acquire the necessary flying skills needed to control the sophisticated machines modern aircraft have become. A simulator provides a safe environment where a pilot can experience an aircraft's behaviour under a wide range of flying conditions. Primarily it is a training system, but it also provides a useful environment for assessing a professional pilot's skills. Plate 32 shows a full-flight simulator for a Boeing 757-200 aircraft.

A flight simulator provides a real-time environment where computer-generated images provide the visual feedback to a pilot as he or she adjusts the flight controls of a simulated plane. The real-time nature of the image generation provides a closed loop system where the pilot is able to interact with the images without any unnatural delays. Although the pilot extracts valuable cues from the images such as position, speed and heading, there can be no personal interaction with them. However, the relative position of the simulator within the virtual 3-D world held in the image generator (IG) does automatically activate various features. Similarly, the training instructor, who is ultimately in control of the simulator, can interact at many levels during the simulation exercise. Such levels of interaction call for high-performance computer systems and image generators, real-time interactive interfaces, and special 3-D modelling strategies.

Accuracy and realism are vital to every aspect of a simulator, which applies to the equations used to simulate an aeroplane's dynamics whilst it is taxiing and flying, the electro-mechanical cockpit controls, the motion of the simulator platform, and the computer-generated images used for creating the virtual airport. If any of these elements fails to accurately simulate their real-world counterparts, the simulator's training role is completely undermined (Scans and Barns 79). Furthermore, one has only to consider the exacting task of simulating taxiing aircraft (Hogg *et al.* 1992) to appreciate the digital complexity of a full flight simulator.

Interacting with Virtual Environments Edited by Lindsay MacDonald and John Vince

The interaction between pilot and plane must occur in real-time, which implies that fast computer systems are employed to compute the parameters driving the cockpit's instrumentation (Burgin 1992). Typically, such data are evaluated at a rate between 15 and 30 Hz. The motion system must also be able to respond in real-time to provide the inertial cues that are vital in simulating the dynamics of the aeroplane, which calls for powerful hydraulic pumps to drive the platform rams (Boothe 1992).

With many types of control systems delays arise through mechanical mechanisms and signal propagation. These also occur in simulation systems, but further delays are introduced by the digital simulation elements. In most cases, these delays are insignificant and in no way interfere with the simulation process. However, the success of a flight simulator does rely upon the synchronous behaviour of the entire system.

As mentioned above, image interaction occurs at two levels: the first is with the training instructor, and is at a personal level; the second is with the virtual plane, and is at a system level. These two modes of interaction are now described in further detail.

16.2   The role of the training instructor

Commercial training instructors are, in general, retired or in-service Line Pilots, and the latter, only instruct in the simulator perhaps once or twice a month; consequently, great attention is given to the design of the instructor station to make it easy to use, and not require excessive familiarisation periods.

The simulator provides a safe environment where an instructor can teach and check other pilots on manoeuvres that would be expensive or dangerous if performed in real aircraft. Pilot examination is performed on behalf of the relevant regulatory authorities, and a typical airline pilot spends less than 18% of his or her total simulator exposure being taught, and more than 82% under "check" conditions (Hall 1992).

A typical simulator mission might include a crew briefing followed by a Captain's Checkride and a First Officer's Checkride. The Checkrides begin with crew preparation followed by events such as taxiing, rejected take-off, take off, or take-off with engine failure, climb, airways routing, instrument landing system procedures, go-round, manual approach, manual approach with one engine in-operative, and landing. These are followed by a debriefing session.

The instructor is seated at the rear of the simulator cockpit where he or she can observe the actions of the crew, and see the computer-generated images through the cockpit windows. The off-board real-time computers used for simulating the plane's dynamics, instrumentation, and the 3-D virtual environment, are interfaced to the simulator via the instructor's station. This is used by the instructor to control the status of every parameter used in the simulation process; such parameters include: wind speed, visibility, time of day, weight of fuel, and mechanical failures.

When the instructor has input a training exercise using the workstation, the crew follow the exercise as if they were in a real plane. Every move they make is monitored by the instructor, who, at any stage, can interrupt them and comment upon their actions. But perhaps the most effective aspect of this training scenario is the level of interaction that takes place at the instructor's station.

16.3 The instructor's station

The instructor's station is located at the rear of the cockpit and consists of two CRTs fitted with touch screens. One CRT is used to display the interactive menus controlling the simulator, whilst the other displays a graphical plan view of the simulated craft in relation to the airport or world environment. Plate 33 is a photograph taken inside the simulator cockpit.

A hierarchical menu system enables the instructor to move through the menus in an arbitrary sequence, or through a pre-selected traversal that ensures that a training session can be prepared in a logical sequence. Colour coding of menu buttons and icons reflect the status of available options, and simply by touching relevant parts of the screen, the instructor can rapidly browse through other menus before altering various system parameters.

The menu layouts have a consistent design for ease of use and rapid working, and will also incorporate graphics where relevant. For example, Figure 16.1 shows a typical text-based menu used for system malfunctions, whereas Figure 16.2 introduces simple graphics and icons to control the visual status of the airfield's lighting. Similarly, another menu is available to control airport ground services, and just by touching different parts of the screen the status of a passenger door can be set open; external power can be left connected, or the gross weight suddenly changed. By altering these parameters without the knowledge of the crew, the instructor can monitor their behaviour, and discover how they react to potentially dangerous scenarios.

Apart from controlling the status of the simulated plane, the instructor can also interact with the parameters associated with the virtual environment, which consists of an airport, the surrounding terrain, and the prevailing weather conditions. For example, before a training session begins, the instructor first selects the airport to be used. The runway conditions can be set to a variety of states such as: dry, wet, wet patches, flooded, snow, slush, icy and patchy ice, which influence the friction parameter used to model the craft's dynamics when taxiing, taking off and landing. Different weather conditions can be selected to control visibility at ground level, airborne visibility and cloud ceiling height. Runway lights can be given different intensities, and the time of the day adjusted to represent day, dusk, and night time.

A familiar simulation exercise involving airports with two runways is to set all the runway landing lights with a common intensity and instruct the pilot to land on one of the runways. Then, unbeknown to the pilot, the intensity of the landing lights on the second runway are increased; the crew is then monitored to see whether this visual cue attracts them to the wrong runway.

Interactive menus provide the instructor with the ability to activate moving features of the database such as ground vehicles and other aircraft. These can be pre-set to interfere with the simulated craft at particular times during a training session, or activated by the instructor on an *ad hoc* basis by touching the relevant icon. Even during the simulated "push back" mode when an aircraft is pushed away from a terminal building to a taxiing position, the crew can be given conflicting information. Even though they have been told that after being pushed backwards they will be left facing west, one touch of the screen by the instructor is sufficient to leave the plane facing in the opposite direction. The crew must recognise these mistakes and know how to recover from such situations.

Although it is possible to interactively control the status of the simulator during a training session, a common practice is to structure the session using a script of events. This consists of a continuous sequence of tasks such as: obtaining clearance for take off, taxiing to a selected runway, taking off, flying to a designated location, obtaining permission to land, and taxiing to a docking point.

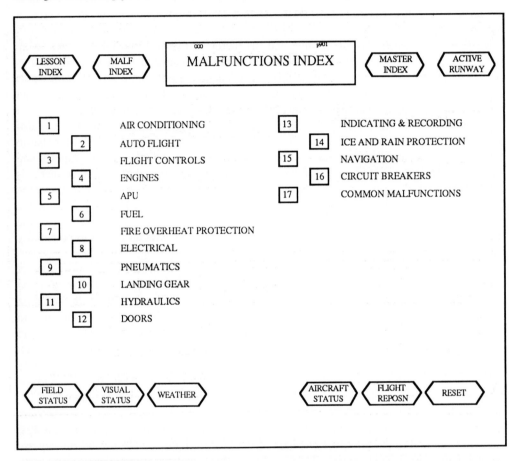

Figure 16.1. A text-based menu, activated via a touch screen.

However, as all of these operational phases are subject to potential dangers, a script can be used to organise them in a sequence and represented graphically upon the instructor's station. This simulated journey is shown as a graph depicting the plane's height at different journey times, with the hazardous events overlaid as menu buttons. During the simulation exercise, the instructor can activate any of the hazards simply by touching the relevant menu button. These events can even be triggered automatically by the elapsed time, flying above or below a given height, or any logical combination of these with other simulated parameters.

Finally, the instructor has the ability to record the status of the simulator during a simulation exercise, and replay its actions back to the training crew. Once more, the touch screen and hierarchical menus provides instantaneous interaction with the simulated craft, and an ideal environment for communicating new skills and observing flying behaviour.

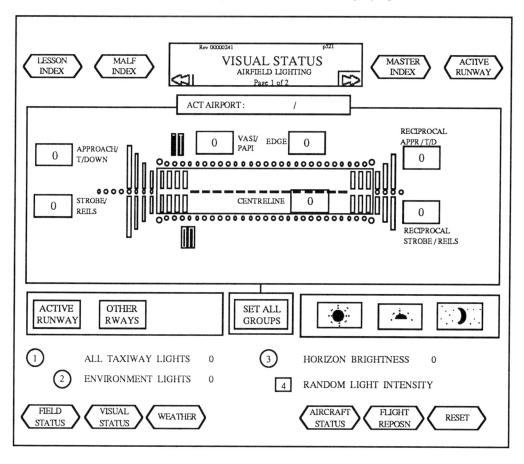

Figure 16.2. A text and icon-based menu, activated via a touch screen

16.4 The 3-D virtual environment

Simulators built in the 1970s relied upon rigid model boards and closed-circuit video cameras to generate the images projected into the simulator cockpit (Rolfe 1986). The model board was a scale model of a generic airport and its surrounding terrain. The model was traversed by a small video camera whose position was determined by the position and heading parameters computed by the central computer. Thus as the pilot manoeuvred away from a terminal building, the camera duplicated the same movement over the scale model, and the pictures were relayed back to monitors mounted on the cockpit windows.

This physical approach to image creation had various advantages and disadvantages; the main advantages were as follows: there was no real limit to the scene complexity, as the model could include houses, hotels, roads, people, traffic, trees, terminal buildings and radar towers - in fact everything one normally associates with a real airport. When illuminated, the model was richly decorated with shadows; surfaces were textured, trees had leaves, and even realistic lights could be fixed to the airport runways.

Unfortunately, there were disadvantages that became increasingly important as the benefits of computer graphics were realised. For example, the model was static - not one feature moved. It was impossible to show another aeroplane landing or taking-off, or even taxiing along a runway. It was impossible to introduce weather effects such as fog, cloud cover, rain, snow, scud and lightning. In fact, because of the model's physical construction, there was no natural mechanism for interactivity, which imposed severe limitations on its use. The model was also physically large and required large levels of illumination.

In the early 1980s the flight simulation industry embraced the technology of real-time IGs. Early systems were only capable of creating primitive images in comparison to the rich detail associated with the rigid model boards. However, the virtual nature of the 3-D digital model quickly revealed the benefits of computer-generated images, and in particular, the modes of interaction that became possible.

Simultaneously with these developments, display technology evolved by moving away from cockpit-mounted monitors to collimated panoramic mirrors. Figure 16.3 shows a schematic of a panoramic display system, where one can identify three projectors on top of the simulator that form a panoramic image upon a translucent back-projection screen. Inside the cockpit one sees a reflection of this image, and because it is collimated, it appears to be located a considerable distance beyond the physical boundary of the simulator. This means that the pilot and co-pilot share a common source of images, whereas with monitor-based systems, each pilot gazes at their own monitor screen, which is a poor substitute for the way the outside world is seen in a real aeroplane.

Nowadays, a single channel IG is capable of rendering a colour scene containing 1000 polygons and 5000 light points at 50 Hz. But as a typical system involves three channels, the scene complexity increases to 3000 polygons and 15000 light points. These figures apply to bright daylight scenes, but for dusk and night scenes, where the level of illumination is much lower, a lower frame update rate of 30 Hz enables 1000 polygons and 15000 light points to be displayed per channel (Vince 1992).

High-performance IGs extend these specifications considerably. For example, the polygon count can be increased to 10000 polygons per channel. Such systems are capable of rendering highly detailed scenes that incorporate real-world satellite and aerial images.

Perhaps the one element that introduces the largest transport delay is found in the display system. This is introduced by the way the computer-generated images are created: typically, this delay is in the order of 60 msec. The pipeline architecture employed in most image generators introduces this delay in three components: the first time slice is needed to prepare the geometric database potentially visible to the pilot; the second time slice creates the perspective projection on this data, and the third slice is used to render a coloured image (Foley *et al.* 1990). If the frame update rate of the image generator is 50 Hz, approximately 60 msec elapses between the start of the first time slice and the end of the third.

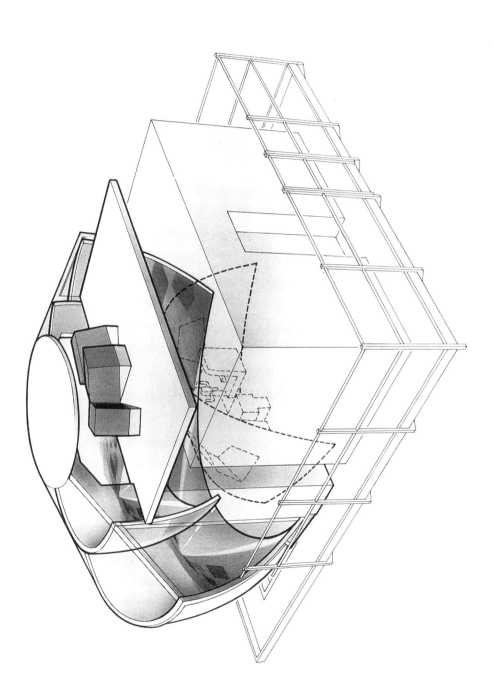

Figure 16.3. This drawing identifies the three calligraphic projectors mounted above the cockpit; the translucent back-projection screen, and the panoramic spherical mirror that provides a collimated image inside the cockpit.   (Courtesy of Hughes Rediffusion Simulation Ltd).

16.5 Interacting with the images

The digital nature of the database and the real-time capacity of the IG means that it is possible to interact with the images in a variety of ways. To begin with, the position and heading parameters supplied by the central computer can be input to the IG to control the perspective view made of the database. As these parameters may be computed at 30 Hz, the IG can interpolate them to identify intermediate values to match its internal frame update rate. The view seen from this position is then computed and rendered and projected into the cockpit after a slight IG transport delay. At this level one has only replaced a physical model board by a virtual 3-D database, however, the real-time channels into the IG permit an unusal range of "on-the-fly" modifications to occur.

Weather effects

Landing and take-off manoeuvres are reasonably difficult without the extra hazards introduced by bad weather conditions. However, such natural phenomena are hazards with which pilots must cope. Fog is particulary dangerous, especially when it is non-homogeneous, and it must be accurately simulated if pilots are going to learn anything from simulator training. Digital fog models provide control over the visibility range which may vary from a few miles where ground haze restricts the viewing range, down to a few tens of feet where pilots must cope with scene detail that suddenly appears with frightening speed. Research still continues into this area to create fog models that have horizontal as well as vertical density structures (Willis 1987).

Rain and snow effects can also be simulated. For example, during the approach to an airport, rain can be simulated by randomly "washing out" parts of the image to create the impression of flying through patchy rain cloud; the projectors can also be slightly defocused to smear the image, especially any light points being displayed. In the case of snow storms, snow flakes are simulated by several thousand light points that fall along random trajectories, and as the plane's speed alters, the familiar sensation of driving through snow is automatically created.

During model building the modeller will identify a range of textures that can be mapped onto certain surfaces. For instance, a concrete runway may be shown with the tyre marks where other aeroplanes have landed, but the Training Captain may also select a runway covered in rain or snow. For extra realism, drifting snow can be shown to blow across the runway by dynamically moving the texture map over the model's surface.

Time of day illumination

The position of the sun is another interactive feature of image generation that increases realism, and some IGs are capable of rendering images based upon this datum. Consequently, when a pilot spends one or two hours in a simulator to rehearse an actual time take-off and landing scenario, the sun's position can be used to modulate the scene brightness from a dusk to night condition that can include a sunset in the form of a horizon glow. Plate 34 shows an airport rendered to simulate daytime and even includes shadows formed by an overhead sun. However, these shadows cannot be computed in real-time, but are introduced as a shadow polygon that remain fixed for buildings, and move over the ground for planes.

At the other extreme, an instantaneous switch can be made from day mode to night mode where light points play an important feature in the images. Although bright light points introduce some valuable visual cues, they can cause problems when displayed upon a raster-based projection system. To overcome the possibility of introducing aliasing artefacts, the light point data is separated from the raster data within the IG and displayed by a calligraphic projector (Elmer 1982) which interleaves raster fields with high-resolution calligraphically drawn light points. Plate 35 shows an airport scene rendered at dusktime and incorporates light points and luminous polygons.

Time of year textures

As a variety of texture maps can be assigned to various model surfaces, the Training Captain can interactively select a family of maps that can simulate different times of the year. This suggests that spring, summer, autumn and winter are all possible to simulate, however, in practice, it is only necessary to include a generic summer and winter set of textures. Plate 36 shows a winter scene where a helicopter is flying low over a landscape decorated with trees modelled from photo-textures. Note that each tree has its own shadow footprint which is also a texture map.

Collision detection

Accidental collisions between camera and the rigid model were a common occurrence on early simulators, but the move from the real into the virtual domain meant that collision detection had to be computed. Collision between the simulated craft and various features of the model are vital parameters if the flight simulator is going to serve any real function. In practice, the tip of an aeroplane's wing or a helicopter's rotor touching a building or another craft could cause a major disaster, and it is vital that such potential strikes or "near misses" are detected in the simulator.

Although it is rare to have two civilian aeroplanes collide whilst flying, "near misses" do occur with some regularity. The simulator provides an ideal place to rehearse such scenarios and can be introduced without the crew's knowledge; the Captain simply programs another craft to fly towards the pilot, and then monitors the pilot's behaviour to see if and when the potential collision is detected.

Accurately computing this type of interaction between craft and environment would be difficult in real-time without involving extra processing power, however, an IG is capable of reporting on the distance between points on the simulated craft and predefined objects in the database. When collisions occur, the simulator can be programmed to behave in various ways, and the Training Captain then has to decide what action to take.

The "height above terrain" parameter is another simulator feature whereby the height above the virtual terrain surface or above database features is automatically monitored; obviously, this is vital when airports are located in mountainous regions.

Visual level of detail

Some databases extend for several hundred square miles which can mean that a pilot's field of view, especially when flying high, is capable of covering a large portion of the database. One automatic strategy that is used to minimize the number of visible polygons is to model features of the database at different levels of detail (Schachter 1983). For example, a terminal building when viewed close up will include all the fine detail that gives it a sufficient level of realism. However, a second model, and perhaps a third, are included in the database when seen at a distance. The IG will automatically select the relevant model as the range between the pilot and the database changes. This is a useful form of interaction and will probably have to become a standard feature of virtual environment systems, especially when using large detailed databases.

An alternative strategy to controlling visual level of detail is found in some IGs where specified surfaces are automatically divided into smaller facets as the range between the ownship (the simulated aeroplane) and the model reaches a critical range. As this distance continues to reduce, vertex positions move, which enables, for example, roof structures to evolve from an original simple flat roof.

16.6 Animation effects

The three main functions of an IG are to identify the portion of the database visible to the pilot, perform a perspective projection after rejecting back-facing surfaces, and render a colour image. To achieve this in real-time, dedicated hardware is required rather than a general-purpose computer. Fortunately, most of the database never moves. For example, runways, terminal buildings, lights, hotels, highways and mountains are fixed elements. However, the very nature of image interaction requires that the database is modified, but to minimise extra computation, the IG restricts the modeller to certain effects.

In the case of another aeroplane landing on a runway, a predefined flight path is prepared, along which the second model is flown. For realism, the flight path is created by flying the simulator in this landing scenario, which permits the IG to record its position and heading parameters that incorporate the flight dynamics of the simulated craft. This pre-processing of data removes the need to compute 3-D flight dynamics in real-time, but it also prevents the simulated aeroplane from interacting with the second aeroplane. For example, if the pilot manoeuvred the simulator onto the runway whilst the second aeroplane was landing, a virtual collision would occur, but the other aeroplane would simply "pass through" the simulator.

Objects that are moved by the IG are known as dynamic coordinate systems (DCSs) and some IGs have the capacity to control up to 4000. In general, DCSs are used to represent other planes, but are also used to animate helicopters, ships, submarines and airport ground vehicles.

Other animation effects, such as a retracting or opening undercarriage, are achieved by storing those parts of the database in its different orientations; this relieves the IG from having to perform unncessary matrix operations. Thus when the animation effect is invoked, the IG automatically cycles through the list of model elements, and renders them into a continuous sequence.

16.7 Lights

Light points play an important part in simulating the reality of airport landscapes, and are frequently separated from the standard polygonal geometry used for model building. When displayed upon a raster-based display system, their small physical dimensions, can cause annoying spatial aliasing. However, special raster/calligraphic projectors can be employed to prevent this from happening, which requires that the IG is capable of supplying two separate outputs for raster and calligraphic data.

Runway lights

Apart from the thousands of lights that delimit different zones of an airport, pilots rely upon the directional information provided by strobe and VASI (Visual Approach Slope Indicator) landing lights. The strobe lights identify the final ground approach to the runway by activating the lights individually in rapid succession to create a linear "strobing" effect. VASI landing lights change in colour depending upon the viewing angle; consequently, a pilot can discover whether the final runway approach is being made too high or low. In order to simulate these effects the IG must monitor the angle the simulator makes with the VASI lights, and make corresponding changes to their colour and intensity. In a further attempt to increase realism, the brightness of the runway lights can be randomly controlled to simulate the intensity distribution caused by dirt, age and malfunction.

Landing lights

An aeroplane's landing lights are vital to runway illumination especially when landing in poor visibility. Computing such effects realistically is a problem in off-line rendering, nevertheless, an IG is capable of computing such illumination footprints in real time. This degree of interaction between simulator, model, pilot and images highlights the real effectiveness of using flight simulators for training purposes.

Vehicle lights

As mentioned above, attention to detail permeates every feature of a flight simulator, and in building the virtual 3-D model there is a creative drive to include features of the real world that will subconciously influence a pilot to accept the IG's images as a realistic substitute. One such feature is found in the simulation of traffic moving along highways, especially at night time when white headlights and red taillights are moving in opposite directions. The IG can simulate this effect by moving strings of lights along paths defined by the modeller. When the light points reach the end of their path they are automatically recycled. Naturally, the relative orientation between the pilot's gaze and the traffic's direction determines whether the light points are displayed as red or white.

Docking aids

Docking aids are another example where the pilot is able to interact with the images and obtain accurate geometric information concerning the relative position of the simulated aeroplane and the terminal building. A docking aid provides the pilot with a visual cue as the aeroplane approaches its final docking position. It is a simple display system mounted on the docking structure at cockpit height, and the pilot positions the aeroplane such that two separate lines beome vertically aligned. An approach to the left, or to the right, results in the lines changing colour and becoming misaligned. Once more, the modeller can exploit charactersitics of the IG to simulate this device.

16.8 Conclusions

Real-time image generation is only just starting to impact upon the way we interact with images. In simulation, real-time image generation has been a vital feature of flight simulators for over a decade, and there exists a wide body of knowledge supporting all aspects of its use. However, during this period the technology associated with image generators has undergone dramatic changes in terms of size, speed, complexity, cost and realism. These changes are still occurring and the next ten years will see even more radical developments in machine architecture, graphic performance and modelling strategies.

With the arrival of multi-processor systems there seems to be a possibility for the "soft" IG, where instead of employing dedicated hardware, which has a relatively short lifetime, software may be capable of emulating all the functions that hitherto have been undertaken in hardware. Hopefully, this will enable new modelling and rendering effects to be incorporated as and when they appear, rather than waiting for the next IG to arrive.

Currently, databases are constructed from the ubiquitous polygon, which imposes severe limitations on the realism of the final image. Planar surfaces are not a natural feature of the real world, and eventually we will have to be able to build a database from free-form surfaces. Perhaps it will be possible to develop models that automatically alter their level of detail depending upon the viewing distance.

Increased image realism will evolve hand-in-hand with computer performance, and with processor speeds doubling every year, it will become possible to simulate highly complex dynamic systems in real-time and observe their results graphically. Together with higher resolution display systems the flight simulator of tomorrow is destined to be a highly sophisticated training system.

References

Boothe E.M., (1992). A Case for Simulator Motion Standards, RAeS Conf. *European Forum on Matching Technology to Training Requirements*, pp. 14.1-14.9.

Burgin P., (1992). Simulator Computer Systems - Technology for the 1990s, RAeS Conf. *European Forum on Matching Technology to Training Requirements*, pp. 2.1-2.7.

Elmer S.J., (1982). A Colour Calligraphic CRT Projector for Flight Simulation, Proc. *SID*, pp. 151-157.

Foley J., Van Dam A., Feiner S. & Hughes J., (1990). *Computer Graphics: Principles and Practice*, 2nd Edn., Addison-Wesley, Reading, MA.

Hall G.E., (1992). The Civilian Simulator - A User's Guide, RAeS Conf. *European Forum on Matching Technology to Training Requirements*, pp. 5.1-5.8.

Hogg C., Self A., Pearce D. & Kapadoukas G., (1992). The Simulation of Taxiing Aircraft, *European Forum on Matching Technology to Training Requirements*, pp. 13.1-13.20.

Rolfe J.M. and Staples K.J. (eds), (1986). *Flight Simulation*, Cambridge University Press.

Scans N.S. & Barns A.G., (1979). Fifty Years of Success and Failure in Flight Simulation, *Fifty Years of Flight Simulation*, Royal Aeronautical Society, London.

Schachter B.J., (1983). *Computer Image Generation*, John Wiley, London.

Vince J.A., (1992). How Real can a Real-time World Be?, *European Simulation Multiconference*, pp. 3-20.

Willis P.J., (1987). Visual Simulation of Atmospheric Haze, *Computer Graphics*, Proc. SIGGRAPH, Vol. 6, No. 1, pp. 35-41.

17

Interacting with Art-ificial Life

Stephen Todd and William Latham

17.1 Abstract

This paper describes the use of life-based rules for the generation of animated surreal art. Rules controlled by the artist define the form of the individual sculptures and how they are coloured and textured. Mutator, an interface based on natural selection, then assists the artist to select preferred sculptures. The film "Mutations" uses these sculptures as actors in an animation. The animation is driven by rules that depict the ideas of parenthood, birth, maturation and decay, and control the timings of these processes.

All the rules are based on concepts of life, but modified and controlled by the artist to express his imagination: the rules use biological inspiration but do not perform biological modelling. The natural basis of the rules gives the works an organic realism, and the artist's imagination imposes a surrealist feel.

The application of rules by the computer removes much labour from the production of works of art, so using the computer as artist's assistant permits the creation of works previously impractical. Beyond that, application of the rules often produces artistic results beyond the artist's expectation and imagination, and so the computer becomes the artist's creative partner.

17.2 Introduction

Life is always a topic that fascinates peoples' scientific and artistic imaginations. Mathematics, though arguably not so important in biology as in physics and chemistry, plays an important role in formalising an understanding of the way life works. To a scientist, understanding life may be an end in itself, but an artist applies this understanding to the production of effective works of art.

Computer technology adds a new dimension to the interaction between scientist, artist and

Interacting with Virtual Environments Edited by Lindsay MacDonald and John Vince
© 1994 John Wiley & Sons Ltd

mathematician. Mathematics is more easily applied in the physical sciences, and so it is in these areas that the technology is more easily exploited. For the physical scientist, computer technology permits automatic application of mathematical rules in **simulation**, and exploration of mathematical ideas in **visualisation**. For the artist, computer technology applies the mathematical rules to remove much of the labour involved in the production of a work of art. Rules of perspective, first explored and exploited by the Renaissance artists, and rules of light and shadow, explored and exploited by Leonardo and by the Dutch school of art, are now routinely included in systems such as the Winsom (Quarendon 1984) renderer we use.

Artificial life is one way of applying mathematical rules to the biological sciences. As with the physical sciences, the ability of computer technology to apply rules consistently and easily is exploited by the scientists both for simulations based on existing rules, and for exploring the effects of new rules. This paper describes how an artist uses a computer to apply rules of life in the production of works of art.

The rules used are based on life, and thus give the work a natural organic feel to which the viewers can relate. However, the rules are not bound by true biology, but are controlled and modified by the artist to express his imagination, and this imposes a surreal feeling.

Computer production of images removes much of the artist's labour, and thus permits the creation of previously impractical works. The use of complex rules goes further, and permits the computer to create results that go beyond even the artists imagination.

The body of this paper shows how the artist uses rules of artificial life to produce art forms. It emphasises the inspiration of biology and artificial life, leaving details of the techniques to the references.

17.3 Techniques used

This section outlines the main tasks involved in our preparation of art works. Most complicated is the creation of an animation, which involves four major creative phases described in this section.

- Creation of the rules that control the form (shape) of the sculptures to appear in the animation. These rules are inspired by models for growing horns, shells, trees and other organic objects.

- Choice of colouring and surface texturing rules, again chosen to mimic natural texturing.

- Selection of individual sculptures generated by the rules above. The selection process is based on an artist controlled version of natural selection.

- Creation of a detailed storyboard, based on rules of birth, growth and death, that defines how these sculptures behave during the animation.

There are also several production phases in rendering an animation and putting it on film or videotape that do not concern us here. We give examples of the rules used, and their relation to biological rules, and end the section with general comments on what makes a good rule.

Figure 17.1. Mathematically generated "biological" forms.

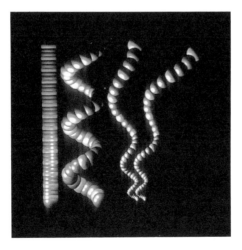

Figure 17.2. Sculptural development of a form: stack, grow, twist and bend.

17.4 Form

Mathematical explanation of the form of biological objects has received much attention, for example the scientist D'Arcy Thompson's investigation of geometry of nature (Thompson 1961). Several people have exploited nature for computer graphics (Kawaguchi 1982, Aono and Kunii 1984, Pickover 1989), including the authors (Latham 1990b, Latham 1988, Latham and Todd 1990).

Our original biologically-based form generation programs used different functions for generation of horns, spiral shells, pumpkin, fan and branching forms (Figure 17.1).

We soon realised that all of these functions were based on taking a simple "primitive" input shape and repeatedly applying a transformation to it. The functions merged into a single iterative function, with parameters to define the primitive object, the transformation to apply, and the number of times to apply it . The transformation parameter gave great flexibility, but as it was difficult to use, it was replaced with sculptural terms such as "stack", "bend" and "twist" (Figure 17.2). This single function no longer refers explicitly to its biological origins, other than its often inappropriate generic name the horn function, but the same interest in organic growth inspires the way it is applied.

The horn function evolved (Latham 1990b) to include variations which permit the generation of more complex organic forms (Plate 37).

- Segmented forms made from a list of horns,
- Horns made by repeatedly transforming input forms that are themselves horns,
- Forms made by recursive (fractal-like) geometry, as used by Barnsley and others to generate trees and ferns.

The horn function so developed became a generative rule used by the artist to create forms. The computer application of the rule not only assisted the artist to render forms, it produced surprising results that assisted his imagination in the creation of forms.

17.5 Texture

All our sculptures are textured using standard computer graphics texturing techniques (Voss 1985, Perlin 1985), implemented as a subsystem (Todd 1990) of the Winsom renderer.

The techniques are based on Fourier generation of filtered white noise, with either fractal or bandpass filters. The filters and textures are often chosen to be suggestive of biological features such as elephant hide or leopard spots (Figure 17.3).

As with many of our rules, our texture generation rules do not attempt to model biological processes, but are chosen to give organic visual results. These results are often close to those generated by reaction diffusion models (Turk 1988) and cellular automata (Li 1989).

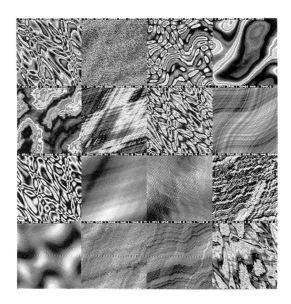

Figure 17.3. Sample textures.

17.6 Mutation and selection

The definition of our forms and textures naturally gives rise to parameterised families of sculptures. Each family is defined by a parameterised program we call a structure. When the program is run with a particular set of parameters, it gives a corresponding sculpture, and the parameters control features such as how much twist a shell has, or how regular a texture pattern is. Thus all the potential members of a family lie in a multidimensional space of forms. Typically we have ten or 20 parameters, and a ten or 20 dimensional space. This is difficult to illustrate, so (Figure 17.4) shows forms in a two-dimensional space.

Mutator (Todd and Latham 1990) is a program to assist exploration of this vast space and selection of artistically interesting members of this huge family. Mutator likens the parameters of our system to genes in a biological system, with the structure and the horn function performing the role of interpretation of the genes by ribosomal expression. It operates by an artist controlled analogue of natural selection.

In its simplest form Mutator has some similarities to Richard Dawkin's Biomorph system (Dawkins 1986). An initial value for all genes is chosen. The computer then "mutates" these values, to give nine sets of genes, and generates and displays a frame of the nine corresponding sculptures. The artist selects a "preferred" sculpture from the frame, and its genes are used as the starting point for a new frame of mutations, and so the loop of computer generation and artist selection continues (Figure 17.5). This dual process follows the natural processes of generation by genetic mutation and selection by survival of the fittest.

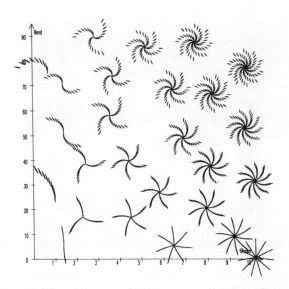

Figure 17.4. Objects in two-dimensional form space: branch number and bend.

The main difference between Biomorph and the basic Mutator is the intended use. Biomorph is a very effective illustration of the power of the dual processes of natural generation and selection. Mutator applies this power to create an artist's interface that uses a series of subjective decisions to select members from a family of sculptures. Because of this, Mutator operates on an artist written structure that produces complex three-dimensional forms, as opposed to Biomorph's fixed structure and two-dimensional forms.

Mutator also provides a variety of additional features.

Figure 17.5. A frame of nine mutations.

Steering

As the artist makes selections, Mutator detects trends in the direction in parameter space of the selected mutations and biases further mutations accordingly. The artist may also make judgements such as "good" or "bad" about mutations other than those selected, and these judgements further influence the generation of mutations. As far as we know this steering technique has no biological analogue, but it relates to the classic "hill climbing" techniques used with Monte Carlo optimisation. The purpose of steering is to speed up the artist's exploration of form space (Figure 17.6).

Marriage

Mutator permits the artist to arrange a marriage between parents, and generates new child sculptures by mixing the genes of the two parents. The artist rejects or selects the children for procreation by further mutation or marriage. This marriage process is clearly derived from sexual reproduction.

The gene mixing may be done in several ways. In random marriage each gene is selected randomly from one or the other parent. In spliced marriage the first so many genes are selected from one parent, and the remainder from the other. Spliced marriage is more effective at generating children with features that closely match those of the parents (Figure 17.7).

We are experimenting with further variations, for example multi-parent marriages, and gene mixing rules based on the ideas of dominant and recessive genes and on averaging.

Family tree

Mutator has various options for displaying and revisiting sculptures. This permits an overview of a family tree (Plate 38). Particularly important is the arrangement of marriages between distant cousins to prevent the generation of uninteresting inbred forms.

Mutation of structure

Mutator as implemented only permits the exploration of members of a family with a fixed number of genes each of which has a fixed interpretation. We intend to extend it to permit mutations of the underlying structure, so that different branches of the Mutator tree will contain members with different numbers and meanings of genes. For example, Mutator might change the structure

```
     horn                 to          horn
        ribs(??)                         ribs(??)
        stack(??)                        stack(??)
        grow(??)                         grow(??)
        bend(??)                         twist(??)        /* <<< */
                                         bend(??)
```

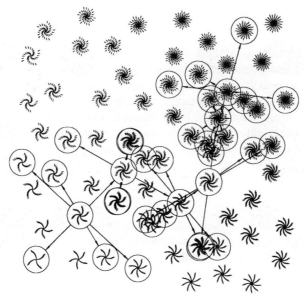

(a) This shows a unsteered attempt to move from the top right into the circle. The heavy line shows the route taken, and the lighter lines mutations offered but ignored. Six moves were required.

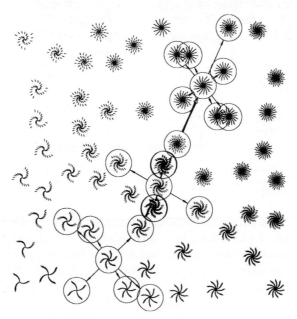

(b) This shows the effect of steering. The mutations offered start collecting around the required direction, and the steps automatically get larger as the direction is established. Three moves were required.

Figure 17.6. Steering used to speed up a search of form space.

Figure 17.7. Marriage, using random and spliced gene mixing rules.

In summary, Mutator is an interface to help an artist select from a family of sculptures. Its rules are derived from an artist controlled analogue of natural selection, but are adapted to make selection as fast and effective as possible.

17.7 Animation

In general, there are two extremes in animation. Conventional animation involves manual drawing of key frames, and the subsequent production of all the in-between frames. It involves a huge amount of human resource, sometimes computer assisted (ACM 1990), but often not (as in Walt Disney's classics). Animations generated to visualise scientific simulations, whether physical (Atiyah *et al.* 1989) or biological (de Reffye *et al.* 1988, Miller 1988), involve human effort in setting up the simulation, and then large computer resources in running the simulation and preparing the pictures. Our animations fall between these extremes (Todd *et al.* 1991). We use rules which are applied by the computer to remove much of the labour of hand animation, but give ourselves considerable control over the rules to give the necessary artistic flexibility. This extends the use a physical rules (Wejchert and Haumnann 1991) and splining of parameters (Steketee and Balder 1985), to allow life inspired rules on animation timing.

The film "Mutations"

The film "Mutations" is an animation of mutation. Rather than mutation being a process used in the selection of static sculptures, as described in the previous section, it becomes the theme of the entire film. Each scene is based on "actors", which are sculptures selected by the artist during a Mutator session. Rules of life control how these actors behave in the scene. These rules control how an actor grows, where it moves, and when it is born and dies.

Rules of growth

As an actor grows and decays, rules of growth define a valid set of gene values at every frame time. The computer uses the rules to compute the genes for that time, and then generates the sculpture using these genes, thus giving a constantly changing form. The genes go through four distinct key sets at specified key times, and interpolation controls gene values at other times (Figure 17.8).

bud   a small simple form for the first introduction of an actor.

fullsize   a fullsize form which does not yet have its own full individuality.

mature   the form as selected by the artist during the Mutator session.

death   the final form before the actor disappears from the screen.

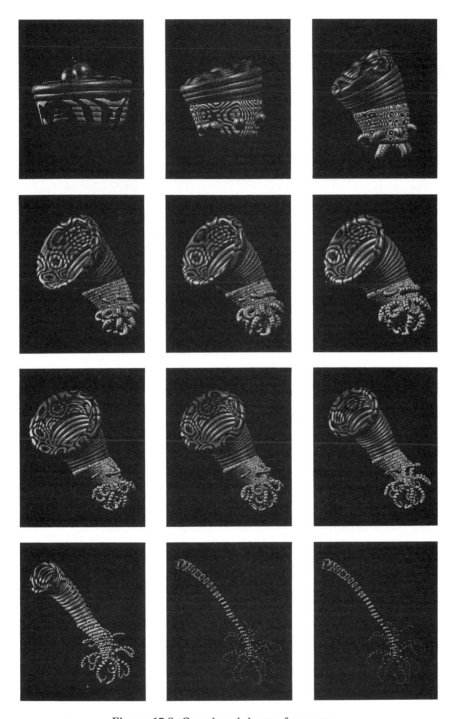

Figure 17.8. Growth and decay of an actor.

The key values for the genes are themselves generated by rules to depict the development of the object. The genes for a all buds are set to zero to give a small, simple member of the family. The fullsize genes are set mid-way between the mature genes of the parent and the actor's own mature genes. The death genes are set from the mature genes by a rule that makes the actor disintegrate and fade away.

All the rules may be manually overwritten. The first actor in a scene generally does not start from a small bud, and the rule for the genes at the fullsize stage is modified for greater artistic variation.

Rules of position

The forms are based around a central "spine" which ends in a flared hollow horn. When an actor is first conceived, it is placed at the start of its parent's spine. It moves down the spine and is born out of the flared end of the horn, a cornucopia depicting birth and parenthood (Figure 17.9). Once born, the child floats away from its parent and falls under the influence of an external whirlwind.

Timing Rules

The life of every actor is thus determined by five key times:

- conceived, when it has bud form and starts its movement down the parent's spine,
- born, when it is released from the parent into the whirlwind,
- fullsize, when it reaches its fullsize form,
- mature, when it reaches its mature form,
- dies, when it reaches its death form and disappears from the screen.

These relate to each other, and to the timings of the actor's parents and children. For example, our rules fail if a child is conceived before its parent. A child may be conceived, or even born, before its parent is born: this is just biologically unrealistic and artistically likely to lead to confusion. Originally these timing values were set manually for each actor, but this became very difficult to control, as slightly delaying the conception of one actor caused a change of times for all descendants. We thus derived Life Cycle, a program consisting of a setof timing rules based on typical intervals:

- conception to birth,
- birth to fullsize,
- fullsize to conception of first child,
- gap between successive children,
- birth of last child to start to decay,
- start of decay to final death.

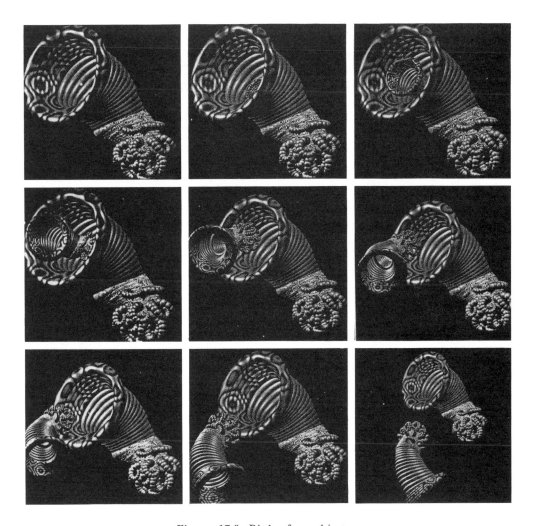

Figure 17.9. Birth of an object.

All of these have default timing values which can easily be overwritten for detailed artistic control, and many of which can be made negative for special effects directed by the artist. Figure 17.10 shows a timing sequence derived from the rules of Life Cycle.

17.8 Artistic rules of life

All the rules are based on biological analogues, modified to our requirements. The main criteria of a good rule is that it should give a natural organic feel and aesthetic results, with interesting composition and timing. Thus our timing rules give a longer life span to actors that have more children: artistically this gives more time to see the "interesting" births, but as far as we are aware the rule has no biological backing.

A good rule gives the artist sufficient control, and has enough variation that it can generate unexpected results. Unexpected results are sometimes an inspiration, but are by no means always good. In particular, we have found that rules that give an interesting variation over animations of a few seconds can lead to chaos or complete boredom when applied to longer scenes. When a rule fails in this kind of way, we generally first override it to create the desired results, and then analyse the final version to derive a new more sophisticated rule.

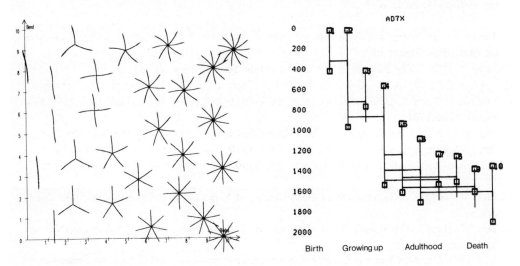

Figure 17.10. Timings generated by Life Cycle.

17.9 Conclusions

We have described the use of mathematical rules in the design of forms and animations. Life is the inspiration behind these rules, and this gives the artworks a realism and relates them to the viewer's experience. Once established, the rules are modified and applied to satisfy aesthetic criteria, and are not rigidly followed to give simulations of life. The results are thus surreal, artificial life, based on life but going beyond it. In all works of art, the artist tries to invest paint or stone to create an illusion of life, for example the Mona Lisa or Rodin's "Burghers of Calais". These however are static; using Mutator and Life Cycle it is possible to evolve forms by a surreal parody of the natural evolutionary process.

The works are a product of the artist's imagination. The artist controls the rules and the parameters that drive them, and the computer applies the rules to produce works impractical to produce in any other way. But the contribution of the computer to the art goes beyond this. Frequently the computer follows the artist's rules to yield results that go not just beyond his practical production capability, but also beyond his conception and imagination. The computer is a creative partner which realises the artist's ideas of growth and evolution. The role of the artist is to be a gardener who prunes, breeds, selects and destroys, his plant sculptures, and who can even change the rules of life of his universe.

References

ACM, *Technological Threat*, ACM Siggraph Film Show, 1990.

Aono M. and Kunii T.L. (1984). Botanical Tree Image Generation, *Computer Graphics and Applications* 4, no.5: 10-34.

Atiyah Sir Michael F., Hitchen N.J., Merlin J.H., Pottinger D.E.L. & Ricketts M.W. (1989). Monopoles in Motion: a study of the low-energy scattering of magnetic monopoles, *Animation and IBM UKSC Report 207*.

Dawkins R. (1986). *The Blind Watchmaker*, Longmans Scientific and Technical.

Kawaguchi Y. (1982). A Morphological Study of the Form of Nature, *Computer Graphics* 16, no.3.

Latham W. & Todd S. (1990). Sculptures in the Void, IBM Systems Journal 28, no.4, 1989 *New Scientist*, no.1701.

Latham W. (1990a). The Conquest of Form, Exhibition at Arnolfini Gallery (Bristol), The Natural History Museum (London) and UK tour, 1988-1990. The Evolution of Form, Exhibition at Melbourne Arts Festival and Australian tour, 1990. The Empire of Form, Exhibition at O-Museum, Tokyo, Japan.

Latham W. (1990b). A Sequence from the Evolution of Form, *SIGGRAPH Film and Video Show*, Dallas.

Latham W. (1990). The Artist's View of Computer Sculpture, *Tutorial at 8th Eurographics UK Conference, Bath*.

Li W. (1989). Complex Patterns Generated by next nearest neighbors cellular automata, *Computers and Graphics* 13, no.3: 531-537.

Miller G.S.P. (1988). The Motion Dynamics of Snakes and Worms, ACM Siggraph 88 Conference Proceedings, *Computer Graphics*, 22, no.4: 169-178.

Perlin K. (1985). An Image Synthesizer, Proceedings of Siggraph Conference San Fransisco, *Computer Graphics*, 19, no.3: 287-296.

Pickover C. (1989). A Short Recipe for Seashell Synthesis, *IEEE Computer Graphics and Applications*, 8-11.

Quarendon P. (1984). WINSOM user's guide, *IBM UK Scientific Centre Report 123*.

de Reffye P., Edelin C., Francon J., Jaeger M. & Peuch C. (1988). Plant Models Faithful to Botanical Structure and Development, ACM Siggraph 88 Conference Proceedings, *Computer Graphics*, 22, no.4: 151-158.

Steketee S. & Balder N.I. (1985). Parametric Key frame interpolation incorporating kinetic adjustments and phrasing control, Journal of Visualization and Computer Animation, ACM Siggraph 85 Conference Proceedings, *Computer Graphics*, 19, no.3: 255-262.

Thompson D. (1961). *On Growth and Form*, Cambridge University Press, Cambridge, UK.

Todd S. & Latham W. (1990). Mutator, a subjective human interface for evolution of computer sculptures, *IBM UKSC report 248*.

Todd S. & Latham W. (1985). *Evolutionary Art and Computers*. (Book). Academic Press Ltd. London, New York.

Todd S. (1990). Winchester Colour and Texture Facilities: WINCAT, *Tutorial at 8th Eurographics UK Conference*, Bath, and *IBM UKSC report 250*.

Todd S., Latham W. & Hughes P. (1991). Computer Sculpture Design and Animation, *Journal of Visualisation and Computer Animation*, 2: 98-105.

Turk G. (1988). Generating Textures on Arbitrary Surfaces Using Reaction Diffusion, ACM Siggraph 91 Conference Proceedings, *Computer Graphics,* 25, no.4: 289-298.

Voss R.F. (1985). Random Fractal Forgeries, Proc. NATO A.S.I 17, *Fundamental Algorithms in Computer Graphics*, Ilkley, UK, ed. R.A. Earnshaw (Springer Verlag, NY).

Wejchert J. & Haumnann D. (1988). Animation Aerodynamics ACM Siggraph 91 Conference Proceedings, *Computer Graphics*, 25, no.4: 19-22.

Index